ON TOUR

presents

Sue Townsend's

the Queen and I

in repertoire with

Jim Cartwright's

BOOKING NOW OPEN

Haymarket Theatre, Leicester: 23 March -16 April
(0533 539797) *
Theatre Royal, Bath: 18 - 23 April
(0225 448844)
New Theatre, Cardiff: 25 - 30 April
(0222 39484)*
New Theatre, Hull: 3 - 7 May
(0482 226655)
New Victoria Theatre, Woking: 9 - 14 May
(0483 761144)
Grand Theatre, Blackpool: 17 - 21 May
(0253 28372)
Theatre Royal, Norwich: 24 - 28 May
(0603 630000)
Royal Court Theatre, London: From 7 June
(071 730 1745)

There will be no performance of ROAD in Leicester or Cardiff.

GRANTA

LOSERS

47

Editor: Bill Buford
Deputy Editor: Ursula Doyle
Managing Editor: Claire Wrathall
Editorial Assistant and Picture Researcher: Cressida Leyshon
Contributing Editor: Robert McSweeney

Managing Director: Catherine Eccles
Financial Controller: Geoffrey Gordon
Marketing and Advertising: Sally Lewis
Circulation Manager: Lesley Palmer
Subscriptions: Leila Sifri
General Assistant: Richard Powley

Picture Editor: Alice Rose George
Executive Editor: Pete de Bolla
US Publisher: Anne Kinard, Granta, 250 West 57th Street, Suite 1316, New York, NY 10107.

Editorial and Subscription Correspondence: Granta, 2–3 Hanover Yard, Noel Road, Islington, London N1 8BE. Telephone: (071) 704 9776. Fax: (071) 704 0474. Subscriptions: (071) 704 0470.
A one-year subscription (four issues) is £21.95 in Britain, £29.95 for the rest of Europe and £36.95 for the rest of the world.

Granta is printed in the United States of America. The paper used in this publication meets the minimum requirements of American National Standard for Information Sciences—Permanence of Paper for Printed Library Materials, ANSI Z39.48-1984 ∞

Granta is published by Granta Publications Ltd and distributed by Penguin Books Ltd, Harmondsworth, Middlesex, England; Viking Penguin, a division of Penguin Books USA Inc, 375 Hudson Street, New York, NY 10014, USA; Penguin Books Australia Ltd, Ringwood, Victoria, Australia; Penguin Books Canada Ltd, 10 Alcorn Avenue, Toronto, Ontario, Canada M4V 3B2; Penguin Books (NZ) Ltd, 182–190 Wairau Road, Auckland 10, New Zealand. This selection copyright © 1994 by Granta Publications Ltd.

Cover by Senate. Cover photograph: FPG International.

Granta 47, Spring 1994
ISBN 0-14-014086-7

GENET

Few people may think a sexual and social deviate – a man accused of killing his intimates and of advocating betrayal, of creating scandal and perpetrating pornography – can provide an example to others; Edmund White's biography shows how this can be in Genet's case and how his state of near canonization came about.

'White's *Genet* is well written and clearly argued throughout... As an orthodox monument to an unorthodox man, *Genet* is unlikely to be surpassed'
GUARDIAN

Paperback May £9.99

BALZAC

The first major English biography of Balzac for over fifty years, Graham Robb's masterpiece of literary biography makes Balzac burst into life on every page.

'*Balzac* is wonderful. The book is very well written, highly original and reads like a thoroughly enjoyable story. The book is one of the very best I have ever read on *Balzac*, if not the best'
JEAN BRUNEAU,
Editor of the Pleiade edition of Flaubert's Letters

Hardback June £20.00

faber and faber

" My sister brought a neurosurgeon over to my place around Christmas – not some V.A. butcher but a guy from the university hospital. He was a slick dude in a nine-hundred-dollar suit. He came down on me hard, like a used-car salesman. He wants to cauterize a small spot in a nerve bundle in my brain. 'It's not a lobotomy, it's a cingulotomy,' he said. **"**

from *The Pugilist At Rest* by Thom Jones

CONTENTS

Losers

Martin Amis Author, Author   9

Neil Steinberg The Spelling Bee   51

Julian Barnes Trap. Dominate. Fuck.   73

Mothers and Fathers

Eugene Richards In the Beginning   103

Susan J. Miller Never Let Me Down   121

Bret Easton Ellis The Up Escalator   135

Jayne Anne Phillips Buddy Carmody   159

Beverly Lowry Patricide   175

The Tragedy of Vukovar

David Owen Introduction   194

Jean Hatzfeld The Fall of Vukovar   196

Gilles Peress Compulsory Departures   223

After the Revolution (Part Two)

Orville Schell Hero of Tiananmen Square   239

Ivan Klíma Progress in Prague   249

Notes on Contributors   256

'If diversity reflects vitality, the American short story comes into the nineties in contentious good health.'
JAY McINERNEY

COWBOYS, INDIANS AND COMMUTERS

THE PENGUIN BOOK OF NEW AMERICAN VOICES

EDITED BY

JAY McINERNEY

SHORT STORIES FROM:
SHERMAN ALEXEI • DOROTHY ALLISON
CHARLES D'AMBROSIO • ROBERT ANTONI • JENNIFER EGAN
JEFF EUGINEDES • PAM HOUSTON • MARK LEYNER
JESS MOWRY • ROBERT O'CONNOR • DALE PECK
ABRAHAM RODRIGUEZ JR • GAIL DONOHUE STOREY
DONNA TARTT • WILLIAM VOLLMANN
DAVID FOSTER WALLACE

VIKING

GRANTA

MARTIN AMIS
AUTHOR, AUTHOR

Cities at night, I feel, contain men who cry in their sleep and then say Nothing. It's nothing. Just sad dreams. Or something like that . . . Swing low in your weep ship, with your sob probes and your tear scans, and you would mark them. Women—and they can be wives, lovers, gaunt muses, fat nurses, obsessions, devourers, exes, nemeses—will wake and turn to these men and ask, with female need-to-know, 'What is it?' And then men say, 'Nothing. No it isn't anything really.'

Just sad dreams.

Richard Royce was crying in his sleep. The woman beside him, his wife, Gina, woke and turned. She came up on him from behind and laid hands on his shaking shoulders. There was a professionalism in her blinks and frowns and whispers: like the person at the poolside, master of mouth-to-mouth; like the figure surging in on the blood-spattered zebra, a striding Christ of first aid.

'What is it?' said Gina.

Richard raised a bent arm to his brow. The sniff he gave was complicated, orchestral. And when he sighed you could hear the distant seagulls in his lungs.

'Nothing. It isn't anything. Just sad dreams.' Or something like that.

Richard awoke at six, as usual. He needed no alarm clock. He was already comprehensively alarmed. Richard felt tired, and not just underslept. Local tiredness was up there above him—the kind of tiredness that sleep might lighten; but there was something else up there over and above it, like a concentration of gravity. That higher tiredness was not so local. It was the tiredness of time lived, with its days and days. No nap or cuppa would ever lighten it. Richard couldn't remember crying in the night. He lay there now, awake, dry-eyed. He was in a terrible state—that of consciousness. Some while ago in his life he had lost the ability to choose what to think about. He slid out of bed in the mornings just to find some peace. He slid out of bed in the mornings just to get a little rest. He was forty tomorrow, and reviewed books.

In the small square kitchen, which stoically and uncritically

awaited him (they had both seen better days), Richard engaged the
electric kettle; then he went next door and looked in on the boys.
These dawn visits to their room had been known to comfort him
after nights such as the one he had just experienced, with all its
unwelcome information. His twin sons in their twin beds. Marco
and Marius were not identical twins. And they weren't fraternal
twins either, Richard often said, in the sense that they showed little
brotherly feeling. But that's all they were, brothers, born at the
same time. It was possible, theoretically, that these boys had
different fathers. They didn't look alike, and were unusually
dissimilar in all their attributes and proclivities. They didn't even
have the same birthday: a sanguinary summer midnight had
interposed itself between the two boys and their (again) very
different parturitional styles: Marius, the elder, subjecting the
delivery room to a systematic and intelligent stare, its negative
judgement suspended by decency and disgust; while Marco just
clucked and sighed to himself contentedly, as if after a successful
journey through freak weather. Now in the dawn, through the
window and through the rain, the streets of London looked like the
insides of an old plug. Richard contemplated the two boys, their
motive bodies reluctantly arrested in sleep, and reef-knotted to their
bedware, and he thought, as an artist might: but the young sleep in
another country, at once very dangerous and out of harm's way,
perennially humid with innocuous libido—there are neutral eagles
out on the window-sill, waiting, offering protection or threat.

Sometimes Richard did think and feel like an artist. He was
an artist when he saw fire, even a match head (he was in his study
now, lighting his first cigarette): an instinct in him acknowledged
its elemental status. He was an artist when he saw society: it never
crossed his mind that society had to be like this, had any right, had
any business being like this. A car in the street. Why? Why *cars*?
This is what an artist has to be: harassed to the point of insanity or
stupefaction by first principles. The difficulty began when he sat
down to write. The difficulty, really, began even earlier.

Richard looked at his watch and thought: I can't call him yet.
Or rather: Can't call him yet. For writers' thoughts now waive the
initial personal pronoun, in deference to Joyce. He'll still be in bed,
not like the boys and their abandonment, but lying there

personably, and smugly sleeping. For him, either there would be no information, or the information, such as it was, would be good.

For an hour (this was his new system) he worked on his latest novel, deliberately but provisionally entitled *Untitled*. Richard Royce wasn't much of a hero. Yet there was something heroic about this early hour of flinching, flickering labour, the pencil-sharpener, the Tippex, the vines outside the open window sallowing not with autumn but with nicotine. In the drawers of his desk or interleaved by now with the bills and summonses on the lower shelves on his bookcases, and even on the floor of the car (a terrible red Escort), swilling around among the Ribena cartons and the dead tennis balls, lay other novels, all of them firmly entitled *Unpublished*. And stacked against him in the future, he knew, were yet further novels, successively entitled *Unfinished*, *Unwritten*, *Unattempted* and, eventually, *Unconceived*.

2

At eleven o'clock Richard Royce dialled the number. He felt the hastening of excitement when Gwyn Barry himself picked up the telephone.

'Hello?'

Richard exhaled and said slowly, 'You fucking old *wreck*.'

Gwyn paused.

'It's all over,' said Richard. 'You're dead.'

Then the elements came together in Gwyn's laugh, which was gradual and indulgent and even quite genuine. 'Richard,' he said.

'Don't laugh. You might break your neck. Forty today. Jesus.'

'Listen,' said Gwyn, 'are you coming to this thing?'

'I am but I don't think you'd better. Sit tight, by the fire. With a blanket over your lap. And an old-boy pill with your hot drink.'

'Yes, all right. Enough now. Are you coming to this thing?'

'Yeah, I suppose so. Why don't I come to you around twelve-thirty and we'll get a cab.'

'Twelve-thirty. Good.'

'Christ,' said Richard. 'You fucking old *wreck*.'

Richard wept briefly and then paid a long and consternated

13

visit to the bathroom mirror. His mind was his own and he accepted full responsibility for it. But his *body*. The rest of the morning he spent backing his way into the first sentence of a 2,000-word piece about the new and expanded edition of the *Nabokov–Wilson Letters*. Like the twins, Richard and Gwyn Barry were born only a day apart in time. Richard would be forty tomorrow. The information would not be carried by *The Times*: *The Times*, the newspaper of record.

Just past noon Richard rang the bell on Holland Park Avenue and preened himself—it felt more like damage control—for the security camera, which jerked round affrontedly at him in its compact gantry above the door. He also strove to prepare himself mentally. The state he sought was one of disparity-readiness. He never found it. Gwyn's set-up always flattened him. He was like the chinless cadet in the atomic-sub movie, small-talking with one of the guys as he untwirled the lock (routine check) on the torpedo bay—and was then floored by a frothing cock of seawater. Deep down out there, with many atmospheres. All that Gwyn had.

To take a heftily looming instance, the house itself. Its mass and scope, its reach and sweep, he knew well, because for a year he had gone to school in an identical building across the street and eight or nine doors up. The school, a cosmopolitan crammer, which was dead now, like Richard's father, who had struggled and scrimped to send him to it, had accommodated a staff of thirty and over 200 pupils; five days a week he had swirled and slumped among them, an ecology of oestrogen and testosterone, Swedes and Turks, bum-fluff, flares, fights, fancyings, first loves. That tiered rotating world was vanished. But now in a place of the same measurements, the same volume, lived Gwyn and Demeter Barry. Oh yeah. And the help . . . Richard moved his head around as if to relieve neck pain. The camera continued to stare at him incredulously. He tried to stare back at it. Richard wasn't guilty of covetousness, funnily enough. In the shops he seldom saw anything that looked much fun to buy. He didn't want all that stuff. But he didn't want Gwyn to have it either.

The door opened, and Richard was shown upstairs, not of

course by Demeter (who at this hour would be unguessably elsewhere in the great house), nor by a maid (though there were maids, called things like Ming and Atrocia, shipped here in crates from São Paulo, from Vientiane), nor by any representative of the home-improvement community (and they were always about: the knighted architect, the overalled stiff with a mouth full of nails): Richard was shown up the stairs by a new order of auxiliary, an American coed or sophomore or grad student, whose straightness of hair, whose strictness of mouth, whose brown-eyed and black-browed intelligence was saying that whatever else Gwyn might be he was now an *operation*, all fax and Xerox and preselect. In the hall Richard saw beneath the square mirror a shelf so infested with cardboard or even plywood invitations . . .

Gwyn Barry was nearing the climax of a combined interview and photo session. Richard entered the room and crossed it in an uneven diagonal with one hand effacingly raised, and sat on a stool, and picked up a magazine. The room—Gwyn's study—was very bad. While in this room it was Richard's usual policy to stare like a hypnotist into Gwyn's repulsively Messianic green eyes, for fear of what he might otherwise confront. He didn't really mind the furniture, the remoteness of the ceiling, the good proportion of the three front windows. What he didn't like seeing were Gwyn's books: Gwyn's books, which multiplied or ramified so crazily now. Look on the floor, look on the table, the desk, and what do you find? The lambent horror of Gwyn in Spanish (*3eo edicione*) or an American book-club or supermarket paperback, or something in Hebrew or Mandarin or cuneiform or pictogram that looked innocent enough but had no reason to be there if it wasn't one of Gwyn's. And then Gallimard and Mondadori and Livro Aberto and Brombergs and Zsolnay and Magveto Konyvkiado. In the past Richard had had several opportunities to snoop around in Gwyn's study, on Gwyn's desk. These opportunities he had readily embraced. Are snoopers in search of pain? Probably. TriStar's terms are, we feel, more than generous. Quite a rarity for a living author to have any, let alone several, works in the Livres de Poche edition. The judges were unanimous. Please find enc. a photograph of the inside of my cunt. I am beginning to be translating your. Her

15

Royal Highness. Richard stopped flipping through the magazine on his lap (it had an interview with Gwyn Barry in it), and stood, and surveyed the bookshelves. They were fiercely alphabetized. Richard's library wasn't alphabetized. He never had the leisure to alphabetize it. He was always far too busy looking for books he couldn't find. He had books heaped under tables, under beds. Books heaped on window-sills so they closed out the sky.

Interviewer and interviewee were winding up some guff about the deceptive simplicity of the interviewee's prose style. The photographer was a woman, a girl, black-clad, Nordic, leggy—how she crouched and teetered for her images of Gwyn. Richard looked on. Being photographed, as an activity, was in itself clearly not worth envying. What was enviable, and unbelievable, was that Gwyn should be worth photographing. Then the boy interviewer said: 'A lot of people think that, because you're the figure you now are, that the obvious next step is politics. What do you . . . ? Do you . . . ?'

'Politics,' said Gwyn. 'Gosh. Well I can't say I've given it that much thought. Thus far. Let's say I wouldn't want to rule it out. As yet.'

'You sound like a politician already, Gwyn.'

This was Richard. The remark went down well—because, as is often pointed out, we are all of us in need of a good laugh. Or any kind of laugh at all. The need is evidently desperate. Richard dropped his head and turned again. No, this really wasn't the kind of thing he wanted to say. Ever. But Gwyn's world was partly public. And Richard's world was dangerously and increasingly private. And some of us are slaves in our own lives.

'They're not incompatible, though, are they?' said Gwyn. 'Novelist and politician are both concerned with human potential.'

'This would be Labour, of course.'

'Obviously.'

'Of course.'

'Of course.'

Of course, thought Richard. Yeah. Of course Gwyn was Labour. It was obvious. Obvious not from the ripply cornices twenty feet above their heads, not from the brass lamps or the military plumpness of the leather-topped desk. Obvious because

Gwyn was what he was, a writer, in England, at the end of the twentieth century. There was nothing else for such a person to be. Richard was Labour, equally obviously. It often seemed to him, moving in the circles he moved in and reading what he read, that everyone in England was Labour, except the government. Gwyn was the son of a Welsh schoolteacher (his subject? Gym. He taught gym). Now he was middle class and Labour. Richard was the son of a son of a Home Counties landowner. Now he was middle class and Labour. All writers, all book people, were Labour, which was one of the reasons why they got on so well, why they didn't keep suing each other and beating each other up. Not like America, where spavined Alabaman must mingle with Virginian nabob, where tormented Lithuanian must extend his hand to the seven-foot Cape Codder with his true-blue eyes. By the way, Richard didn't mind Gwyn being rich and Labour. Richard didn't mind Gwyn being rich. It is important to establish the nature of the antipathy (to free it from distractions), before everything gets really awful, all ripped and torn. He made me hit my little one, thought Richard incensedly, for the twentieth time that morning. Rich and Labour: that was OK. Having always been poor was a good preparation for being rich—better than having always been rich. Let the socialist drink champagne. At least he was new to it. Anyway, who cared? Richard had even been a member of the Communist Party, in his twenties, for all the fucking good *that* did him.

The interviewer had concluded his official business. He was now staring at his tape recorder with what seemed to be incredulous sorrow, but then nodded to himself and got to his feet. Richard understood: he too had spent a lot of time staring at tape recorders. Round about here the photographer's presence started to gather and expand—her height, her health. She said, 'Now if I could just have *three minutes* of your time over on that window seat over there.'

'I don't pose,' said Gwyn. 'The deal was you snap away while we talked. But no posing.'

'Three minutes. Oh please. Two minutes. The light's so perfect there.'

Gwyn acquiesced. He acquiesced in the manner of someone who had similarly acquiesced many times before, perhaps too many: the well and all its sweet water would surely one day run dry.

'Who's coming, Richard?' Gwyn called, from beyond, as the photographer's strap and pouch-swathed figure interposed itself between the two men.

'Not sure.' Richard named some names. 'Thanks for coming along. On your birthday and everything.'

But now without turning to him the photographer with frantic fingers was making quelling gestures behind her back and saying, 'Good, good. I'm getting something. That's very good. Hold it. Higher. Stay. Oh, wow. That's very good. That's very good. That's beautiful.'

On the way out they encountered Demeter Barry in the hall. She was twenty-eight, and comparatively disorganized for someone with so much money. Like Gina Royce, she had no connection with literature other than marriage to one of its supposed practitioners.

She said, 'Hello Richard.'

'My dear Demi,' said Richard, giving a brief stiff bow before kissing her on either cheek.

3

An hour into lunch in this fish restaurant for rich old men, and something extraordinary was about to happen. Nothing from the outside world. It was just that Richard was on the verge of passionate speech. Yes: passionate speech.

You don't think that's extraordinary? Oh, but it is, it is! Try and think of the last time you did it. And I don't just mean 'Well I think it's absolutely disgraceful' or 'You're the one who brought it up in the first place' or 'Get straight back into your room and get into bed.' I'm talking speech: passionate speech. *Speeches* hardly ever happen. We hardly ever give them or hear them. See how bad we are at it. See how we fuck it up. We salivate and iterate. Women can do it, or they get further, but when the chance of tears presents itself they usually take it. Not having this option, men just shut up. They are all *esprit de l'escalier*. Men are spirits on the staircase, wishing they'd said . . . Before he spoke, there in the buttoned plush, Richard hurriedly wondered whether this had been a natural resource of men and women—passionate speech—before 1700 or whenever Eliot said it was, before thought and feeling got dissociated. The sensibility of men was evidently much more dissociated than the sensibility of women. Maybe, for women, it just never happened. Compared with men, women were Metaphysicals, Donnes and Marvells of brain and heart.

So: his passionate speech. Passionate speech, which unrolls, with thoughts and feelings dramatized in words.

The place. A private room full of food and drink and smoke—full of mouths. Someone rich paying.

The company. Financier, male columnist, female columnist, publisher, diarist, photographer, captain of industry, Shadow Minister for the Arts, Gwyn Barry.

The alcohol consumed. Richard had been very good, managing to get through a Virgin Mary and a lite beer before his pre-lunch whisky. Then a ton of wine.

The provocation. Considerable, some might think. Sufficient, in any case.

London's weather was bound to play an important part: a hot noon gloom. Like night falling on the interior of the church, the lunchers gathered . . . Gwyn Barry had his photograph taken. The financier had his photograph taken. Gwyn Barry was photographed with the financier. The publisher was photographed with Gwyn Barry and the captain of industry. The captain of industry was photographed with the Shadow Minister for the Arts and Gwyn Barry. Two speeches were given, read from pieces of paper—neither of them passionate. The captain of industry, whose wife was interested enough in literature for both of them (Gwyn often dined with them, Richard knew), gave a speech in praise of Gwyn Barry on this, his fortieth birthday. That took about ninety seconds. Then the financier gave a speech during which Richard smoked three cigarettes and stared tearfully at his empty glass. So the financier was trying to get his money's worth. It wasn't just going to be a free meal with some slurred shop over coffee. The financier spoke about the kind of literary magazine he would like to be associated with—the kind of magazine he was prepared to be the financier of. Not so much like magazine A. Not so much like magazine B. More like magazine C (defunct) or magazine D (published in New York). Gwyn Barry was then asked about the kind of magazine *he* would like to be associated with (the kind that had high standards). Ditto the captain of industry, the Shadow Minister for the Arts, the female columnist, the male columnist. The diarist was not consulted. Neither was the photographer, who was leaving anyway. Neither was Richard Royce. Richard found that he was being consulted only on technical matters (print runs, break-even points and so on); he found, moreover, that he knew nothing about these things, or about anything else, though his answers were fluent and bold. Rather, Richard found that he was increasingly absorbed in the many minor tragedies that were unfolding inside his body, his body, and nobody else's.

Would there be any point, the financier, Sebby, was saying (and his general popularity owed a great deal to this bandied diminutive: never mind, for now, all the fellow sharks and bastards he had left shivering over their visual display units), would there be any point in getting some market research underway? Richard?

Richard suddenly looked rather worryingly short-necked. He was in fact coping with a digestive matter, or at least he was sitting there until the digestive matter resolved itself one way or the other.

'What, reader profile stuff?' he asked. He had no idea what to say. He said, 'Age? Sex? I don't know. The *TLS* did something like that and it just made everyone incredibly depressed.'

'Oh? Why?'

'The only thing they found out was that all their readers were ninety years old.'

Sebby paused, as if waiting for more, and then said, 'This would be more prospective, obviously. I thought we might press a questionnaire on, say . . . students reading English at London? Something of that kind?'

'Find out what they're looking for,' said the publisher.

'Targeting,' said the male columnist, who was about twenty-eight and sparsely bearded, with a school-dinner look about him. The column he wrote was political. 'Come on, this isn't America. Where, you know, the magazine market is completely balkanized. Where they have magazines,' he said, already looking round the table to garner any smiles that might soon be cropping up, 'for the gay South Moluccan scuba diver.'

'Still, there are more predictable preferences,' said the publisher. 'Not many men read *Ms.*'

There was a silence. To fill it, Richard said, 'Has anyone ever established whether more men or women buy literary magazines?'

'Oh please. What is this?' said the female columnist. 'Men or women? This is a *literary magazine* for God's sake!'

Even when he was in familiar company it sometimes seemed to Richard that those gathered in the room were not authentic selves—that they had gone away somewhere and come back not quite right, half remade or reborn by some blasphemous, cack-handed and above all inexpensive process in a sinister circus or horror-flick funhouse. All flaky and carny. Not quite themselves. Him included.

Richard said, 'Is all this without interest? Nabokov said he was "frankly homosexual" in his literary tastes. I don't think men and women write the same way. They go at it differently. I don't think they read the same way either.'

'And I suppose,' she said, 'I suppose you think Africans and Chinese read and write differently too.'

'Probably. Almost certainly. Yes.'

'I can't believe I'm hearing this. I thought we came here today to talk about *literature*. What's the matter with you? Are you drunk?'

He turned his senses on her, which were indeed pretty sclerotic by this time in his life, old and dimmed and thin. (He didn't really want to do this. And he didn't really want to talk in that antique editorial voice.) The woman: gruff, sizeable, stately handsome, always barging through to her share of the truth. Richard knew the type—because literature knew the type. Like the smug boiler in the Pritchett story, the Labour politician, up north, proud of her brusqueness and her good big bum.

The Shadow Minister for the Arts said, 'Isn't this what literature's about? Transcending human difference?'

The female columnist said, 'Exactly. Me? I don't give a damn whether people are male, female, black, white, pink or polka-dotted.'

'Don't say that,' said Richard. 'No. No. Don't say that.' And he looked up at Gwyn, not for rescue but for acknowledgement of pain.

Addressing the Shadow Minister for the Arts, Gwyn said: 'I don't think in terms of men or of women. I think in terms of . . . people.'

It was that little rapt pause before *people* that did it. Richard exhaled in the consensual silence and began, 'A very *low-level* remark, if I may say so. Shall I tell you what you remind me of? A quiz in a colour mag—you know, Are You Cut Out To Be a Teacher? Final question: would you rather teach: (a) history, (b) geography, or (c) *children*. Well of course you're going to be teaching *children*. You don't get a choice about that. But there is a difference between history and geography. It must be a great relief to deny all the evidence of your faculties and say that being a man means nothing and being a woman means nothing and what matters is being a *person*. Hey, how about being a spider, Gwyn, you Taff dunce? Say you get away with your life after your first big date and look over your shoulder and there's the girlfriend eating one of your legs like it was a chicken drumstick. What would you say? I know. You'd say: I don't think in terms of male spiders or of female spiders. I just think in terms of *spiders*.'

He sank back, rhythmically sighing or whinnying with all that this had cost him. He didn't have the will to look up, to look up into that unanimity of downward-revision. So he stared at the tarnished tablecloth, and saw only the rising—no, the plunging—seahorses that lived behind his eyes.

4

Gwyn had been quiet in the cab going home. The light outside, the sky, was the same as the driver's treated windscreen, the upper half all charcoal and oil, the lower palely glowing. Richard pulled the side window down to validate this; and of course the glass loomed slowly up again, interposing its own medium. Here perhaps was the only way to see London truly, swinging low over it in a cab, in darkness-at-noon July. How beautiful it made the colour of the traffic lights, he thought, beneath their meshed glass: the anger of their crimson, the jaundice of their amber, the jealousy of their green.

'Could you believe that woman,' said Richard. 'You know—she really thinks she's *authentic*. Whereas . . . ' He paused. Whereas to him she had seemed almost horrifically otherwise. 'Unmarried, I assume. She reeked of spinst.'

Gwyn turned to him.

'Spinst. Like unmarried men reek of batch.'

Gwyn turned away, shaking his head slowly, sadly. 'You can't say such things. And not just for public reasons.' Richard assumed (perhaps wrongly) that Gwyn meant something more like: you can't say such things because the whole area has been seen to be contaminated, fouled by men who really do hate women.

Anyway Richard went ahead and said, 'Great gusts of spinst. A miasma of spinst.'

'Would you just pull in at the corner here please.'

Nothing. Gwyn was just buying an evening paper from the boy. He left the door open when he slid out. Jesus, the light looked like the end of London, the end of everything; its guttering glow was livid now, and something you wouldn't want to touch, like the human-hued legs of pigeons beneath their dirty overcoats.

Gwyn sank back as the cab resumed its endless journey—its journey of hurry up and wait, hurry up and wait. He opened the paper and turned to the Diary and eventually said, 'Well there's nothing about it here.'

Richard was staring at him. 'Nothing about what?'

'About the lunch. Your little outburst.'

Richard stared harder. 'Relieved about that, are you?'

Gwyn spoke with restraint. He said: 'It's quite a while since anyone talked to me like that.'

'Is it? Well this time you won't have so long to wait. Get ready, because someone's going to talk to you like that again. That's the lunchtime edition. You think the guy just phones it on to the news-stands? It's lucky no one knows how fucking thick you are. That really would be a scoop.'

'Nothing about the job offer either,' said Gwyn, his bright eyes still scanning the page.

'There wasn't any job offer.'

'Yes there was. While you were making one of your visits to

the toilet. I turned it down of course. I mean, as if *I* . . . '

The first drop of rain greyly kissed him on his baldspot as he climbed out of the cab and into the shoplit dungeon of Marylebone High Street. The clouds cracked: they could hold it no longer. And then it all came down.

R ound about now, in time, the emotions lose lucidity and definition, and become qualified by something bodily. Something coarse and coarse-haired in the fury, something rancid and pulmonary in the grief, something toxic and long-toothed in the hate . . . Richard put his thoughts in delivery order, as a writer might: stuff to be *got in*. And at the same time he experienced one of those uncovenanted expansions that every novelist knows, when, almost audibly to the inner ear, things swivel and realign, they transform (the cube comes good), and all is clear. You don't do this. Your talent does it. He sat up. His state was one of equilibrium, neither pleasant nor unpleasant in itself, but steady. He gave a sudden nod. It was all so simple now. At last Richard had found a literary project that he passionately believed in and could deeply commit himself to.

He was going to fuck Gwyn up.

A nd of course after that he felt so full of life that he got up and went out to the Canal Diner and drank seven Zombies . . . *That's it*, said the barman. *Uh-oh*, said the bedroom floorboard beneath the sleeping wife. *Tsk tsk*, said the watch by his ear . . . That night he cried in his sleep again. Gina didn't hear it. Nobody knew: only the sleepless, the omniscient, the someone watching over him. Why do the men cry?

Why do the men cry in their sleep? Because of fights and feats and preferment, because of jobs and money, because of all that men have done. Because they can't be happy or sad any more—only smashed or nuts. And because they don't know how to do it when they're awake.

And then there is the information.

5

The next day it was *his* turn: Richard turned forty. Turned is right. Like a half-cooked steak, like a wired cop, like an old leaf, like milk, Richard turned. And nothing changed. He was still a wreck. Richard Royce—I mean, Richard Royce was a *wreck*.

Who's who?

At twenty-eight, living off book reviews, social security and copywriting for ad firms, pale and thin and interestingly dissolute, most typically to be seen wearing a collarless white shirt and jeans tucked into misshapen brown boots—looking the kind of ex-public schoolboy who, perhaps, drunkenly carpentered or landscape-gardened for the good and the great—with his fiery politics and his riveting love affairs in which he was usually the crueller, Richard Royce published his first novel, *Aforethought*, in Britain and America. If in order to arrive at a consensus you homogenized all the reviews (still kept, somewhere, in a withered and thinning brown envelope), allowing for the many grades of generosity and IQ (the flailing turk, the frowning has-been, the one who likes everything or at least dislikes nothing, the one who dislikes everything including the regular exceptions he pretends to like), then the verdict on *Aforethought* was as follows: nobody understood it or even finished it, but, equally, nobody was sure it was shit. Richard flourished. He stopped getting social security. He appeared on *Better Read*: the three critics in their breakfast nook, Richard behind a desk with an unseen Gauloise fuming unseen in his trembling hand—he looked as though his trousers were on fire. Three years later, by which time he had become books and arts editor of a little magazine called the *Little Magazine* (little then, and littler now), Richard published his second novel, *Dreams Don't Mean Anything*, in Britain but not in America. His third novel wasn't published anywhere. Neither was his fourth. Neither was his fifth. In those three brief sentences we adumbrate a *Mahabharata* of pain. He had plenty of offers for his sixth because, by that time, during a period of cretinous urges and vacillations, he had started responding to the kind of advertisements that plainly came out with it and said, WE WILL PUBLISH YOUR BOOK and

AUTHORS WANTED (or was it NEEDED?) BY LONDON PUBLISHER. Of course, these publishers, crying out for words on paper like pining dogs under a plangent moon, weren't like normal publishers. You paid them, for example. And, perhaps more importantly, no one ever read you. Richard stayed with it and ended up going to see a Mr Cohen in Border Mews off Marylebone High Street. He came out of there, his sixth novel still unplaced, but with a new job, that of Special Director of the Tantalus Press, where he went on to work about a day a week, soliciting and marking up illiterate novels, total-recall autobiographies in which no one ever went anywhere or did anything, collections of primitive verse, very long laments for dead relatives, crackpot scientific treatises and, increasingly, it seemed to him, 'found' dramatic monologues about manic depression and schizophrenia. *Aforethought* and *Dreams Don't Mean Anything* still existed somewhere, on the window-sills of seaside boarding houses, at the bottom of tea chests in storage, going for ten pee in cardboard boxes at provincial book fairs . . . Like the lady who was of course still there between the mortar board and the prosthetic legs (and what a moving acceptance speech she gave), like the laughing athlete who, after that mishap in the car park, awoke to find himself in life-choice traction and now runs a network of charities from his padded rack, Richard had to see whether the experience of disappointment was going to make him bitter or better. And it made him bitter. He was sorry: there was nothing he could do about it. He wasn't up to better. Richard continued to review books. He was very good at book reviewing. When he reviewed a book, it stayed reviewed. Otherwise he was an ex-novelist (or not ex so much as void or phantom), the literary editor of *The Little Magazine* and a Special Director of the Tantalus Press.

Bitter is manageable. Look how we all manage it. But worse happened, and the real trouble began. It was a viscous autumn, and Richard had stopped dating girls (he was married now), and Gina was expecting not just one baby but two, and the rejection slips were coming in on novel number four, *Invisible Worms* (does it merit these italics, having never been born?), and his overdraft practically trepanned him every time he dared think about it: imagine, then, Richard's delight when his oldest and stupidest friend, Gwyn Barry, announced that his first novel, *Summertown*, had just been accepted by a leading London house. Because Richard at least partly understood that the things you hate most always have to go ahead and happen, he was ready for this—or was expecting it, anyway. He had long been an amused confidant of Gwyn's literary aspirations, and had chortled his way through *Summertown*—plus a couple of its abandoned predecessors—in earlier drafts. *Summertown*? *Summertown* was about Oxford, where the two writers had met; where they had shared, first, a set of rooms in the mighty hideousness of Keble College and, later, a rude flatlet off the Woodstock Road, in Summertown, twenty years ago. Twenty years, thought Richard, forty today: oh, where had they all *gone*? Gwyn's first novel was no less autobiographical than most first novels. Richard was in it, clumsily and perfunctorily disguised (still the promiscuous columnist with his poetry and his ponytail), but affectionately and even romantically rendered. The Gwyn figure, who narrated, was wan and Welsh, the sort of character who, according to novelistic convention, quietly does all the noticing—whereas reality usually sees to it that the perspiring mute is just a perspiring mute, with nothing to contribute. Still, the Gwyn figure, Richard thought, was the book's only strength: an authentic dud, a dud insider, who brought back real news from the dud world. *Summertown* duly appeared, to modest sales and (Richard again) disgracefully unmalicious reviews. The following year a small paperback edition limped along for a month or two . . . We might have said that Richard was tasting fresh failure, except that failure is never fresh, and always stale, and weakly fizzes, like old yoghurt, with his sixth novel when Gwyn sent him a bound proof of his second, entitled *Stumbling on Melons*. If Richard had chortled his way through *Summertown*, he cackled and yodelled his way through *Stumbling on Melons*: its cuteness, its blandness, its naïvely pompous semi-colons, its hand-me-down imagery, the almost endearing transparency of its little colour-schemes and tinkertoy symmetries. What was it 'about', *Stumbling on Melons*? It certainly wasn't autobiographical: it was about a group of fair-minded young people who, in an unnamed country, strove to establish a rural community. And they succeeded. And then it ended. Not worth writing in the first place, the finished book was, in Richard's view, a ridiculous failure. He was impatient for publication day.

With this mention of patience, or its opposite, I think we might switch for a moment to the point of view of Richard's twin sons—to the point of view of Marius, and of Marco. There was in Richard a fatherly latitude or laxity that the boys would, I believe, agree to call *patience*. Richard wasn't the one who went on at them about duties and dress codes and, above all, toy tidying—Gina had to do all that. Richard didn't scream or storm or spank. Gina had to do all that. On the contrary, with Richard in sole charge, they could gorge themselves on ice-cream and packets of Wotsits and watch TV for hour after hour and wreck all the furniture, while he sat slumped over his desk in his mysterious study. But then Daddy's patience changed . . . *Stumbling on Melons* had been out for about a month. No stir had been caused by it, and therefore no particular pall had fallen over the Royce maisonette. The reviews, while hardly the pyrotechnic display of sarcasm and contempt for which Richard hoped, had nonetheless been laudably condescending, and unanimous, and brief. With any luck, Gwyn was finished. It was a Sunday morning. To the boys this meant a near-eternity of unmonitored delectation, followed by an outing to Dogshit Park or better (the zoo or the museum, with one or other tranced and speechless parent) and at least two hired tapes of cartoons, because even Gina was TV-patient on Sunday nights, after a weekend in their company, and was often in bed before they were.

So. Daddy in the kitchen, enjoying a late breakfast. The twins, their legs further slenderized by the baggy bermudas they both sported, were to be found on the sitting-room carpet, Marius ably constructing sea- and space-faring vessels with plastic stickle-bricks, Marco more dreamily occupied: with the twinned cords of the telephone and angle lamp which shared the low round table by the fireplace, Marco was ensnaring and entwining various animal figurines, here a stegosaurus, there a piglet, with transformation on his mind, thus arranging things—how did the fable end?—so that the lion might lie down with the lamb . . . The boys heard a loud, bedraggled wail from across the passage. This sound, its register of pain or grief, was unconnectable with their father or anyone else they knew, so perhaps some stranger or creature? Marco sat back, thus tugging at his tangle of duckling and velociraptor, and the little table slewed; his eyes had time to widen before it fell, had time to glaze with tears of contrition and pre-emption before Richard came into the room. On patient days he might have just said, 'Now what have we here?' or 'This is a sorry tangle' or, more simply (and more likely) 'Jesus Christ.' But not this Sunday morning. Instead, Richard strode forward at about the speed that one recoils from the touch of flame and with a single swoop of his open hand dealt Marco the heaviest blow he had ever felt. Marius, sitting utterly still, noticed how the air in the room went on rolling, like the heaving surface of the swimming-pool even after the children had all climbed out.

Twenty or thirty years from now, by which time the twins would have become grown men themselves, this incident would be something they could lie back and tell their psychiatrists about: the day Daddy's patience went away. And never returned, not fully, not in its original form. No one except Richard will ever know what happened that Sunday morning, the ragged wail, the fiercely crenellated lips, the rocking boy on the sitting-room floor—though Gina might have pieced it together, for the same night Richard was impotent with her and never really got that back either. What happened that Sunday morning was this: Gwyn Barry's *Stumbling on Melons* entered the bestseller list, at number nine.

But before he did anything else, before he did anything grand and ambitious like pressing on with *Untitled* or rewriting his review of the new Swift biography or getting started on fucking Gwyn up (and he had, he thought, a good opening move), Richard had to take the vacuum cleaner in . . . That's right. He had to take the vacuum cleaner in. This is how I account for the darkness, the melancholy and the alienation of twentieth-century literature: in a servantless world, writers are always having to do things like taking the vacuum cleaner in. When she proposed the errand to him, Gina used the words 'nip' and 'pop': 'Could you nip round to the electrician's and pop the Hoover in,' she had said. But Richard's nipping and popping days were definitely over. He stood in the passage staring at the vacuum cleaner for perhaps half a minute. Then his eyes closed slowly . . . The visit to the electrician's would also involve him in a visit to the bathroom (to shave: he was too mired internally now to let the world see him with his surface unclean; he too much resembled the figure he feared he would become: the terrible old man in a callbox wanting something very badly—cash, work, information). In the bathroom mirror, of course, he would be reduced to two dimensions; so the bathroom mirror was no place to go if what you wanted was depth. *By the age of forty everyone has the face they deserve.* Like *the eyes are the window to the soul.* Good fun to say, good fun even to believe, when you're eighteen, when you're thirty-two. Looking in the mirror now, on the morning of his fortieth birthday, Richard thought that *no one* deserved the face *he* had. No one. No one in the history of the planet. There was nothing on the planet it was that bad to do. What happened? Oh, what have I *done*? His hair, scattered here and there over his crown in assorted hanks and clumps, looked as though it had just concluded a course of prolonged and nauseating (and entirely futile) chemotherapy. Then the eyes, each perched on its little blood-rimmed beer gut, beneath luxuriantly piebald brows. If the eyes were the window to the soul then the view stopped at the window, which was walled up behind rusty wire netting. All over his body there were whispered rumours of pain. His cough sounded like a wiper on a dry windscreen. These days he drank and smoked largely to solace himself for what smoking and drinking had done to him—but they had done a lot to him, so he smoked and drank a lot. He indulged, furthermore, in any other drug he could get his hands on. At any given moment, whatever he was doing, at least two of his limbs were immovably numb. In fact, physically, at all times, he felt epiphanically tragic. His doctor had died six years ago—and that, in Richard's mature opinion, was definitely that. He had a large and weirdly lucent lump on the back of his neck. This he dealt with himself, by the following means: he kept his hair quite long, so no one could see it. If you told Richard Royce he was in denial, he would deny it. But not hotly.

Nevertheless, he still had to take the vacuum cleaner in. He *had* to take it in, because even Richard (who was, of course, being a man and everything, a prodigious slob) could tell that the quality of life, in 47 Calchalk Street, had dramatically declined without it. Oh, *you* know: dust of such feathery ubiquity that it made Richard suspect, quite wrongly for a change, that he was due another liver attack; Gina's grieving reminders; Marco's life-threatening allergies. By the time he had wrestled the vacuum cleaner from its sentry box beside the boiler Richard had long been weeping with rage and self-pity. By the time he was out of the apartment with it he was wondering if he had ever suffered so. By the time he reached the hall downstairs he was busy concluding that Samuel Beckett, at some key juncture in his life, had been obliged to take a vacuum cleaner in. Richard gave himself a loud breather while he looked through his mail. His mail he no longer feared. The worst was over. Why should a man fear his mail, when, not long ago, he had received a solicitor's letter from his own solicitor? When, rather less recently, in response to a request for more freelance work, he had been summarily fired, through the post, by his own literary agent? When he was being sued (for advances paid on unwritten books) by both his ex-publishers? Most of the time, though, his mail was just junk. Once, in the street, on an agitated April afternoon, on his way back from lunch with some travel editor in some tragic trattoria, he had seen a city cyclone of junk mail—flying fliers, circling circulars—and had nodded, and thought: me, my life. And a lot of the time he got no mail at all. Now, on the morning of this his fortieth birthday, he received one small cheque and two large bills—and a brown envelope, hand-delivered (no address, no stamp), featuring his own name in tortured block capitals, with the accurate but unfamiliar addendum, 'MA (Oxon)'. He put it in his pocket, and once more shouldered his load.

A vacuum cleaner is designed to cruise grandly round a carpet. It is not designed to be humped half a mile through a wet London Wednesday, with the cars trailing their capes of mist. Cruelly encumbered, Richard staggered on, the brown base under his arm as heavy as a soaked log, the T-shaped plastic adjunct in his free hand, the tartan flux-tube round his neck like a fat scarf, and then the plug, freed from its broken catchlet, incensingly adangle between his legs. The 'freshness and sheer optimism', the 'unembarrassed belief in human fulfilment and, if not "perfectibility", then at least robust improvement' for which *Stumbling on Melons* was now being retrospectively praised would presumably reach new orders of flame-eyed unction when its successor appeared later in the year—now that Gwyn Barry no longer had to take the vacuum cleaner in. Richard lurched sideways into Ladbroke Grove. The plug and lead snarled his ankles like a hurled bolero. The tartan tube clutched his neck in a pythonic embrace.

Once in the shop he let the whole contraption crash down on to the low counter. Behind it stood a tall young man who looked at the vacuum cleaner and then its owner with an inexpert eye before reaching for a foolscap document. Richard sobbed out his name and address. Make, model, registration number. Eventually they came to the section headed TYPE OF MALFUNCTION. The young man said, 'What's wrong with it?'

'*I* don't know,' said Richard. 'It doesn't clean carpets. It cuts out all the time and it makes this screeching sound and the bag leaks so all the crap keeps coming out the back.'

The young man considered Richard, and this information. His eyes returned to the form, where, after due thought, under TYPE OF MALFUNCTION, he wrote: 'Not working.'

'Yeah,' said Richard. 'Yeah, well that ought to cover it.'

In the streets outside the old divisions of race and class were giving way to the new divisions: good shoes as opposed to bad shoes, the paleface as opposed to the redskin (blocked pallor versus the visage far fierier than any Tabasco), different preparedness for the form that urbanity was currently taking (the city-tuned as opposed to the starer, the secular holyman, the marooned rustic). The young man stared at Richard, with weak hostility, or pain. Looking into these eyes, eyes as dim and marginal as the lights of a cheap car left on all night, Richard was presented with another divide, the universal, to do with words, and words are all we have. Richard had provoked this stare but he couldn't meet it, not today: the display fixtures on the wall, decorative or labour-saving, white cones and spheres—and then in the back of the shop, valved like the wet city, all the junk that wasn't working, the unrecompleted, the undescribed, the unwritten.

On the way home he stopped at a stall under the Westway and ordered a cup of tea to accompany the cigarettes he was trying to smoke in the dousing rain. He took from his pocket the brown envelope—MA (Oxon)—and took from it a single sheet of paper that might have been torn from a child's exercise book:

blue-lined, softly creased, an air of much effort, little progress. The letter had been heavily corrected by another pen in another hand, but it still said:

Dear Richard
You are the writer of a 'novel'. Aforethought. Congratulations! Nice one. Hows it done. First you get the topic. Next, you package it. Then comes the hipe.
I am thinking of becoming 'an author'. Snap. If you want to meet and discuss these issues over a few 'jars' feel free to give me a bell.
Yours sincerely,
N. Bishop

Well-known writers get this kind of letter every other day. Usually more sensible; sometimes less sensible, all about devils and electricity. But Richard was not a well-known writer, and he got this kind of letter every other year (and they were normally about book-reviewing anyway). So he looked at it with rather more care than a well-known writer would have done. And his scrutiny was rewarded. In the lower left-hand corner of the half-filled sheet, half hidden by the fringe of the rip, were the letters: TPO. Richard turned the page over.

I know the wierd girl, Diva. Shes the one they all wan't. Christ what a looker. You're mate Gwyn Barry, is in love with her of TV fame.

This was puzzling, but sounded, on the whole, like excellent news. What he was looking at, here, might turn out to be a good plan B. Though as it happened he was feeling exceptionally upbeat about plan A. With the intention of getting moving on it Richard finished his tea and his cigarette and sloped off home through the leaning rain.

6

Richard's opening move, in his plan to ruin Gwyn's life, was not intended to be in itself decisive, or even dramatic. On the other hand it did demand from Richard a great deal of trouble and expense—and internal wear (slow, disaffected, heavy-footed, life-ruining: the stuff that brings about all the bread-and-butter deaths). All these phone calls and stunned crosstown journeys, and talentless grapplings with brown paper and string . . . Nonetheless, he was decided. He even raised his chin for a moment in quiet pride, and inhaled richly. Richard had resolved to send Gwyn Barry a copy of the Sunday *New York Times*. With a note. And that was all.

He was quite clear about it in his own mind . . . Richard sat at his desk; he had just put *Untitled* away for the morning, after completing a hysterically fluent passage of tautly leashed prose, and was now assembling his notes (which were widely dispersed) for a 700-word review of a 700-page novel by a prize-winning Panamanian. In the interim he was taking his own pulse. Meanwhile too his smaller son Marco, who had failed Gina's dawn fitness test and was taking another day off school, was at his father's side, balancing a rubber troll or goblin on various roughly horizontal surfaces: Richard's forearm, Richard's shoulder, Richard's baldspot. And from outside through the shivery window came the sound of fiercely propelled metal as it ground against stone, shearing into the sore calcified struts and buttresses with sadistic persistence: the house, the street, the whole city, taking it deep in the root canal.

For instance, it had to be the *NYT*. The *LA Times* was even bigger, Richard knew, but in his judgement Gwyn wasn't quite nuts enough for the *LAT*. But he was surely nuts enough for the *NYT*. Richard would have staked his reputation on it. If Gwyn wasn't nuts enough for the *NYT* then Richard was losing his grip. Now he reached backwards for his jacket, hooked over the chair, and dug out the frayed cheque book on which he hoped he might have written a few words about the big novel from Panama. He had: *epic sheep-dip scene p.536ff*. The cheque-book joined his other notes, loosely gathered on the heaped desk: a credit-card slip, a torn envelope, an empty matchbook. And the slab of the novel itself. He hated it as a physical object. He had read every page (in such matters Richard was psychotically conscientious) and he had hated every page. But now he just hated its solidity and mass.

Turning to the back flap, intending to energize himself with a glimpse of the obscenely handsome author, he disturbed the empty matchbook, which fell to the floor. Marco retrieved it and repositioned it, sighing carefully.

'Helping Daddy,' said Marco, 'in whatever he does. Each day.'

The idea was this: Richard would send Gwyn Barry a copy of the Sunday *NYT*, all of it, that forest-slaying suitcase of smeared print, accompanied by a typed note that would read, in its entirety:

> Dear Gwyn,
> Something in here to interest you. The price of fame!
> Yours ever,
> John

There would, of course, be no indication of where this interesting something was to be found. Sitting back, sitting back in the alphabet soup of his study, Richard imagined Gwyn opening the package, frowning at the note, looking first, with a slight smile, at the Books section, then, rather less equably, at the Arts section, then . . .

'Marco, what's the point of doing that?'

Either Marco didn't hear or he didn't understand. He said: 'Wot?' There is of course this difficulty of rendering childish speech. But how do you get around it? Marco didn't say 'What?' He said 'Wot?'—definitely a humbler and shorter word, and entirely unaspirated.

'Balancing that toy on my arm,' said Richard. 'Why? What for?'

'Does it bolla you?'

'Yes.'

'Does *that* bolla you?' he asked, balancing the toy on Richard's head.

'Yes.'

'Does *that* bolla you?' he asked, balancing the toy on Richard's shoulder.

The ups and downs of a Panamanian goatherd, thought Richard, *don't obviously demand . . . can't be said to cry out for the epic frame, but Enrique Murillo in this, his seventh and longest . . .* How would he deliver the *NYT*? Leave it on the doorstep?

Richard rang the London offices of the *NYT*. They *did* keep a copy of the Sunday paper, and Richard was free to come in there to consult or admire it; but he couldn't take it away. They told him, rather, to go to International Dispatches in north Islington, which was known to sell copies of the Sunday *NYT*, which cost lots of money. With his mac and his hangover and his book (a biography of William Davenant, Shakespeare's bastard: 700 words by Thursday week), Richard embarked at Ladbroke Grove, changed at Notting Hill Gate and Oxford Circus, and rode in the slatted light to Islington, whose streets he roamed for fifty-five minutes in tears of rage before stumbling upon International Dispatches where an old man in what looked like a crofter's cottage thatched with *Frankfurter Zeitung*s and *El País*es and *India Today*s and many other journals daubed in exclamatory Farsi or Sanskrit told him that they no longer stocked the *SNYT*: only the daily. Pressure of space. Richard came home again. A couple of days later, when he had calmed down, he rang the London offices of the *NYT*: they told him to ring the distributors, in Cheapside. He rang the distributors: they said that such copies of the *SNYT* as came their way were all subscription copies, though occasionally (true) there was a spare . . . Richard used all his charm on the young woman at the other end of the line. But the trouble was that he didn't have any charm, not any longer, and she told him he would just have to turn up one Monday morning on the off-chance, like anybody else. So began his weekly journeys to the warehouse in Cheapside, where they would typically pass him round from Portakabin to van mouth to storage room and back again, before sending him on his way (to the *Little Magazine*, in fact, where in the dawn he would start subbing the book reviews over a papercupful of tomato soup). It was on his seventh visit that he revealed, to the assistant manager's intense sneer of puzzlement, that he didn't necessarily want a copy of *that week's SNYT*. Any Sunday *NYT* would do. Contritely Richard followed the assistant manager to another storage room, one never seen before; here, any number of *SNYT*s lay about in stacks and heaps, along with unwanted Sunday *Boston Globe*s and Sunday *San Francisco Chronicle*s. Richard listed faintly on his feet. In the pleasure and nausea he felt there was an element of straightforward incomprehension, at the sadness and greyness and dampness and deadness of old newsprint—and at human profligacy and clamour. Christ: shut up! Anyway, he cracked, and went for size. That day he came home with the Sunday *LA Times* cradled tenderly in his arms . . . Brown paper and a ball of string took about a week each to purchase and assemble. Then Richard was ready to move.

7

Before he delivered it, but after he had wrapped it, Richard was struck by an unpleasant thought: what if there *was* something to interest Gwyn Barry in this particular issue of the Sunday *LA Times*? An eight-page symposium on his work, for example. Or a whole Gwyn Barry section. As in the UK, *Stumbling* had first been a flop, then a sleeper and finally a smash in the United States. Brought to Richard's attention by a patriotic item in a London newspaper, this wound still out-throbbed all others: the general battering meted out by the book's evident popularity in Germany, France, Spain, Italy and Japan, which he got to hear about through Gwyn's offhand complaints about foreign camera crews, sudden five-city whistle-stop tours and so on. Such information drew Richard's mind to a place where it didn't want to go: to the universal. He dealt with it as follows. Had Gwyn found that voice which speaks to and for the human soul, in all places, in all times? No (Richard argued): he had just stumbled on the LCD. The multitudes of the humourless, the well-intentioned, the bland, the abashed: they had stopped reading Herman Hesse and started reading Gwyn.

It was seven o'clock in the evening. Richard had actually cleared a space on his desk for the package containing the *LAT*—in itself a stunning achievement. His desktop was so untidy that his desktop phone often stopped ringing before he found it. Now he eyed the great brown knapsack, weakly supposing that he had better glance through its contents, prior to delivery. True, it would require incredible skill, but if he could slip the thing out while preserving at least some of the wrapping . . . He picked at the fused knot of string; he worried the folds of the creased paper: in the end he tore it all apart with a roar so savage that his children, in the next room, looked up from their GI Joes and stared at one another with clean round eyes and shrugged theatrically, palms opened at right angles to the wrist.

With care and dread Richard inspected Book World (including Briefly Noted, Points of Interest and Information, Please), Arts and Entertainments (in case something of Gwyn's had been harrowingly translated to screen or stage), the main Magazine (a profile, perhaps, or Faces to Watch, or Bedside Reading), and the Week in Review (the Gwyn Barry phenomenon). In a rather more relaxed spirit, he then thoroughly skimmed the Update section, the Style section, the Briefing section, the Flair section, the You section and the Poise section. Feeling, by now, laughably rigorous (and hugely vindicated), he checked the Op-Ed page of the News section: multiculturalism? the redefined syllabus? whither publishing? The Business sections, the Fashion section, the Appointments section, the Lawnmower pull-out and the Curtain Rail supplement: these he disdainfully ignored.

At midnight Richard was deciding that the last five hours had been pleasurably and profitably spent. If Gwyn Barry was such a big cheese, you wouldn't know it from the *LAT*. Richard never doubted that Gwyn was nuts enough to read the whole thing at least twice, right down to the recipes and the crossword clues. He imagined his friend three weeks from now, drinking instant coffee and rubbing his eyes as he readdressed himself to the opening pages of the Deckchair section . . .

As he was putting the paper back together again Richard mysteriously ran out of whisky and went to the kitchen to find something more to drink. Anything alcoholic would do. He experienced a thud of surprise, from temple to temple, when instead of the usual striplit void he confronted his wife. She was not a large woman, but the size of her presence was dramatically augmented by the lateness of the hour. And by marriage, and beauty, and neglect. Her hair was up and back; her face glowed with half-assimilated night-cream; her towel dressing-gown revealed an inverted triangle of rosy throat. Richard abruptly realized what had happened to her, what she had done: she had become a grown-up. And Richard hadn't.

'How many hours a day,' she said, 'do you spend on your novels?'

'What?' said Richard, who had his whole head in the drinks cupboard.

'How many hours a day do you spend on your novels?'

'I don't know. Depends.'

'You usually do it first thing, don't you? Except Sundays. How many hours, on average?'

'Two. Maybe three.'

Richard realized what this reminded him of, distantly: being interviewed. There she sat across the table with her pencil and her notebook and her green tea. Pretty soon she would be asking him if he relied, for his material, on real life or on the crucible of the imagination, how he selected his subjects and themes, and whether or not he used a word-processor. Well, maybe. But first she asked: 'How much money have they earned you? Your novels.'

'In my life?'

She nodded.

Richard thought he had better sit down. The calculation didn't take him very long. There were only three figures to be added together. He told her what they amounted to.

'Give us a minute,' she said.

Richard watched. Her pencil softly slid and scraped, then seemed to hover in thought, then softly scraped again.

'And you've been at it for how long?' she murmured to herself: good at sums. 'Right. Your novels earn you about sixty pence an hour. A cleaning lady would expect to make seven or eight times that. From your novels you get a fiver a day. Or thirty quid a week. Or fifteen hundred a year. That means every time you buy a gram of coke—which is what?'

Richard didn't know she knew about the coke. 'Hardly ever.'

'How much is coke? Seventy? Every time you buy a gram of coke . . . that's more than a hundred man hours. About six weeks' work.'

While Gina gave him, in monotonous declarative sentences, a précis of their financial situation, like something offered to test his powers of mental arithmetic, Richard stared at the tabletop and thought of the first time he had seen her: behind a tabletop counting money, in a literary setting. His blood had slowed and wearied with hurt. He was so hurt he wasn't even drinking.

'Now,' she said. 'When was the last time you received actual payment for your novels?'

'Eight years ago. So I give them up, right?'

'Well it does look like the one to go.'

There followed a minute's silence—perhaps to mark the passing of Richard's fiction. Richard spent it exploring his own numbness. He was impressed by its density. Emotion recollected in tranquillity, said Wordsworth, describing or defining the creative act. To Richard, as he wrote, it felt more like emotion invented in tranquillity. But here was emotion. It would fill the sky if there was a sky to fill, instead of a kitchen. Upstairs, Marco was pleading in his sleep. They could hear him—pleading with his nightmares.

She said, 'You could review more books.'

'I can't review more books.' There on the table lay a slablike biography of Swinburne. Richard had to write 2,000 words about it for a famously low-paying literary monthly, by next Friday. 'I already review about a book a day. I can't review more. There aren't enough books. I do them all.'

'What about all this *non*-fiction you keep agreeing to write? What about that Siberia trip?'

'I'm not going.'

'I don't like to say this, because at least it's regular, but you could give up the *LM*.'

'It's only a day a week.'

'But then you spend forever writing those "middles". For nothing.'

'It's part of the job. The literary editor has always written the middles.' And he thought of their names, in a wedge, like an honours board: Eric Henley, J. C. Partridge, Roland Davenport. They all wrote the middles. Richard Royce. Surely you remember J. C. Partridge's controversial attack on the Movement poets? J. C. Partridge was still alive, unbelievably. Richard kept seeing him, in Red Lion Street, in the callbox, staring with terrible purpose at the student-clogged entrance of the language school. Or flapping around on his hands and knees in the passage behind the Merry Old Soul.

'For nothing,' said Gina.

'Yeah, that's right.'

'No one reads the *LM*.'

'Yeah, that's right.'

One of Richard's middles had been about writers' wives—a typology of writers' wives. The pin was a biography of Hemingway, who, Richard argued, had married one of each. (Stoutly or fogeyishly resistant to clever headlines, Richard had in this case submitted to the inevitable 'For Whom the Bells Toll'.) How did they go? The Muse, the Rival, the Soulmate, the Drudge, the Judge . . .

'You can't give up the Tantalus thing, which is pretty decent as well as regular. You tell me. You could give up smoking and drinking and drugs. And clothes. It's not that you spend. You don't earn.'

'I can't give up novels.'

'Why not?'

Because . . . because then he would be left with experience, with untranslated and unmediated experience. Because then he would be left with life. Christ . . .

'Because then I'd just have this.' The kitchen—the blue plastic tub filled with the boys' white pants and vests, the stiff black handbag on the chair with its upturned mouth open wanting to be fed, the bowls and spoons and mats laid out on the table for the morning and the eight-pack of cereal boxes in its Cellophane: all this became the figure for what he meant. 'Days. Life,' he added.

And this was a disastrous word to say to a woman—to women, who bear life, who bring it into the world, screaming, and so will never let it come second to anything.

Her breasts and her eyes—for a moment they all swelled up. Then she blinked and said, 'The alternative is I go full time.' She told him what they would pay her: a chastening sum. 'That means you get the twins up every morning and get them down every night. I do weekends. You shop. You clean. And you cook.'

'I can't cook.'

'I can't either.'

'Jesus.'

'That way,' she said, 'you'll be getting plenty of life. You won't be going short on life.' Gina paused. 'I tell you what,' she said. 'How near are you to finishing the one you're doing now?'

Richard creased his face. One of the troubles with his novels was that they didn't really get finished. They just stopped. The new one was already very long. 'Hard to say. Couple of months?'

'OK. Finish that and see if it makes any money. Then we'll decide. What's it called?'

'*Untitled.*'

'When will it be?'

'No, it's *called Untitled.*'

'You mean you can't even think what to call it?'

'No. It's *called Untitled.*'

'How can it be *called Untitled?*'

'It just is. Because I said so.'

'Well that's a bloody stupid name for it. You know, you might be a lot happier, without them. It might be a big relief. Gwyn and everything. That's not you. That's a whole other story. Demi says it's *frightening* how the money comes in. I wonder if you still really believe in it. Your fiction. Because you never . . . Because what you . . . Ah I'm sorry. I'm so sorry.'

Because you never found an audience—you never found the universal. Because what you come up with in there, in your study, is of no general interest. End of story: your story.

Using a kilometre of string and about four rolls of Sellotape, as if in a field hospital, Richard bandaged his package together. The *LAT* was now ready to go. Over a contemplative cognac he squared up to the fateful, exalted challenge of delivery.

8

The heat was stiffling, read Richard. 'Jesus,' he said.

> The heat was stiffling. Moodly he looked out of his bedroom window. Yes, the day was far too hot to be sleepy. The time had come. He *had* to chose.

Richard wasn't reading this in a speculative spirit. He was marking it up for the printer. He said, 'Now there's a first sentence that gets you by the lapels. *The heat was stiffling.*'

Balfour Cohen came and looked over Richard's shoulder. He smiled understandingly and said, 'Ah yes. That's his second novel.'

'Did we publish his first?'

'We did.'

'How did that start? Let's think. *It was biterly cold.*'

Balfour smiled understandingly. 'It's probably a pretty good yarn.'

Richard read on:

He *had* to chose. To win, to suceed, would be incredulous. But to fail, to loose, would be contemptuous!

'What I don't understand,' said Richard, 'is what these people have against dictionaries. Maybe they don't even know they can't spell.'

As he said this he found he was sweating, and even crying. Another thing he didn't understand was why he had to correct the spelling. I mean, why bother? Who cared? No one was ever going to read this stuff, except the author, and the author's mum. What if it was alphabet soup?

'I'm amazed he spelt the title right.'

'What is the title?'

'*Another Gift from Genius.* By Alexander P. O'Boye. That's assuming he spelt his name right. What was his first one called?'

'One moment.' Balfour tapped his keys. '*A Gift from Genius,*' he said.

'Jesus. How old is he?'

'Guess,' said Balfour.

'Nine,' said Richard.

'Actually he's in his late sixties.'

'Pitiful, isn't it? What's the matter with him? I mean is he *insane?*'

'Many of our authors are retired. This is one of the services we perform. They have to have something to do.'

Or something to be, thought Richard. Sitting in the pub all day with a dog on your lap would be more creative, and more dignified, than nine-to-fiving it on the illiterate delusion. He glanced sideways. It was possible that Balfour regarded Alexander P. O'Boye as one of the flowers of his list. He was always more hushed and pious when it came to the fiction and the poetry. In any case it was Richard who was now Fiction and Poetry Editor at the Tantalus Press. He didn't have to do what Balfour did, which was mark up the biographies of pet goldfish and prize gherkins, the thousand-page treatises that supposedly whipped the carpet out from under Freud and Marx and Einstein, the revisionist histories of disbanded regiments and twilit trade-union outposts, the non-fictional explorations of remote planets, and all the other screams for help.

'One should remind oneself,' said Balfour, as he said every week, 'that James Joyce initially favoured private publication.' Then he added: 'Proust, too, by the way.'

'But that was . . . Wasn't that just a manoeuvre. To avoid a homosexuality scandal,' said Richard carefully. 'Suggested by Gide. Before Proust went to Gallimard.'

'Nabokov,' suggested Balfour.

'Yeah, but that was just a book of love poems. When he was a schoolboy.'

'Nevertheless. Philip Larkin. And of course James Joyce.'

Balfour was always doing this. Richard expected to learn that Shakespeare got his big break with a vanity press; that Homer responded to some ad whining for fresh dross. The Tantalus Press, it went without saying, was not a springboard to literary success. The Tantalus Press was a springboard to more of the same: to *Another Gift from Genius*. 'Private' publishing was not organized crime exactly, but it had close links with prostitution. The Tantalus Press was the brothel. Balfour was the madame. Richard helped the madame out. Their writers paid them to publish—or at any rate print—their trex. And a writer should be able to claim that he had never paid for it—never in his life.

'What have you got?' said Richard.

'Second World War. It looks rather controversial.'

'The myth of the six million?'

'He goes further. He argues that the concentration camps were run by Jews and that the prisoners were all Aryan Germans.'

'Come on, Balfour. You're not taking that, are you?'

Had he been around for the Holocaust in which all four of his grandparents were enslaved and then murdered, Balfour would have been dead half-a-dozen times over. Pink triangle, yellow star: it would have been a complicated badge he wore, in his last days. Racially subhuman (Jewish), sexually perverted (homosexual), mentally unsound (schizophrenic), physically deformed (club-footed) and politically deviant (communist). He was also a vanity publisher; he was also entirely uncynical. Furthermore—and as it were disinterestedly—Cohen was a serious collector of anti-Semitic propaganda. Look at him. There never was a gentler face, Richard thought: the bald brown head, the warm brown eyes, the humour and humanity gathered in the creases beneath his all-forgiving orbits.

'It's not my business to question an author's views or his findings.'

'Findings? What *findings*? Oh, think how horrible he must be. It's amazing,' Richard offered, 'the urge to get the Jews wrong. No one sends you stuff about, I don't know, Stalin devoting his life to handicapped children. Or blacks putting white Alabamans to work in the cottonfields.'

'That's true.'

'Anyway, don't publish it. Destroy it unread.'

The office was comfortable, even tasteful, but diligently unluxurious (Balfour enjoyed saying, as an ordinary publisher would not enjoy saying, that his operation was non-profit-making), and you were allowed to smoke in it. A communist could hardly forbid smoking. As well as communists, sick people, the racially inferior—the unnecessary mouths, the life unworthy of life—the German state killed malingerers, trouble-makers, shirkers and grumblers. But not smokers. Richard might have faced the ultimate penalty for grumbling, but not for smoking. Hitler disapproved of smoking. Stalin didn't, apparently. When the Russians were repatriating the wanderers of Europe, when the war was over, every itinerant under their care was granted an astonishingly—almost an unsmokably—generous allowance of tobacco: even children, even babies. Balfour paid Richard very generously for his one day a week.

45

'I think we might have found a rather promising poet. Rather striking, for a first collection.'

'Sling it over,' said Richard.

Who was aware that if he worked here two days a week instead of one he would be finished, humanly, within a year. Braced at first by the Saharas and Gobis of talentlessness which hourly confronted him, Richard now knew this stuff for what it was. It wasn't bad literature. It was anti-literature. Propaganda, aimed at the self. Richard's novels might have been unreadable, but they were novels. Whereas the finished typescripts, print-outs and flabby exercise books that lay around him here just hadn't made it out of some more primitive form: diary, dreamjournal, dialectic. As in a ward for the half-born, Richard heard these creatures' cries, and felt their unviewable spasms, convulsed in an earlier version of being. They shouldn't be looked at. They really shouldn't be looked at.

Balfour said with infinite circumspection, 'And how is your—how is your latest?'

'Nearly done.' And he didn't go on to add—because he couldn't see that far ahead, because men can't see further than the next fight or fuck—that his latest might be his last. Not just couldn't see: couldn't look. That couldn't be looked at either.

'If for any reason you don't find a home for it, I would of course be proud to publish it under the Tantalus imprint.'

Richard could see himself ending his days with Balfour. This presentiment was becoming more and more common—habitual, reflexive. Endings his days with Balfour, with Anstice, with J. C. Squires, that bus-conductress, that postman, that meter maid. Richard the haggard and neurotic ex-prettyboy, in an airless pool of batch or spinst, sparing and unpredictable with his sexual favours, vain, hideous and sullen, and very fussy about his China tea.

'I know you would, Balfour.'

'We could do it on subscription. Make a list. Starting with your friends.'

'Thanks. Thanks. But it's got to take its chances. It's got to sink or swim.'

Sink or swim in what? In the universal.

9

In the octagonal library, seated in a French armchair, Gwyn
Barry *frowned down* at the chessboard. Frowned down at it, as if
some gangly photographer had just said, 'Could you like *frown
down* at it? Like you're really concentrating?' Actually there were
no photographers present. Only Richard, who, seated opposite,
and playing black, made a move, N (QB5)–K6 in the old notation,
N(c4)–e5 in the new, and let his peripheral vision feast on the
Sunday *LAT*, which lay on a nearby sofa in encouraging disarray.
The room was tall and narrow, something of a miniature folly; it
felt like the chamber of a beautiful gun or antique missile—the six
facets of inlaid bookcases, and then the two facing windows, like
blanks. Now Richard gave Gwyn's hair an exasperated glance (so
thick and pewtery—the hair of a palpable charlatan) before his
eyes returned, in brief innocence, to the board. He was a pawn up.

'Do you take the *LAT*?' he said wonderingly.

Gwyn seemed to lose the tempo, or the opposition—he paused
awkwardly before replying. Richard's last move was of the kind
that presents the adversary with a strictly local, and eventually
soluble, problem. An adequate—a more than adequate—answer
was available. Richard had seen it as his fingers retreated from the
piece. Gwyn would see it, too, in time.

'No,' said Gwyn. 'Some stupid bugger sent it to me.'

'Why?'

'With a note saying, "Something here to interest you." No
page-number, mind. No marks or anything. And look at it. It's
like a bloody knapsack.'

'How ridiculous. Who was it?' said Richard.

'I don't know. Signed "John". Big help that is. I know loads
of people called John.'

'I always thought it must be quite handy being called John.'

'Why?'

'You can tell when you're going nuts.'

Gwyn looked at him.

'I mean, a real sign of megalomania, when a John starts
thinking that "John" will do. "Hi. It's John." Or: "Yours ever,

John." So what? *Everybody's* called John.'

Gwyn found and made the best reply. The move was not just expedient; it had the accidental effect of clarifying White's position. Richard nodded and shuddered to himself. He had forced Gwyn into making a good move: this seemed to happen more and more frequently, as if Richard was somehow out of time, as if Gwyn was playing in the new notation while Richard toiled along with the old.

'It being LA,' said Gwyn, 'I thought there may be an item about the movie deal. On *Stumbling*.'

'What "movie" deal?'

'TCT are doing it.'

' . . . Gwyn. That's Welsh for John, isn't it?'

'No. Euan. That's Welsh for John.'

'Spelt?'

'E, u, a, n.'

'How perfectly disgusting,' said Richard.

He looked down at the sixty-four squares—at this playing field of free intelligence. Oh yeah? So the intelligence was free, then, was it? Well it didn't *feel* free. The chess set before them on the glass table happened to be the most beautiful that Richard had ever used, or ever seen. For some reason he had neglected to ask how Gwyn acquired it, and anxiously assumed it was an heirloom of Demi's. For surely Gwyn, left to his own devices (his taste, and many thousands of pounds) would have come up with something rather different: in which the pieces consist of thirty-two more or less identical slabs of quartz/onyx/osmium; or else are wincingly florid and detailed—the Windsor castles, the knights with rearing forelegs and full horsebrass, the practically life-sized bishops with crooks and pointy hats and filigreed bibles. No. The set was in the austere measure, the chessmen delightfully solid and firmly moored on their felt (even the pawns were as heavy as revolvers), and the board of such proportion that you did indeed feel like a warrior prince on a hilltop, dispatching your riders with their scrolled messages, and pointing through the morning mist, telescope raised. And not a drop of blood being shed. That's how the valley had looked two minutes ago: Field of the Cloth of Gold. Now it resembled some sanguinary disgrace from a disease-rich era, all pressed men, all rabble, the drunken cripples reeling, the lopped tramps twitching and retching in the ditch. Richard was now staring at what any reasonable player would recognize as a lost position. But he would not lose. He had never lost to Gwyn. He could go on smoking and drinking and failing and hating for decades yet, and never lose to Gwyn.

They exchanged knights.

'So what happened? I suppose you could have just chucked the whole thing out . . . The *LAT*. What's the matter with you?'

In formulating this last question Richard had slightly stressed the personal pronoun. For Gwyn was doing something that he did more and more often, these days, something that made Richard's neck throb with sudden mumps of loathing. Gwyn was inspecting an object—in this case, the black knight—as if he had never seen it before. With infant wonder in his eyes. As a *writer* might. Richard really couldn't sit there: opposite someone pretending to be innocent.

'It's a chess piece,' said Richard. 'It's a knight. It's made of wood. It looks like a horse.'

'No,' said Gwyn, placing the piece with his other captures, 'I found it in the end.'

'Found what?'

Gwyn looked up. 'The thing about me. The thing that was meant to interest me in the *LAT*.'

Richard ducked back to the board.

'My glance just fell on it. Luckily. I could have been slaving through that thing all bloody week.'

Demi was entering the room, or crossing it: the library lay between the two drawing-rooms. She moved past them with reverent stealth, actually tiptoeing for the central few strides, with knees naïvely raised. Big, blonde, unbohemian, unsatirical, but not quite the other thing either (unburnished, unrefined), Demi performed her tiptoe without ease and without talent. Like the not so natural parent, playing a children's game. Richard thought of the flash accountant he had unnecessarily and temporarily hired, after the American sale of *Aforethought*: how, during the appointment at his place, he had made a show of jovially chasing his daughter from the room, with a jangle of keys and coins, with knees raised, past the modern first editions and the texts of tax . . .

She paused at the far door.

'Brrr,' said Demi.

'Hi, Demi.'

'It's not very warm in here.'

Gwyn turned her way, his eyes bulging uxoriously. To Richard he looked like a clairvoyant who, as a matter of policy, was keen to demystify his profession.

'Why not put a cardy on, love.'

'Brrr,' said Demi.

Richard got his head down and, with infinite grief, started working to a different plan.

For the next ten days, with almost unprecedented clarity and focus, Richard worked hard: reading the *LAT*.

No, he didn't get Gwyn's copy off him ('Are you finished with that?'), nor did he crouch each midnight by the Barry dustbins, waiting for the significant ten-gallon bag. He was of course prepared for such stratagems. Instead he went and bought another one, incurring the familiar inconvenience and expense, down in Blackfriars.

He knew the thing backwards by now anyway. But here it came again. Books, Arts, Entertainment. Real Estate, Appointments, Sports. Poise, Style, Flair. Where next? He read everything from the cookery column (egg and chips à la mode de Gwyn Barry?) to the crossword clues (Wry grab stumbles to NY? 4,5). Every ten or fifteen minutes with a bedraggled gesture he flung aside whatever section he happened to be busying himself with, convinced that he had been rumbled and finessed—that the *LAT* was innocently, was poutingly Gwyn-free. And the little Taff had pulled a flanker on him. But Richard persisted. During this period he reviewed no books: not a single slim volume, or tremulous novella, no quickie socio-cultural pamphlet, no brief life.

Late in the evening of the tenth day he found it. Page eleven, column three: the personals page, in Classified. It went like this:

'Stephanie'. Pet Adoptions. Rottweiler 1 yr. Gentle girl. Summertown. Wanted. First ed. of novel by G. Barry. Swap-Meet Garage Yard Sale. All welc.

GRANTA

NEIL STEINBERG
THE SPELLING BEE

A t kindergarten, we make milk into butter. We locate our homes on a map with coloured pins. We dress up for Hallowe'en and parade through the school in our costumes. We sit cross-legged on the floor and sing songs while our teacher plays the piano. On rainy days, we make a big boat out of blocks.

And one day, we are given mimeographed sheets of paper with an outline of the letter 'A', surrounded by illustrations of an apple, an airplane and other 'A' words. The mimeographed sheet is a vague purplish blue, and smells wonderful. We take out our jumbo crayons and begin to colour it.

Up to that point, we are all equal in the eyes of the school. Though differing wildly in our background, ability and potential, we find ourselves kneeling at the same starting line. There are no slow learners, no gifted classes. No one has failed, and no one has been singled out for honour. We receive our 'A' hand-outs, hold them up to our noses, sniff their narcotic chemical air and begin to colour. And we are never equal again.

1

The National Spelling Bee is a contest open to all students under the age of sixteen who have not passed beyond the eighth grade. It is sponsored by the Scripps Howard newspaper chain, with another 200 or so other newspapers as local and regional sponsors.

Each year, about nine million children enter the bee, attracted by the prospect of scholarships, prizes and trips to Washington, DC. Out of the nine million children, 8,999,999 will lose, and they will lose in a public and humiliating fashion. It would be hard to think of a way of making failure more demeaning, short of letting a quartet of circus clowns drive deficient spellers from the stage with flappy paddles.

The first spelling bee I attend, at the Northwood Junior High School, outside of Chicago, is one of the preliminary rounds. In the hallway is a poster. IF YOU CAN SPELL, YOU CAN WIN. THE 1993 CHICAGO TRIBUNE CHICAGOLAND SPELLING BEE. The poster, done in *Tribune* blue, has bees and honeycombs on it, and is intriguing in some way I can't immediately identify. Then it hits me. The *Tribune*. Simplified Spelling. In 1934, the owner of the *Tribune*, Colonel Robert McCormick, decided that the language of Shakespeare, Poe and Whitman was too idiosyncratic and sloppy for his fine publication ('The World's Greatest Newspaper') and that, in the name of efficiency (a quality the *Tribune* so admired in the Germans), it should be cleaned up. Thus was a new, efficient vocabulary created: 'fantom', 'lether', 'crum', 'tho', 'trafic', 'dialog', 'frate' and seventy-three other simplified words. The policy governed the *Tribune*'s spelling until McCormick died more than twenty years later (although even then it clung to certain spellings—'tho', 'thru', 'thoro', 'cigaret'—which, from the lofty height of Tribune Tower, 'appear to have won widespread acceptance'—according to its editorial of 21 August 1955; it was not until the late 1970s that the *Tribune* abandoned its dream).

No one in the Northwood Junior High School auditorium seems to appreciate the irony of the *Tribune*'s sponsorship. The auditorium is where the bee is to be held. It is already full of students: classes from each grade level have filled the seven sets of bleachers pulled out from the cinderblock wall.

Neil Codell, the principal, appears—a friendly, small and handsome man with oiled hair, like a basketball coach. His eyes are dark and alert, scanning the room, ready to spot trouble. After his school has settled down, he delivers a brief speech.

'We want to welcome all of you today to observe and enjoy this year's school spelling bee. In the spirit of competition and participation, you as students know what our expectations are. If we find that you cannot live up to our expectations as an audience member, you will find yourself removed from today's assembly and a parent will be called. I need not say more. Please remember we do not want you cheering wildly, or at all, for any individual students.'

The principal introduces the contestants. When the name Jonathan Niehof is announced, it is greeted with wild cheering. Sruti Nadimpalli also gets her share of applause. I know Sruti—the local champion—and have met her family. The principal utters a dark warning: 'Remember, your noise influence could cause a contestant to make a mistake.'

Contestants can ask for a word to be defined and for its

nation of origin. They can also ask to have its root confirmed—for instance, whether the root of 'humanitarian' is 'human'. In round eleven, one contestant asks for the definition of 'existential'. I lean forward slightly in anticipation. The best understanding I have involves Sartre wanting to puke whenever he sees an oak tree, and that can't be right. But I get no closer to the truth. 'A state or fact of being, of existence, of existentialism,' the teacher reads, none too helpfully, stumbling three times over the last word.

By round twelve, only Jon Niehof and Sruti Nadimpalli are left. They duel through rounds thirteen, fourteen, fifteen, sixteen and seventeen; and in round eighteen, Jon blows 'relinquish'. To win, Sruti must now spell two words correctly: one to match Jon, and the other to defeat him. The auditorium is quiet as Sruti spells 'melancholy' and then knocks off 'authentic' for the victory. There is a loud howl from Jon's supporters, while Sruti gets wild cheers from hers.

As the students begin to leave, the principal makes another little speech.

'Congratulations to all the contestants. And we now know that next year we will finally have a new champ. But this year, three years straight, Sruti Nadimpalli, defending her crown . . . '

In the hall, dense with children, a teacher scolds one of her charges: 'You're entitled to your opinion, but you should congratulate her anyway.'

2

Three weeks after the bee at Northwood, I have followed Sruti to the next round and to another affluent suburb. This is the County finals, which are being held at South Park Elementary School.

Students are met in the teacher's lounge by the principal, Mrs Denise Nielsen-Hall, a very large woman, who checks their names off in a register and hands out name tags and numbered white cards to be hung around the neck along with a fancy little flower arrangement.

'It makes it a little festive,' she explains of the boutonnières.

Each has a little bee alighting on the flowers. The bees, she adds, were ordered especially for her by a florist.

Despite this enthusiastic flourish, Mrs Nielsen-Hall has reservations about spelling bees. 'They're public and traumatic, and I don't like them very much,' she says. 'There were maybe twenty kids at the last bee we had. We got down to the last four children. I gave a word to one of the little girls, and she misspelled it. She became so frantic she ran from the stage into the audience, into her parents' arms. We carried on, and when I gave the next word, she turned around and in front of two hundred people she screamed at me: "That word is easier than the word you gave me!" It was terrible.'

In her opening address, Mrs Nielsen-Hall tells the students, 'You're all winners, because you're here tonight,' a concept parroted again and again by bee officials, and one at complete cross-purposes with what the bee is doing—that is, weeding out the losers and creating increasingly smaller sets of winners who move on to lose at higher levels.

I wonder about the necessity of the lie. Children are smart; they know they are not all winners. They will not all win and move on to the state championship. What they have done is win to get here, and thus they have accomplished something whether they move on or not. Too bad Mrs Nielsen-Hall couldn't just come out and say that—'By the time tonight is over, most of you will have lost, but just because you have lost do not feel like a loser, because by struggling to get here you will have attained a private victory.' It seems a much healthier sentiment. And a more honest one.

As a bee unfolds, one is always confronted with some previously unimagined marvel, and tonight it is in the form of Mr Bill Cloud, an older ruddy-faced man, introduced as 'a professional spelling bee pronouncer.' Mr Cloud introduces his wife, Madge, who is also a pronouncer and will share his duties. He then begins an earnest explanation of every aspect of the bee rules delivered in a mellifluous, calm, bell-clear voice.

'I cannot tell you how many unexpected things can occur,' he says.

There is a practice round. The second speller, Sunnie Levin, who holds a lucky troll is given the word 'nozzle'. 'Nozzle?'

Sunnie asks.

Mr Cloud repeats the word, in an achingly precise way. Sunnie then spells it correctly.

Mr Cloud turns to address the audience. 'You will notice that when she said "nozzle" in a questioning way, I did not say "Yes",' he says. 'Mrs Cloud and I will never say "Yes"; we will only repeat the word. The reason is that we might not be thinking of the same word the contestant said. So we'll never verify anything you say. We'll always just repeat the word if you wish us to repeat it.'

Round one of the bee proper is a killer. George Holdcroft adds an 'e' to 'ransom', takes his certificate and is out before seven o'clock. The programme states that all contestants are required to remain until the contest is completed, but the rule is ignored. John Evans, a dignified, husky-voiced fat boy with a buzz haircut, misses 'worthwhile'. He has a vacant, stunned expression as he slowly walks down the centre aisle. I want to follow him, ask him something, probe his emotional state, but I can't do it. I watch John and his family put on their coats and leave. No point in holding a mirror to their misery; it's all too clear.

Matthew Briddell misspells 'dullard' and goes to sit by his mom. She rubs his back comfortingly. 'It's OK,' she says. Together they examine the certificate, as if it is an object of great detail and interest.

To my surprise, no child reacts violently to defeat, although each conveys some small message of disappointment or sadness. Winifred Alves gives a slight nervous smile when she misses 'resistible'. Patrick Putnam misspells 'pleurisy' and does a sort of rolling turn away from the microphone, leading with his head, as if he has been shot.

During a break, I seek out Mr and Mrs Cloud. They are teachers from a high school in a distant suburb of Chicago. They've taken many courses in linguistics and phonetics and the history of language. They get paid well for their work this evening—600 dollars for the pair. Over time, Mr Cloud says, he has observed that the winners are usually those who have worked the hardest. He also imparts a bit of insider cut-throat spelling-bee strategy. Sometimes, he says, a speller will ask the derivation of a word just to see what part of the dictionary it is in—whether Mr

Cloud turns to the front for 'f' or more towards the back for 'ph', for instance.

George Holdcroft's mom comes up, almost laughing.

'My poor guy,' she says. 'He studied all those words. He knew all the advanced words. He goes to me, "Oh, I knew ransom." He was the first one out.'

Mr Cloud is used to this. 'That's too bad,' he coos. 'What grade is he in? Fifth? Oh, he'll be back.'

Unable to contain myself, I ask her how her son felt to be the first one out. 'Awful, probably,' she says, dismissively. 'He was sitting there with me, he could spell all the other words.' Then Mrs Holdcroft reveals her true purpose—would a list of the words used in the bee be available? Mr Cloud tells her no.

By round four, most of the contestants have been eliminated. Robert Zwirner, a kid who looks as though he's wearing a frown mask, is given 'succotash', which he pronounces crisply and begins spelling confidently. 'C-U . . . ' He stops. He knows. He shakes his head disbelievingly. You cannot correct yourself at the bee. The end of the word is spelled quickly, in a crushed whisper, 'C-C-O-T-A-S-H.'

Mr Cloud is sympathetic. 'The correct spelling is—by the way, you knew that, didn't you?—the correct spelling is S-U-C-C-O-T-A-S-H.'

The bee proceeds, but on Robert's face, an amazing thing happens. He smiles, for the first time that night, a big, bright smile, his expression transforming him back into a child as he takes his seat in the audience.

Four contestants are left by round twelve. Number twenty-two, Bob Berman, a chubby little boy in a blue and white striped shirt, buttoned at the wrists but untucked at the waist, is shaping up to be Sruti's toughest competition. He stands very straight, almost at attention, shoulders square, head level, his little fists on his hips, and methodically spells 'encroachment'. In the next round, he spells 'lanolated'. He is a rock.

There is a break before round sixteen. The students return to a much tougher world. A spelling bee is, first and foremost, a show, and should it begin to drag, the organizers are quick to bring out the heavy artillery to slay the stragglers. Sruti starts the round carefully spelling 'armigerous', but 'kaolinize' hangs in the air in front of Jordanna Grant like a palpable menace. She asks for a definition and is told that it is to convert a feldspar mineral into a fine white clay. She doesn't get close. Foluso Williams misses 'exaration'—an act or a product of writing—and, looking glum, is out.

Two are left, Bob and Sruti. There is a pause, and I imagine the tough words being slipped out of their lead-lined cases. The silent atmosphere of expectation is broken, however, as Mr Cloud stumbles on the first monster word, 'decumbiture'. When asked, he gives the definition as 'the time of taking to one's bed because of sickness.'

Bob works out the word, squeezing his eyes shut, and then spells it correctly. There are gasps and whoops and applause from the audience. Bob looks around, beaming, as if he can't believe it himself.

Mr Cloud again stumbles, over 'cruciferous', and Sruti knocks it down with a minimum of fuss. Bob is given 'nictitant', adds an initial 'k' and is out. Sruti must spell one more word, 'scurrilous'. It is too easy. She receives long, hearty applause, and the bee is over.

There is a quick ceremony. The runner-up gets a trophy and his school gets an identical one, so the accomplishment 'will be long remembered there.'

3

The state championships are held on a greyish spring day in an auditorium on the seventh floor of the Tribune Tower, a gothic horror show of a building, festooned with flying buttresses, peaked cornices, fleurs-de-lis and vaulted doorways.

With an hour to go before the bee, there's time to wander around the dark wood-panelled hallways. A mother is amazed that all spelling lists have to be checked in at the door, like guns in a Western saloon. 'What's the idea?' she says to her son, who is eating a big cookie. 'They think I'm going to cheat for you? That I could tell you the right spellings by sign language?' She wiggles her fingers in imitation of some complicated sign code.

I discover Mr Cloud lounging with other officials. We strike up a conversation, and Mr Cloud asks me what I'm writing about. I have barely uttered a sentence when a red-faced, portly man butts in. He turns out to be Casey Banas, education correspondent from the *Tribune* and one of the judges. 'You're going to say spelling bees are a failure,' he sputters angrily, his fists doubled up as though he is about to punch me. I try to reassure him that what I hope to write about is how kids cope with failure, then beat a hasty retreat, marvelling that a man with such a stevedore temperament can cover anything, let alone education.

I sit down and scope out the room, which is richly appointed with *Tribune* lucre. Twenty-one brass chairs with green cushions are arranged before a brown velvet curtain.

Behind me, two people are talking. One is complaining.

'Look how close we are to the front row,' she says, in a flat, nasal voice, referring to the distance between the audience and the contestants' chairs. 'I don't like this.'

'You're just going to have to block us out,' says an older woman—her mother, I assume. 'Look over people's heads.'

I turn in my chair, as though casually scanning the room, to see who it is behind me. It is number nineteen, Janelle Jensen, who has a disconcertingly adult look to her, a pinched, sour expression, set off by her hooded eyes and her secretary's outfit: blouse, skirt, hoop earrings, high heels. She could pass for forty.

The contestants take their chairs at the front. Maureen Martino, from the *Tribune*'s public relations department, trots out the standard bee philosophy of universal victory.

'Whoever wins the championship, we all go home winners,' she says. 'Just remember that.' Then she warns parents not to mouth words, even to themselves, lest their children be disqualified.

Mr Cloud is looking more like a banker than a teacher—expensive loafers, a charcoal suit. He paces as he gives his introductory speech.

'Good luck to all of you,' he concludes and then turns to the audience. 'They really are all winners, and by the way, so are you, parents and teachers.'

Round one passes without incident. 'Madge, would you go

get us a hotel room. This is going to take a couple of weeks,' Mr Cloud jokes.

The first person out is number eight, Shawna Hammons from downstate. She misses 'conveyance' and, showing no emotion, sits down in the front row.

The competition proceeds, with students dropping out in every round, none in any dramatic way. In round three, Byron Barnes is given 'pompadour'. His mom purses her lips tight, clamps her right hand across her chest and rocks to and fro. Byron stands very still. He asks for the definition, for the sentence, for the origin. He thinks, then spells the word correctly. He smiles broadly. His mother lets out her breath. Byron has inherited her nerves. In between turns at the microphone, he makes gentle, silent clapping motions with his hands, as if to dry them off.

Fifteen people are left at the beginning of round five.

Sruti spells 'perennate'. Jacob Gordon Schlosburg, who has a haughty, bored expression, snaps out 'repêchage' as if he has a train to catch.

Sruti spells 'feracious'. In round seven, Byron Barnes goes out on 'dodecuplet'. He has a hazy, faraway smile as he takes his seat next to his parents. Sruti spells 'smorgasbord'. Jacob spells 'idiosyncratically' and nods at the 'That is correct,' as if to say, 'Damn right that is correct, lady.'

Nine are left at round eight. Sruti spells 'tatami'. She spells 'prejudicial'. She spells 'phosphorescence'. She spells 'pterodactyl'. She spells 'cronyism'. Fellow contestant Jessica Delfert looks at her in something like wonder as she spells 'adjuvant'.

The bee grinds on. Sruti spells 'jurimetrician'.

Before round seventeen there is a short break. Casey Banas stands up, hitches his pants around his gut and grunts dismissively, 'All girls left.'

There are six contestants remaining, and they hold out, round after round. Sruti spells 'psychrometer'. She spells 'pignorate'.

Before round twenty-three, Mrs Cloud visits the judges. I anticipate a fusillade of lethal words and am not disappointed. Contestants spell 'suspirious', 'caladium', 'paranee', 'bilander'. Finally, Jessica Delfert goes out on 'enfilade'. She sits down next to her mom and cries.

It happens in round twenty-seven. Sruti gets 'desinence'. She stammeringly asks for the word to be used in a sentence and takes a stab at it. 'I'm sorry, that is incorrect,' says Mrs Cloud. Sruti, glumly playing with her bracelet, goes back to her seat in the front row and puts her head on her mother's shoulder. She starts to weep.

In round thirty-six, Leah Petrusiak, a red-haired girl with bumblebee earrings who delivers her spellings in a flat monotone, is faced with 'transcendental'. Leah goes through the routines. She asks for the word to be repeated. She asks for a definition, for it to be used in a sentence, its word origin. She then asks for it to be repeated again. And again.

She spells the word, apparently without the 'c', yet it is deemed correct. A murmur breaks out in the audience, and the judges quickly ask for the tape to be played back. A moment later it booms in perfect clarity, from expensive *Tribune* speakers. Leah sits with her hands at the sides of her face, agonizing. The 'c' is clearly dropped. Mr Cloud asks for the tape to be played again. The phrase 'torturing her' is heard from a member of the audience. Finally, Mrs Cloud says, 'I'm sorry, that is incorrect,' and gives the correct spelling.

In round thirty-eight, Cheryl Oliver misses 'bastion'. Jo Marie Sison spells 'metamorphosis' and 'jingoistic' and is the champion.

The *Tribune*'s Maureen Martino has returned to hand out certificates to the contestants. She leaves the audience with this thought: 'You're all going home winners, just remember that. On behalf of the *Chicago Tribune*, I'd like to thank you for supporting the Chicagoland Tribune Spelling Bee.'

Sruti is still crying. I quiz a few of the losers and beat it.

4

In Washington DC, the afternoon before the 66th Annual Scripps Howard National Spelling Bee, the Presidential Ballroom at the Capital Hilton is all set up. It has an eerie, empty stillness. The 235 spellers will sit in four long rows of beigish pink chairs that stretch across the entire length of the ballroom, elevated on bleachers. Just in front is some sort of dais, for the judges and pronouncer. Then there are the long tables covered in white linen, with water pitchers and glasses. This is where the members of the press will sit. The parents will be exiled to an ancillary room, cut off by a square proscenium arch. They will follow the action on four big televisions.

In the press room, I find three Scripps Howard staffers—college kids in bee T-shirts. They are hanging out, and, identifying myself and my purpose, I join them. 'You have to meet Mr Bee,' says Ellen Morrison, a DePauw University senior, taking me up to a three-foot-high wooden and wire bee fetish. Mr Bee has a pleasing, 1950s feel.

We have a wide-ranging conversation about the bee. The staffers are surprisingly loose with what they say. Joel Pipkin, a recent graduate from Midwestern State University, suggests that the bee is a good way for junior high kids to pick each other up—he has seen contestants holding hands. Just joking, he adds quickly. They tell me about kids falling off the stage, and about the Comfort Room, a chamber off the ballroom where the failed contestants are immediately led to compose themselves after missing their words.

'You won't be allowed in because the kids will be upset,' says Shannon Harris, another DePauw student.

'And because you're a journalist,' adds Ellen Morrison, who seems to have a thing against journalists.

They are so forthcoming with damning details that I find myself laboriously warning them that I am a journalist. 'You understand,' I keep saying, 'that I'm a writer. I'm talking to you because I'm writing an article which will be published and which the general public will then read.' Normally, this speech is reserved for people I suspect of having limited mental capacity, given in the hope of helping them understand that I am listening to everything they say and reducing the chances of their being surprised when they see their words in print later on.

The next morning, I get to the bee early. The first person I run into is Ellen Morrison, barely recognizable in her peach publicist's suit and done-up hair. She flaps up to me, a flurry of concern, worried that I will quote her candid comments of the day before 'out of context'.

The concept of being quoted out of context was invented, I believe, by people who blurt out ill-advised statements and then regret them. I try to reassure Ellen that most journalists are not out to skewer innocent subjects. The beauty of the profession is that the guilty always find a way to hang themselves.

As if to prove my point, Ellen takes me into the Comfort Room, which I had asked to see beforehand since I will not be allowed to enter it once the bee begins.

She gives me a quick tour of the narrow, elegant little room. Her narration, in the best and most in-context transcription I can make off my tape, is as follows, beginning with her pointing out a few objects in the room: 'Mr Bee. Food. Dictionary. Parents are allowed back here. No journalists are allowed back here. We'll have some upset kids back here. Usually we have a curtain across the middle so that the ones who are crying hide behind it and shiver like rhesus monkeys. You know: *wooo, ooo, ooo*.'

I ask about the punching bags rumoured to be a Comfort Room feature, intended to dissipate excess zeal.

'We normally have punching bags, but last year the bag we used deflated—someone punched it too hard—so I'm not sure if they're going to replace it this year,' she says.

At this point, she decides that we have lingered, and signals that the interview is over by snapping, 'Enough? Enough?' In the hallway, she gives me permission to sit on the ballroom steps and again expresses concern about what I'm going to write. 'We're proud of our bee, and we think it will measure up—we can take on anyone!' she says, the last part in a triumphant, emphatic whisper. Immediately, she has second thoughts about what she has just said. 'Don't quote me! Don't quote me!' she urges. I assure her that it wasn't such a bad thing to say. We discuss the possibility that a vindictive Scripps Howard will track her down and 'get' her, and I reassure her that by the time the public gets to read the piece, she will have probably moved beyond the grasp of that organization and into somebody else's employment. She agrees, and we part company.

By eight a.m., the action is getting underway. The parents' section is packed. How early, I wonder, does one have to stake out seats to get one in the front row?

The answer turns out to be 5.45 a.m.

By eight-fifteen, the 235 spellers are in their neat rows. None seems particularly tense—you don't get this far without seriously mastering your emotions. There are opening statements. The tame concept of 'winner' has been abandoned in favour of the more regal 'champion'.

'No matter what happens today and tomorrow, each is already a champion,' a bee official tells the assembled company. This constant reinterpretation of the meaning of victory, coupled with the utter disregard for the definition of the words being spelled, reinforces my growing view of the bee as a near-Orwellian mockery of the idea that words convey meaning. It is like a contest where people hold books at arm's length and guess their weight.

Today's pronouncer, Dr Alex J. Cameron, has a forbidding, wall-eyed look to him, but his opening remarks are soothing and intelligent.

'I suppose the real purpose of my standing here for a few minutes is to begin to let the spellers get used to the sound of my voice,' he begins, in a clear, though not exaggerated, manner. 'They will eventually hear entirely too much of that sound.'

He explains how the English language is peculiarly constructed to make spelling both possible and challenging, and how American society developed as to bring about so unusual a phenomenon as spelling bees.

'They came out of grass-roots beginnings, mostly small communities,' he says. 'I have begun to suspect that for the nineteenth-century, the upwardly mobile lower-middle class with ambitions saw the bee as a way of asserting their access to education and to the American Dream.'

Cameron doesn't mention it, but what was true for the nineteenth century is also true for the end of the twentieth. The bee retains its appeal as a symbol of the American Dream. A full quarter of the contestants come from ethnic immigrant families—Chinese, Koreans, Thais, Cambodians, Hispanics and subcontinental Indians. They are the same crowd that excels at schools across the country, their families having instilled in them the fierce drive to succeed.

Cameron finishes with a more thoughtful version of the

'you're all winners' speech, recounting the awesome arithmetic of the culling process performed by the bee.

'A few short months ago there were ten million of you. Somewhere along the line that number got cut down to the relatively few people who showed up at your regional bees. The regional bees contained less than one per cent of that original nine or ten million people. By the time you get to this stage, that percentage is down to a much, much smaller number . . .

'You've won. You've moved all the way to the top. From this point, who is second, twenty-sixth and two hundredth is, well, part of the game you are going to play to show off for your parents.' Here there is grateful laughter. 'Our point here is to have a little fun. As soon as breakfast settles down at least, have a little fun.'

Shortly before nine, the bee commences, with an appropriately dramatic flourish.

'Are we ready on the tapes? Are we ready on the records desk? Dr Cameron, are you ready?' says a bee official. 'All right then, will speller number one, April Donahower, representing the *Intelligencer Journal* from Lancaster, Pennsylvania, please step to the microphone.'

With a little hesitation, April spells her word, 'bulimic'. The word is actually something of an anomaly, because most of the words in the first round are of the sort never encountered by speakers of the English language: 'thanatophidia', 'abiogenist', 'strongylid', 'deunsere', 'toolach', 'sacalait', 'nastaliq'. These are the words that get cut when dictionaries are abridged. A full quarter of the group are knocked out in the first round.

The speller after April Donahower is the first out. Number two, a small girl from Maryland named Jennifer Sri, mangles 'chalaza'. She gives a brave smile and, hands straight at her sides, walks the fifty feet between the microphones and the door, where she is greeted by a bee staffer whose job it is to smile, shake her hand, throw a sisterly arm over her shoulder and lead her to the Comfort Room. It is 9.02 a.m., the first day.

There is only so much one can take of this. After a few dozen contestants, I head out into the hall and track down Jennifer Sri. She is guarded and candid at the same time. 'I kinda knew I spelled it wrong because it didn't sound right,' she says. 'I didn't really feel anything. I just kinda felt really bad. I studied that word. I remembered that word. I just didn't spell it right.'

The spellers all seem to gauge their defeats by whether they knew the word and had studied it, or whether the word was utterly unfamiliar, the latter case being the much easier to live with.

Passing by the Comfort Room, the entrance to which is shielded by a blue curtain, I sometimes hear the sound of compressing, air-sucking sobs. It occurs to me that not only does the Comfort Room protect the overwrought contestants from the prying eye of the media, but it also eliminates the possibility of embarrassing footage of hysterical children appearing on the evening news.

From time to time, I encounter one of the college volunteers. Ellen Morrison is smiling at somebody's baby, happy in a carrier. 'We're grooming him for a future bee,' she says casually. Then she realizes she is talking to a journalist, and her mood swings into wild alarm. 'No! No we're not!' she babbles, and then, as if making an official statement: 'We do not groom babies for spelling bees.'

I spend the lunch break outside, under a lovely blue sky, and I find it almost impossible to return for the afternoon session. Re-entering the ballroom, I have a feeling of horror. The beads of moisture condensed on the cold metallic sides of the water pitchers. The stark, numbered signs, held by blue string. The children, inert, poised, waiting, staring vacantly into the distance, pounded into a fugue state by boredom. The media, most following their local champion, keeping score, writing down the spelling of each word as if they were going to compile them, as if the bee didn't have two people doing that already, documenting each misspelled letter for posterity.

I struggle to find meaning, some utility in this vast expenditure of effort. A child could learn to play the violin in the studying time it takes to get to the national bee. The best rationalization I can come up with is that the contestants are preparing themselves to be grilled by Senate sub-committees. The lights, the sombre judges, the give-and-take of pro forma questioning, the lob of the word, the return of the correct spelling.

By now I am getting up every ten minutes to walk through the halls. I run into Shannon Harris, the graduate from DePauw. She greets my observation that the bee has sunk into tedium by chirping, 'It never drags; it's spelling!' I look at her, astonished. A reporter meets lots of people in a state of debasement—coke-addict moms and their deformed children, crusty drunks in emergency wards, slobbering hookers wearing T-shirts as dresses—but none do I sympathize with less than the ambitious college grad who has sold her soul for a bad job.

The next day, the last one, the bee atmosphere is supercharged by the presence of the Cable News Network. In the hall, a table is loaded with equipment, mounds of black, snakelike connections, tiny intriguing monitors, joysticks and fade levers, around which no fewer than six people are always clustered, talking into headsets and flipping switches. The televisions set up in the hall and in the parents' ancillary room are no longer showing pictures from a single, amateur bee camera, but are now receiving the official CNN feed, which means that there are secondary shots of the loser walking towards the Comfort Room. Energized by the presence of CNN, the Scripps Howard people have regained their professional equilibrium and are leaving me alone.

Inside the ballroom, CNN has set up nineteen blinding lights, so bright that at least one speller puts on sunglasses, as do several members of the audience.

The Chicago city winner, Sophoan Khoeun, who escaped the Khmer Rouge with his family in 1984, misspells 'barbarism' and is out. He looks puzzled and walks off the stage.

Shortly after eleven, I notice a face I recognize in the audience. A careful study of my bee materials reveals she is Amanda Goad, fourteen, last year's bee winner. Bee rules forbid the winner from competing again, but she is back, anyway, in the audience with her mother. They wince simultaneously as number fourteen blows 'exhilarate' and sadly shake their heads. Both have pads of paper and pencils—Amanda is working out the words before the spellers, testing herself—and this, coupled with their air of wise serenity, gives them the look of a pair of racetrack touts.

Above: contestants in round one of the final of the 66th National Spelling Bee in Washington.

By 4.17 p.m., the eighth round, nineteen kids remain. One by one they go, defeated by 'dystopia', 'shandry', 'bathyscaphe', 'censer'. Number 138, David Urban from Amarillo, is given the word 'desiccation'. He asks, 'Does it come from the Latin word *desiccus*, meaning "dry"?' I want to cheer; for me, this seems the intellectual high point of the bee.

By the time only seven kids are left, the bee stops to prepare for the final moments. The rules are reviewed, and the families and official newspaper escorts are asked to come up and wait at the far right of the stage. A bee official informs everyone 'exactly what will happen at the moment a champion is crowned,' and I wonder if a real crown will be involved. I hope so.

There are three spellers left by round twelve and the pressure is high. Geoff Hooper spells 'phrasaical'. David spells 'contumelious'. Yuni Kim can't spell 'solipsism' quickly enough—she obviously knows it. In the next round she goes out on 'apotheosize'.

In round fifteen, Geoff is given 'enchilada', to groans and

Photo: J. Scott Applewhite (AP/Wide World Photos)

laughter from the audience. He asks for a definition anyway.

David misses 'renascent'.

Geoff needs one more word, and Dr Cameron gives him 'kamikaze'. Again, groans break out in the audience. He spells it, hands in pockets, laconically. A big, protracted cheer goes up.

The room dissolves into activity. Someone sets up three fat velvet ropes on pedestals in front of Geoff. He is handed an old-fashioned loving cup trophy. A stool is produced for him to sit on. No crown. About two dozen reporters and cameramen crowd in front of him to shout the standard questions.

I step on to the stage, fifty feet from where Geoff is being questioned, and turn to survey the audience, trying to gain some elevation, some perspective. Suddenly Ellen Morrison is at my elbow. 'No reporters on the stage,' she intones, in such a serious, emphatic way that for a moment I think she is joking. I decide not to give ground—let them come and arrest me. Take me to bee jail. Then I see Shannon Harris having the same conversation with the reporters closer to the fat velvet ropes, and it takes the fight right out of me. I move off, humiliated. Once I am on the floor, I look up at Ellen Morrison, trying to figure out what to say. 'No reporters on the stage,' she repeats, smiling maliciously. *I'm on the stage and you're not, nyah, nyah, nyay-nyah-nyah.*

I move into the audience and run into Amanda Goad and her mother. We talk about the bee. Both mother and daughter have an air of weary, concealed knowledge, giving the impression they could tell you a lot if they wanted to. Mrs Goad says her daughter would not have competed even if she had been allowed to. 'Once you reach the top in this, you don't want to try it again.'

They introduce me to Linda Tarrant, a woman who has devised a programme that takes the Scripps Howard 'Words of the Champions' list and pairs it with pronunciations and definitions.

'When my daughter in the third grade started spelling bees, I decided I didn't want her learning to spell words that are meaningless to her,' says Tarrant. 'It's pointless to learn words the Scripps Howard way. You'd be better off learning the

Opposite: Geoff Hooper, 14, winner of the 1993 Spelling Bee, with his parents and the vice-president of Scripps Howard.

telephone directory. At least you'd know who to call.'

Scripps Howard is claiming that its list of difficult words is in its copyright, and that Linda Tarrant is ripping it off.

As I leave the hotel, I run into a woman with an astronaut's wife hairdo and the emaciated, kohl-eyed look of a woman who smokes four packs a day and is going politely crazy. 'You have to wonder when he is given words like "enchilada" and "kamikaze",' she says meaningfully, in the tone people usually reserve for discussing second gunmen and grassy knolls. 'Did the pronouncer use a set list? And if not, what are we doing?'

She is just pointing out that the winner is—wouldn't you know? wink, wink—*from a Scripps Howard newspaper*, when I make my escape, explaining that I have a train to catch.

A t kindergarten, after the initial 'A' sheet, we get another letter to colour each day, and slowly we move forward, first as a pack, then separating ourselves into one of two groups: one consisting of the brighter kids, who will cruise through the Pilgrims, Henry Hudson, cursive and long division; and the other of the less bright, who will struggle in a desperate rearguard action to keep up.

We don't have a lot in common, and our wildly differing levels of ability become clearer day by day, but we are still kept together as a class, all in the same room, the same thirty people, for the first seven years of our education.

I was a bright kid, perhaps because of my own diligent efforts and deep intrinsic personal worth, or perhaps because my father was a nuclear physicist who crammed our house with books, and my mother marched me to the library and made me read.

The spelling bee is not the baroque horror I imagined, but it is a large-scale version of what goes on in schools all the time. And it is a sad process, a strange, adult ritual that magnifies the natural disappointments and frustrations of childhood to no discernible end. Good spelling is a handy skill, but ninety-nine per cent of good spelling is knowing when to use a dictionary. If I am a little shaky on the second vowel in 'separate', as I am from time to time, I don't squint my eyes and try to dredge the proper spelling out of some inner core. I look it up.

GRANTA

JULIAN BARNES
TRAP. DOMINATE. FUCK.

Sceptics maintain that live chess is as enthralling as watching paint dry. Ultra-sceptics reply: unfair to paint. As a theatrical experience it is austere and minimalist: two men, two chairs, a table and no dialogue. Yet for three months the cheapest seats at the Savoy were, by a long way, the most expensive cheap seats in any London theatre. Twenty pounds to watch *The Times* World Chess Championship from the stalls, thirty-five pounds from the upper circle, fifty-five pounds from the dress circle. This wasn't just greed speaking, or desperation on the part of Times Newspapers to recoup some of their estimated four-to-five-million-pound investment. It was also a genuine anticipation of domestic interest. For the first time in the modern history of the championship— deemed to have started with the 1886 match between Steinitz and Zukertort—a Briton had emerged as title contender. Nigel Short was also the first Westerner to contest the final since Bobby Fischer in 1972. Pre-Fischer, you had to go back to 1937 to find another Westerner, the Dutchman Max Euwe, post-Fischer, the only way to get into any of the seven World Championship matches was to be a Russian whose name began with K: Karpov, Korchnoi, Kasparov. Now, at last, there was a local boy to root for, and a serious underdog as well. Kasparov is constantly referred to as the strongest player in the history of the game; Short wasn't in the top ten. The size of his task could be estimated by the fact that even one of Kasparov's seconds, the Georgian grandmaster Zurab Azmaiparashvali, was ranked above him.

Gary Kasparov was, or was thought to be, a known quantity. He was the dynamic, aggressive and moody champion, much photographed lifting weights, thumping a punch bag, playing football and swimming on his 'Croatian island retreat'. He was the new-style Russian, from 'war-torn Baku'—the chum of Gorbachev, then of Yeltsin; easily packageable, and with the zippy nickname Gazza (by analogy with another Gazza). Nigel Short was the harder case for packaging, since, like many chess players, what he had mostly done in his twenty-eight years was play chess. Only two things appeared known about him: that he had once played in a teenage rock band called the Urge (originally titled Pelvic Thrust),

Opposite: Nigel Short.

and that he was now married to a Greek drama therapist seven years his senior. But then the phrase 'chess biography' is—as Truffaut once cattily remarked of the expression 'British film'—a contradiction in terms. Chess is, famously, an activity entirely unrelated to the rest of life: from this springs its fragile profundity. Biography theoretically links the private to the public in such a way that the former illuminates the latter. But in chess no such connection, or reductiveness, applies. Does grandmaster X prefer the French defence because his mother left his father when he was as yet a small child? Does bed-wetting lead to the Grunfeld? And so on. Freudians may see chess as Oedipal: an activity whose ultimate aim is to kill the king, and in which the sexy queen is dominant. But attempted match-ups between on-board and off-board character produce as many counter-indicators as corroborations.

Ruthless gutting of Cathy Forbes's *Nigel Short: Quest for the Crown* therefore added only a few small, irrelevant embellishments. Nigel had fallen into an Amsterdam canal as a child, and been mugged in his home city of Manchester at the age of twenty; his parents had separated when he was thirteen, and his frequently stated ambition was to become a Tory MP. It is an indicator of how scarily scant the record is when Ms Forbes is driven to record that, as a teenager, Nigel 'alarmed acquaintances by threatening to dye his hair blue.' An empty threat, as it turned out, though perhaps not entirely unhelpful to the putative psychobiographer, given that blue is the emblematic colour of the Conservative Party.

These exiguous and banal details were widely reproduced. Since chess players are on the whole neither charismatic nor polymorphous, it was comic to see the varying journalistic templates into which Short was excitedly fitted. For *Hello!* magazine, that tinned rice pudding of the newsstand, it was Nigel the family man, posing happily in his Greek retreat with wife, Rea, and little daughter, Kyveli. For the *Sun*, it was Nigel as modern British hero, who 'loves rock music and a pint with his mates . . . He stormed up the ranks but he didn't ignore his other passions— women and music.' Short dutifully posed for a laddish photo, hoof to plume in black leather, strutting his stuff among knee-high chess pieces while toting an electric guitar. Headline? IT'S ONLY ROOK AND ROLL BUT I LIKE IT. Harmless fun, and all that, but, at the same time, deeply unconvincing. Nigel, too, has a nickname, by the way. If Gary is Gazza, Nigel is Nosher. Etymology? 'Nigel Short' anagrams out schoolboyishly into Nosher L. Git.

Short is twenty-eight, Kasparov thirty, but judging from their pre-match press conferences you would guess at a much wider age differential. Short, a boyish figure in a bottle-green suit, with boffinish specs and cropped hair, cut a nervous, adolescent, halting figure, and spoke with the slightly strangulated vowels of one who has had speech therapy. He was accompanied on the podium by his manager and accountant, grandmaster Michael Stean (of whom it was once said that he thought about chess all the time except when he was actually playing it); Stean would occasionally lean over and deflect the trickier questions. There is, of course, no reason at all why a chess player should be good at PR; even so, the difference between Short and Kasparov was remarkable. For a start, the Russian has much better English than Nigel. He handled the conference by himself and with presidential ease; was just as much at home with geo-politics as with chess; attended courteously to questions he was mightily familiar with; and generally came across as a highly intelligent, worldly, rounded human being. In his many interviews and appearances, Short, by contrast, gave the impression of being thoughtful, considered, wise and precise when talking about chess, and barely adult when talking about anything other than chess. He brought to mind the remark of the great world champion Emanuel Lasker in his *Manual of Chess*: 'In life we are all duffers.'

The talking-up and colouring-in of the match entailed a certain half-hearted attempt at demonizing Kasparov. It has been a feature of all world championship matches since Fischer v Spassky that there has to be some goody–baddy, them-or-us aspect for the non-aficionado to get a handle on. So now the champion—hitherto presented as the applaudable outsider who had taken on Moscow Centre—was restyled as 'the last great beneficiary of the Soviet machine.' (Linguistic note: we may occasionally have had a 'programme'; they always had a 'machine'.) And the fact that Kasparov had assembled a strong team of ex-Soviet seconds was put down not just to the sinister continuance of 'the machine' but also to the money Kasparov had amassed during his reign. Short could therefore be depicted as the cash-strapped Western individualist, though in fact he was paying his coach Lubomir Kavalek 125,000 dollars for twenty weeks of work, with a promised victory bonus of the same amount. The political angle was also rejigged. The fact that Kasparov had moved on from being a Gorbachevian to a Yeltsinite prompted Short, the Tory hopeful, to denounce his opponent's politics as 'a fake'. The Englishman also chose a Reds-under-the-beds line in pre-match interviews by emphasizing the 'KGB connection'. This stated, first, that Kasparov had enjoyed the friendship and protection of a local KGB boss back in Azerbaijan; and, secondly, that he had received special training from the master manipulators in how to unsettle opponents. 'The story may be nonsense,' Short said of the latter claim, while happily rebroadcasting it to *The Times*, 'but it would be absolutely consistent.'

Nor was this all. Short and his camp deliberately promoted their man's personal dislike of Kasparov as a factor in the encounter. 'I find it hard to pinpoint the exact moment when Nigel Short first began to loathe Gary Kasparov,' Dominic Lawson, editor of the *Spectator* and a close friend of Short's, wrote in his own magazine. He made a pretty good job of it nonetheless, identifying an incident during a tournament in Andalucia in 1991, when Short had played a certain move against Kasparov and the world champion had responded by laughing. The Russian, Lawson revealed, also 'glares' at opponents and, according to Nigel, walks up and down in their line of vision 'deliberately . . . like a baboon.' Not that Short needed his friend as a mouthpiece. He was already on record as calling the champion an 'Asiatic despot', saying that Kasparov 'wasn't spanked enough as a child,' labelling his seconds as 'lackeys and slaves' and pugilistically lamenting that when it came to the World Championship final, 'I don't want to sink to the level of the animal to beat the animal.' At the pre-match press conference, Short was asked about the fact that he had once called Kasparov an 'ape'. Although the journalist gave him an out by admitting that it was an 'old quote', Short replied with schoolboy jauntiness: 'Anyone who has seen Kasparov by the swimming-pool will know that he is very hairy.' When this drew a chuckle, Short backed up his 'old quote' by pointing out that 'the Norwegian women's team refer to Kasparov as "the Rug".'

One could certainly rule out the idea that Short's low abuse of Kasparov might have been a nervous miscalculation by one unused to the spotlight. Ever since Short was first declared a boy wonder, nearly twenty years ago, he has been skin-bleached by flashbulbs and had his tonsils scoured by microphones. More to the point, Short has a history of graceless behaviour. Interviewed for the tournament bulletin of the World Junior Championships in Belfort, the eighteen-year-old Nigel delivered this view of his host country: 'France represents everything I detest most in life. Your country's only useful products are porn films.' Perhaps it was a wonky joke (or even an early attempt to suck up to Mrs Thatcher), but a couple of years and several rescinded invitations later, Short was obliged to grovel to *Europe Echecs*. 'Would you believe me if I told you that I love France and that I dream of being able to play there again?' Cathy Forbes finds a neat formula for Short's verbal manner, which can be shy, awkward, polite or aggressive, and sometimes all four: 'He seems to use speech to conceal thought.'

Kasparov himself had made only a single pre-match verbal strike, just before Short played the Dutchman Jan Timman for the right to challenge for the title. Asked whom he expected to meet, and how he expected the final to go, the champion had replied, 'It will be Short, and it will be short.' But Kasparov's serious—and scary—response to Nigel's taunts came, quite properly, across the chessboard at the Savoy. Watched closely in the early games, he failed to glower, he failed to smirk at Nigel's moves, failed to pace up and down like a baboon. He behaved impeccably. And at the same time he played cruel and destructive chess.

The first four games of the twenty-four-game match were catastrophic for Short. Setting off for the Strand in a state of rather wan patriotism that first Tuesday in September, I thought: two–two after the first four; we'll settle for that. No, we'd be *thrilled* with that. Short is a notoriously bad starter in big matches. So (this was my modest plan) Short should attempt to slow down the champion, frustrate him, not let him play the way he wants to. Eight days later, Short had made almost the worst possible beginning, with three losses and a draw. It was bad not just because of the brute score but for various and cumulative reasons. Short lost the first game after running out of time in a frenetic scramble and ignoring the offer of a draw. He drew the second after missing a chance to create a passed pawn, which some said might have given him winning chances. He lost the third despite a furious, flamboyant attack on Kasparov's king. And he lost the fourth despite laying out a lengthy and impressive opening preparation. The preliminary conclusion seemed to be this: that Short was showing he could set Kasparov problems, but the champion was showing that he could answer them in style.

I followed the opening games in the Grandmasters' Analysis Room, a couple of doors away from the Savoy, at Simpson's-in-the-Strand, a place with historic chess associations. During the last century, patzers and pros met upstairs, at Simpson's Divan, to drink coffee, play chess and gamble for shillings; here in 1851 Anderssen played his so-called 'immortal game', a classic of sacrificial attack, against Kieseritzky. This location no longer exists, but a curved brass plaque reading 'Simpson's Divan Tavern' hangs like an armorial shield on the wall of the downstairs smoking bar, which has been commandeered for grandmasters and their hangers-on. The atmosphere is part senior common-room, part sweaty-socks rumpus area. Here, away from the formality and actuality of play, are the basic necessities for following the game: two large display boards flashing out the moves as they happen, a television link with a fixed long-shot of the players at work, a television whose live commentary allows colleagues to be gently or not so gently mocked, an array of chessboards on which to thump out possible continuations, power points for databases and the *Official Bulletin* laptop, ashtrays and a half-price bar. Here also are the luxuries: space to roar and burble, chunter and chatter, rage and wail. A roomful of grandmasters in a state of busy analysis recalls some wildlife clip of lion cubs scuffling among one another. There are snarls and spats and ear-chewing expressions of territoriality; only when the camera pulls back do we realize that the lion and lioness themselves are lolling higher up the hill.

When you eavesdrop on the chatter of chess, you discover that it reproduces and confirms the game's compelling mixture of violence and intellectuality. As pieces are finger-flipped around demonstration boards in swift refutation of some other grandmaster's naïve proposition, half the language has a street-fighting quality to it. You don't just attack a piece, you *hit* it. You don't merely take a piece when you can *chop it off, hack it off* or *snap it off*. Pawns may advance, but they prefer to *stomp* down the board like storm troopers. Getting your opponent into time trouble, you try to *flag* him; playing a sacrifice, you *sack* a piece, as you might sack a city. And since violent verbs require victims, your opponent's bits of wood are personified into living matter: 'I want to hit *this guy* and *this guy*.'

Aggression involves contempt. So an opponent's strategy which seems passive or unadventurous is dismissed as *vegetarian*. (Hitler was a vegetarian, of course, but no matter. So too is Jon Speelman, the British number four.) Here is Nigel Short reflecting before the title-match on some of the off-beat lines he had played against Karpov: 'Kasparov could destroy such openings at the board, and then I'd be fucked. I must play a real man's opening. No quiche.' Real men are macho, as is shown by these examples of Shortian language, taken from Dominic Lawson's book of the match, *The Inner Game*. 'I'm going to give it to him good and hard.' 'I'm going to give the guy a good rogering.' 'I'm going to give it to him good and hard, right up him.' 'I want to rape and mate him.' Lawson recalls the moment in Barcelona in 1987 when he first heard Short use the acronym 'TDF', which he took as shorthand for some complex strategical ploy. At first he didn't want to confess his chessic ignorance, but after Short and the American grandmaster Yasser Seirawan had used the expression several times, he finally cracked and inquired. 'Trap. Dominate. Fuck,' the two grandmasters chanted back at him.

Interwoven with all this is a more polysyllabic language of theory and aspiration. A move may be *natural* or *artificial*, *positional* or *anti-positional*, *intuitive* or *anti-intuitive*, *thematic* or *dysfunctional*. If its aim is to inhibit the opponent rather than strike menace on its own behalf, then it is said to be *prophylactic*. And what are the two players seeking? The *truth of the position*; or sometimes, the *absolute truth of the position*. They are struggling to prove something; though an outside observer might not *believe in* it. This makes each game a courtroom scene, and a world championship match a Day of Judgement. Another analogy is with the philosophical symposium: as in, 'The players are *continuing their discussion* of the Bc4 variation of the Najdorf.' Thus high ambition combines with low brutality; there seems to be no middle vocabulary developed by the players.

Strategic verbal violence is a factor in daily life off the board as well. You only have to sit among top chess players for a while to learn that they tend to divide one another into two categories: 'nutters' and 'traitors'. These terms were widely deployed in the global institutional wrangling that preceded the London match, and which hung over it like weather cloud. For decades, the world championships had been run under the auspices of FIDE, the International Chess Federation, the second-largest governing body in sport. Collisions between high ego, high financial expectations and this sort of established bureaucracy are hardly surprising: in 1975, Bobby Fischer had laid down several million and five demands as a condition for defending his title, FIDE had accepted several million and four, whereupon the American had scowled off into the sunset never to push a public pawn again until his grey-haired rematch last year with Boris Spassky. Since 1982, when Florencio Campomanes became president of FIDE, relations with some of the top players have deteriorated sharply. I asked one English grandmaster what he thought of Campomanes. He replied that he found him charming, intelligent and very likeable; the only problem was that he should have been running a small Marxist state with a large military budget rather than a sports federation.

The latest rumble began in 1985, when Campomanes called off the first Karpov–Kasparov match on the spurious grounds that both players were exhausted (though both said they wished to continue). In 1987, top players dissatisfied with FIDE set up the Grandmasters' Association (first president: Gary Kasparov), which ran its own tournaments and had its own World Cup while continuing to cooperate with FIDE for the world championship qualifying cycle. But by 1990 many grandmasters were fed up, some with the quarrelling, some with Kasparov's bossiness, and they signed a peace treaty with FIDE. Kasparov resigned from the Grandmasters' Association and was left without a power base. His long-term plan at this time was to play (and win) the 1993 final under the FIDE rules: 'Then, in 1996 I will take the championship away from FIDE, make an independent promotion . . . Campomanes will create a new world champion, but who will care about him?'

In fact, his chance came much sooner, and from a surprising source. After Short had qualified for the final, FIDE called for bids from interested cities to host the match. Various organizational ineptitudes and divagations ensued before Campomanes awarded the match to Short's home city of Manchester, which had offered 1.15 million pounds in prize-money. FIDE had, however, failed to inform Short or discuss the matter with him, whereupon Short proposed to Kasparov that they organize the match themselves. 'FIDE thought I was a little bunny rabbit because I smile a lot and look fairly inoffensive,' the Englishman later recalled. 'But I'm a bunny rabbit with sharp teeth, and they got bitten.'

Thus came into being the Professional Chess Association, a body so ad hoc that it consisted—and still consists at the time of writing—only of Short, Kasparov and Kasparov's lawyer. It was formed, in Raymond Keene's often-repeated phrase, 'to bring chess into the modern world.' This meant 'giving fans maximum enjoyment and sponsors full value for money,' according to one of the Association's rare public statements; it also meant 'better-focused marketing'. Nigel Short at his opening press conference spoke of the need 'to professionalize and commercialize the sport, as has been done in the past with tennis and golf.' This sounds fair enough, but there is also a certain amount of humbug in the Association's proclamations. Creeping bureaucratese, too. Try this for size: 'The PCA is the first governing body to be co-founded by a world champion and to be vested by him with the ability to further confer the title through competitions organized by it. As a result, the PCA has an organic right to do so not enjoyed by any previous sanctioning body.' In playground terms, this means: I've got the biggest conker, come and get it, ya ya ya.

Professionalize and commercialize . . . tennis and golf. This meant, in part, television, and the medium responded with enthusiasm. Channel 4 (as co-backer) put out three transmissions on every match day, and the BBC one. Television close-ups roundly emphasized the physiognomic and gestural differences between the two players: Kasparov fizzingly coiled, scowling, frowning, grimacing, lip-scrunching, head-scratching, nose-pulling, chin-rubbing, occasionally slumping down over his crossed paws like a melodramatically puzzled dog; Short more impassive, bland-faced, sharp-elbowed and stiff-postured, as if he'd forgotten to take the coat-hanger out of his jacket. But this repertoire of tics, plus the undifferentiated way of playing the moves (not much room for commentary on the back-lift, pick-up or follow-through of the arm) does not amount to much in the pantheon of sports images. Experts did their best with junior-anthropology interpretations of body language ('Nigel's got his knuckles pressed up to his chin—he's really concentrating') but were too often reduced to valorous attempts to talk up the action. 'We're actually seeing two people thinking in public!' enthused the aptly named Mr Keene at one point. 'Thinking incarnate on the TV screen!' The camera did provide one shot that gave a powerful idea of the force field of a chess game: an overhead view of both players straining forward across the board, with only two ranks separating them from a Maori nose-rub or, more likely, a head-butt. Still, when all is said and done, the basic and constant visuals in television chess are of two seated players pushing wood.

Or, too often for comfort, not pushing it. Channel 4 carried the first hour of each game live, and wandered into quasi-philosophical problems of being and nothingness. What invariably happened was that the players would in the first few minutes rattle out a familiar opening, until one produced a prepared variation from the known line. The player who had been varied against would then settle down for a long and slumberous ponder while the innovator went off and made himself a cup of tea. The high point of such on-air 'thinking incarnate' came during Game 9, itself a facsimile of Game 5 in its opening moves. After the first eleven moves had been flicked out in a couple of minutes, Kasparov varied. Short thought. And thought. Commercial break.

And thought. And thought. Second commercial break. And thought. Finally, after using up forty-five minutes of live television time, he castled. Tennis and golf? Forget it.

Another reason chess is unlikely to take off (and the support of the ignorant couch potato plus know-nothing stadium-clogger are an important financial factor) is the variable charisma of those who play the game. If all players were as intelligent, voluble and linguistically assured as Gary Kasparov, the game could print its own cheque-books. But the truth is that pawn pushers *en masse* tend to belong to the train-spotter tendency. Anoraks, plastic bags, old sandwiches and an introverted excitement are some of their characteristics. Television did its chivvying best with the species: two of Channel 4's resident grandmasters were Daniel King, whose shoulder-length hair and colourful shirts looked positively *vie de Bohème* in the context, and the bankerish figure of Raymond Keene (nicknamed 'the Penguin' for his well-lunched stomach and the rather Antarctic set of his head on his shoulders). The third, however, was the far more compelling—or, if you were a ratings-bothered television channel controller, uncompelling—figure of Jon Speelman.

Speelman is a very strong player indeed, who beat Short in the Candidates' cycle in 1988 and was currently acting as one of the Englishman's seconds. Some, indeed, take the view that Speelman's mazily unfathomable style might have given Kasparov more trouble than Short's more directly aggressive manner; though when I tentatively put this theory to grandmaster James Plaskett in the bar of the Analysis Room he looked at me as if I had just played some nutter's opening (say, 1h4), and replied, 'Gazza beats everyone, doesn't he?' To add my own penn'orth of tribute: I once played Speelman in a charity simultaneous, and he handled my attacking verve and prepared innovations very well, especially given that he was also taking on thirty-nine other opponents at the same time. (To come clean, what happens is this: you sit there trembling at the board, hideously alone, knowing that you are obliged to have your move ready the moment the grandmaster arrives before you. This is fine at the start, when the chance of going humiliatingly wrong is less, and you have some time to think as he strolls round the other thirty-nine boards; but as the game goes on, other players drop out and the position complicates, your tormentor comes whizzing along with ever-increasing frequency. At moments like this you feel the tiniest inkling of what it must be like to be subjected to full-time, high-level pressure from across the board. The other humiliating aspect is that you swiftly realize that the flurrying figure who gazes briefly at the position, bangs out a move and flurries on, isn't really playing *you*; he's playing the board. You are not just one-fortieth of his thinking time, you are also merely the equivalent of some practice position set up by one of his trainers to get the sleep out of his eyes.

But Speelman, for all his great savvy on the board, and the affectionate respect in which he is held, is never going to be the Agassi of the sixty-four squares. His name was once misprinted in *The Times* as Specimen, and the sobriquet is still remembered and apt. Tall, gawky and shy, with downcast eyes, thick-lensed spectacles and a circular shrubbery of comb-free hair, Specimen is the ultimate boffin version of the chess player. His other nickname, from the days when he had a wild beard as well, was Speelwolf. There exists rare footage of him on the dance-floor after a chess Olympiad. Unwinding is what he seems almost literally to be doing: a sort of frenetic, uncoordinated whirling response to all the self-imposed discipline of the previous days. Boadicea with knives on her chariot wheels cleared less space around her than the grandmaster on the dance-floor. Despite his regular appearances on television over a period of three months, it would be a fair bet that no clothing chain has subsequently approached him with the suggestion of a sponsoring deal. He is, in brief, a sports marketer's worst nightmare. This is, of course, all to the greater and more serious glory of the sport he takes part in. But the alarming and true presence of Specimen stands like an emblematic bar to the popularizer's dreams.

As Game 5 began, with Short already three clear points down, the bookmaker William Hill was declining to take any money on Kasparov. Local cheerleaders ransacked the records to discover that Steinitz had once been one–four down in a world championship. Fischer had trailed Spassky zero–two, and Smyslov in 1954 had been in exactly the same mess (half to three-and-a-half) against Botvinnik before fighting back to level at twelve–twelve. By Game 9, however, Short was five clear points down, and we were all staring at another famous deficit instead: Kasparov's own zero–five against Karpov in their first title match of 1984–85, a score that, by a rare coincidence, was also reached after nine games.

What the brute statistics failed to reveal, however, was that the chess had been vivid and thrilling, as it would continue to be until almost the very end of the match. Both players favoured sharp, open positions, which—apart from anything else—meant that the amateur observer could see much more clearly what was going on. Not all professional observers approved. US grandmaster Larry Evans was in the Savoy Theatre commentary box during Game 6, and through the earphones you could practically hear his neck crack from incredulous head shaking. 'Looks like a position out of Hack Attack in *Kingpin* magazine. It doesn't look like a world championship game. It looks like a coffee-house game.'

Game 8, a street-fighting draw, was further enlivened by the news that Nigel Short had sacked his coach at the end of the first week's play. Lubomir Kavalek had been paid off after Game 3 and was now back in the States. The surprise was all the greater given the unremitting public praise of 'Lubosh' right up to the opening pawn-push. He was, we were told, Nigel's secret weapon; he had an unrivalled database of a million games; he was 'the Czech who loved beating Russians' (having left Prague in 1968, he had resurfaced four years later in Reykjavik as Fischer's unofficial second). He had coached Short since the start of the Englishman's run at the title and was variously described as his mentor, guru, father-figure and Svengali. The extent of his influence may be judged from this delicate revelation from Cathy Forbes: that Kavalek 'also pays attention to the regulation of his charge's bodily functions. After Short has let off steam by playing his guitar before a game, Kavalek will remind him to empty his bladder.'

Kavalek was sacked, it later emerged, because he had stopped coming up with new ideas, was enjoying the free hotel life too much and had become a 'depressing influence' according to Short. Though the Short camp tried to make light of the event, with

Dominic Lawson talking about Nigel finally getting 'the team he wants,' the same journalist's subsequent account of Short's anger and dismay is revealing; 'Tomorrow I must kill Kasparov. But today I am killing my father . . . He was my mentor. In the past year I have seen as much of him as I have of my wife. No, in fact I have spent more time with him than I have with Rea . . . Don't you feel the brutality of this moment? It's parricide.' Listening to this plaint, Lawson 'began to feel like an extra in *Oedipus Rex*.' It is, no doubt, never quite the right moment for parricide, but the timing of Kavalek's departure seemed inept: comforting to the enemy, dispiriting to the home supporters. Besides, who was now reminding Nigel to pee before each game?

By the first Saturday in October, the match had reached its halfway point, Short had yet to win a game and was still trailing by five clear points. In one sense, the match was dead, and the bookmakers rated a Short victory as improbable an event as proof of the Loch Ness Monster's existence within the next year. Ambitions for Short were readjusted: he was aiming, as a starting-point, to register a single victory; he was 'learning to play' Kasparov with the longer-term ambition of doing better next time. A far cry from the apprehension that he might have to 'sink to the level of the animal to beat the animal.' But in terms of excitement things were far from dead, and Short had just had his best week of the match. In Game 10, he built his most powerful attack so far with white, then missed a completely clear win and had to settle for a draw. In Game 11, Kasparov cleverly played on the expected demoralization the missed win would have caused, but Short defended astutely and gained his first draw with black. Game 12 went in a sharp blast from opening to endgame, leaving a position that to the chess duffer looked awful for Short: he had a bishop for three pawns and the champion had four passed and interconnected pawns on the kingside, which looked all set to pile down the board like space invaders. Still, duffers shouldn't underestimate the power of a sole bishop or the defensive usefulness of a mobile king, and Short got his third half point of the week.

That afternoon the Analysis Room was bustling: grandmasters, hangers-on, journalists, drinkers, wives and

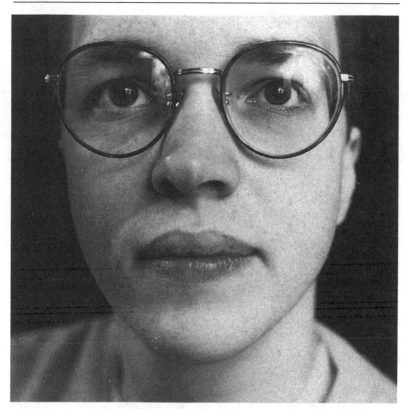

Photo: Steve Pyke (Network)

children, traitors and nutters. Rea and Kyveli were in evidence; the small and studious nephew of *The Times*'s literary editor, in Fair Isle jumper and Short-ish glasses, was bashing out the move on a plastic set; while Stephen Fry, the chessoholic actor, wandered in to unleash his own bit of literary home preparation about Short's plight (*Antony and Cleopatra* II.iii, Soothsayer to Antony: 'If thou dost play with him at any game/Thou art sure to lose, and, of that natural luck/He beats thee 'gainst the odds.') The atmosphere should have been genial, but there was a distinct edge of rattiness. The grandmasters' table was voluble, opinionated and largely pro-Short. But those around it were also watching something which they themselves would certainly never achieve: a challenge for the world title. And, given that chess is a game of extreme competitiveness, a further edge may develop towards the person who is there instead of you—namely Nigel Short. Patriotism (or support for the underdog, or politeness to one's hosts) can therefore give way to 'Christ, what did he do *that* for?' When Short blocked a long diagonal bishop attack with a knight, a roar of disbelief went up from the table; but in fact it proved the start of a solid defence. Throughout the match, experts, whether on television, over headphones at the Savoy or in the Analysis Room, constantly mis-predicted the two players' next moves. Only a few were prepared to say, 'I don't understand what's going on,' or, 'We'll only know when we get the players' analysis of the position.' But to those in the grandmasters' circle, tapping into their databases, flicking out possible continuations and then taking them back, freed from the stress of actual play, shuttling to the bar for drinks, fizzing with rivalry yet safe from the highest rivalry two doors away, there was often an exaggerated certainty about what is going on. 'Well, there's *this*,' snapped Tony Miles (the first-ever British grandmaster and a 'traitor' for having apparently offered his services to Kasparov), bossing a couple of pawns around, 'but it's a bailout.' Not a bailout that was followed by Nigel Short, as it happened. At times I was reminded of a remark by the writer Clive James, who had once provided captions to a set of photographs in the *Observer* magazine. A helpful sub-editor generously restyled them for him, pointing up the wit and taking out the longueurs. 'Listen,' James cruelly explained to the sub while making him restore the original text, 'if I wrote like that, I'd be *you*.'

In Game 13 violence was expected. Kasparov considers thirteen to be his lucky number—he was born on the thirteenth and achieved his grandmaster rating on the thirteenth and is the thirteenth world champion. Gary, the whisper went, would really be going for it today with the white pieces. Nigel had no chance of winning—you had to go back two years to find the last occasion Kasparov was beaten playing white. But there was no explosion. Kasparov looked weary, Short fresh, and they ground out a solid, dull, professional draw. This disappointed some but pleased others. 'They're playing world-championship chess now,' said one international master.

There were good extraneous reasons for both players to be comparatively docile. Between the twelfth and thirteenth games, the attempted coup against Yeltsin had taken place; Kasparov had to sit and watch tanks blast his parliament building. 'Frankly speaking,' he admitted, 'I spent more time looking at CNN than at the chess books.' Short's worries were more parochial. While Kasparov contemplated the future of democracy in Russia, Short consulted libel lawyers over a *Sunday Times* article alleging that the Englishman was 'near to collapse'; that there were 'deep divisions' in his camp; and that, after the departure of Kavalek, Short's friend Dominic Lawson was exercising 'too much influence'. Most insultingly, if not most libellously, Short, hitherto compared to a David taking on Goliath, was now held to resemble Eddie 'the Eagle' Edwards, the British ski-jumper who became a comic national mascot by cheerily finishing last—and usually a very long way last—in various major competitions up to and including the Winter Olympics.

Short's reaction has its ironic side. Here was someone who had breezily trashed the moral character, political integrity and physical appearance of the world champion coming on all sensitive and writ-happy when offered a forkful of rough abuse himself. More to the point, he was finding out a little of the cost of 'professionalizing and commercializing' the game, of putting it up there with tennis and golf. Marketing a sport involves changing it to suit the people who pay the bills. Marketing means making your sport more accessible to people who are only half-interested in it, and thus coarsening either it or the process by which it is described, or both. Marketing means getting written about by people who understand your sport even less than those who normally write about it do. Marketing means playing up inherent nationalism and chauvinism: witness Corey Pavin wearing a Desert Storm cap during the Ryder Cup. Marketing means betraying the subtlety of your sport, and the subtlety of human character; it means Heroes and Villains, and pratting around in black leather for the cameras. It means extravagant praise leading to extravagant blame: the tall-poppy syndrome, as it's known in Australia. Marketing can mean earning a lot more money, and marketing surely and finally means, unless you are very lucky, getting dumped on. The comparison between Nigel Short and Eddie 'the Eagle' Edwards is, apart from anything else, severely inaccurate: Short—to take the Olympic analogy—was already assured of the silver medal when he met Kasparov. But you can't expect to be written about with fastidious accuracy once you 'professionalize and commercialize' your sport. As an early warning of what might come, when Short and Kasparov opened the bids for their match at Simpson's-in-the-Strand, the Englishman sat Kyveli on his lap. This harmless gesture was publicly derided by Dutch grandmaster Hans Ree as 'Saddam Hussein-like'. Short for once had the lightness of touch to respond: 'It's a long time since I invaded Kuwait.' Some might think being compared to Saddam *and* Eddie the Eagle is a bit tough. But that's marketing.

Between the fourteenth and fifteenth games of the London match, I lunched some observations out of William Hartston who had been at school with me back in the days when chess was a very amateur business in this country, and the notion of a British grandmaster was as speculative as the yeti. At our school, there were two reliable ways of getting out of the playground rain at lunchtime. The uncompetitive joined the stamp club, the competitive the chess club. (I joined the stamp club.) Thereafter I followed Hartston's progress from a distance: International Master, top board for England, chess correspondent of the *Independent*, resident BBC chess sage.

Hartston has a positive lifetime score against Nigel Short of two–one, though he admits that both victories came before Nigel started shaving. Hartston also works as an industrial psychologist and tends to take a broader and more amused view of proceedings, thereby attracting the 'traitor' rather than 'nutter' label. For instance, he was sceptical of the new official line about Short: that since he was not going to stage a miracle recovery, he was now 'learning to play' Kasparov for the next time round. In Hartston's opinion, there won't be a next time: 'If you put Short back into the ratings, he would be ninth, with five younger players above him.'

This assumes that the Professional Chess Association will still be there next time round. Hartston was not as dismissive as I had expected about the marketing possibilities of chess . . . But tennis and golf? Why not, he replied. He reckons that the players are just as promotable as golfers (who admittedly are not all charismatic totems), and points out that the last game of the 1987 Karpov–Kasparov match, in Seville, drew an astonishing live television audience of eighteen million Spaniards. When I asked him to assess the chances of other grandmasters abandoning FIDE and throwing in their lot with the Professional Chess Association, he replied, with a sort of benign cynicism, 'The way to a chess player's heart is through his wallet.' This doesn't, of course, make chess players much different from anybody else; indeed, in their case the cardio-economic link is all the more understandable. The very best players have always been able to make a living, but in few other professions (except perhaps poetry) does the earnings graph go so suddenly into free fall when set against the graph of ability. International master Colin Crouch, who is around number thirty in the country, spent nine days away from the London match at a tournament in the Isle of Man. The top prize was a mere 600 pounds, and despite a bright start Crouch came home with only his expenses. This is the reality of even a strong player's life: small tournaments, small money, local fame. A couple of years ago, Hartston did the following calculation during a grandmaster tournament in Spain: assuming that all the prize money on offer was split between the grandmasters (and there were some powerful IMs there as well), their average earnings worked out at between two and three pounds an hour. The basic rate for the female industrial mushroom pickers in the North of England who demonstrated outside last year's Booker Prize ceremony was three pounds seventy-four an hour.

Hartston certainly thinks that the money and the politicking were serious distractions to Short's first-time title challenge. Indeed, he goes further, believing (as does Cathy Forbes) that at some level Short recognized he wasn't going to beat Kasparov and therefore put his energy into getting the best possible payday that he could. In Hartston's view, this fundamental self-disbelief had also leached into the Englishman's play. 'I get the feeling that Short is trying to prove to himself that he isn't afraid of Kasparov—*but he is.*'

Hartston admires what he calls Short's 'classical, correct chess style,' and praised his tactics against Karpov, when he varied his openings in such a way as to provoke damagingly long periods of reflection in that Russian. This is a fundamental part of successful match play. 'The history of the world chess championship,' Hartston maintains, 'shows that the way to beat a great player is to allow him to indulge his strengths in unfavourable circumstances.' I asked Hartston what strength-cum-weakness Short might play on against Kasparov, and he replied, 'Impatience.'

With apt timing, Game 15 arrived to annotate this theme. Short, with the black pieces for the eighth time, played a solid, traditional defence which he knew well and had played in all his candidate's matches but had not so far offered to Kasparov. Observing the opening moves, international master Malcolm Pein praised 'a sound, sensible Nigel Short not trying to strangle Gary Kasparov from the beginning.' David Norwood, Hartston's co-commentator in the BBC studio and fellow-critic of Short's Panzerism, enthused over what he saw as 'normal chess'. The game would turn, ultimately, on whether Kasparov's two central pawns were weak or strong, but the truth of the position would not be swiftly yielded up. Indeed it wasn't: Kasparov wheeled and probed, Short adjusted and secured. Kasparov had the choice—the eventual choice—of attacking either kingside or queenside; black's job was to stay patient, shore up the sea wall and wait to find out from which direction the waves would break. Short seemed to do this admirably: there were none of the wide-open spaces and forced piece-trading of earlier games. Then, fascinatingly, the game developed as 'normal chess' sometimes does: that is to say, a rather closed, quiescent position, with no material gains and only a half-square or so advantage to either side, opens up into a thrilling, charging attack. The answer to the question as to whether Kasparov's central pawns were strong or weak was disclosed: they were strong, not least because they belonged to Kasparov. In ten brutal moves, the world champion jemmied his way into Short's position and ripped the place to bits. Short had not gone on a rash strangling trip, and Kasparov had been obliged to wait a long time for the right moment. Yet he had shown no signs of self-

KASPAROV   **SHORT**

Photo: Greg Williams (Select)

destructive 'impatience'. On the contrary, he had displayed exemplary patience, then perfectly-calculated aggression.

Subsequent analysis of Game 15 showed, not surprisingly, that the above description is too neat, too thematic. Kasparov may have jemmied open Short's front door, but the householder had lifted the latch himself. Moments like this—when subsequent analysis acts like gravy thickener on the game you thought you knew—are part of chess's fascination. If you watch a video of an old Wimbledon final or Ryder Cup match, you aren't really re-analysing, you are merely reminding yourself of what happened and suffusing yourself again with the emotions provoked by the original events. But a chess game, after it has happened, continues in organic life, changing and growing as it is examined. In Game 6, for instance, when Short opted for what he called 'the most violent method of smashing Kasparov's defences,' sacrificing a bishop on move twenty-six, it was generally thought that he had 'missed a win'. Analysis of the game continued, however, and by the time the players were hunched over Game 15 a defence had been found which would have given Kasparov a draw. On the other hand, at the time of playing neither player had seen this possible defence, so in a sense it didn't exist. This is one of the aspects of chess that gives it a sense of high and oscillating peril:

the tension between objectivity and subjectivity, between some coldly ascertainable, finally provable 'truth of the position' and the clammy-handed actuality of play, with half a dozen different half-truths running through your head while the clock ticks, while the footlights and your opponent glare.

Eventually, some final truth about a position may emerge, months or years down the track. The immediate post-mortems, while appearing to start this process, may in fact work more as a continuation of the struggle on the board, and thus be more psychologically freighted. What normally happens when a game finishes is that the players discuss between themselves the final position and the key moves that led to it. This is not just from sadistic or masochistic interest but also from lucid need. (Kasparov used to do this after games with Karpov, even though he loathed and despised him. 'I am talking chess with the number two in the world,' he explained. 'I wouldn't go to a restaurant with him, but who else can I really talk to about these games? Spassky?') Such analysis continued for television and the press, with Short showing himself at his best: straight, rueful, likeable, self-critical, still fretting about the truth of the position. Kasparov, by contrast, the supreme strategist and consummate psychological bruiser, seemed to treat the follow-up discussion as part of the match. Avuncular, dismissive, unfretted, he played the wise don to Nigel's anxious student. Yes, on the one hand there was this, this and this; but then I have that, and maybe that, and then that; and if Rb8, then Nc5; and of course that move of Nigel's was a big blunder, so really I think the position is equal; perhaps I even have the better chances. Kasparov's analyses often seemed craftily to diminish Short's (and everybody else's) assessment of what had happened. 'Nigel's problem was hesitation,' Kasparov announced in a lordly way after the débâcle of Game 4. 'He has big psychological problems, and I am curious to see how he deals with them.' In Game 10, when Short had played a dramatic queen sacrifice and missed a clear win, *The Times* headline the next day was 'DEMON' KASPAROV DODGES KILLER BLOW; but if you looked to the end of *The Times* report, you came to the champion's laconic summary: 'An exciting but exhausting game. Both of us missed chances to win.' With Game 14, Kasparov initially agreed with his challenger's analysis: yes, the logic of the position demanded that Short push the pawn to c5; yes, Nigel missed a win. Who would quarrel with the finest calculating mind in chess? Except that by the next day the champion had demoralizingly changed his mind: no, c5 wouldn't have led to victory after all, and Nigel hadn't, as we might have imagined, nearly scored his first win.

Arriving for the sixteenth game, with Kasparov six points clear and needing only three draws to retain his title, I ran into one of the rumpus room's senior figures, Professor Nathan Divinsky. Benign and epigrammatic, he is President of the Canadian Chess Federation (and, among other achievements, was once married to Canada's prime minister). I observed that the match might be over that week.

'It's been over for six weeks,' he responded.

What about the idea that after the match was settled they might play a few exhibition games for fun?

'It's been an exhibition game since the beginning.' As a transatlantic observer sitting day after day at the grandmasters' table, Divinsky confessed himself disappointed with the narrowly partisan attitudes of the local analysts, with their 'Nigel-this, Nigel-that' approach to the match. Here, after all, was a rare and privileged opportunity to watch in action the strongest player in the history of the game: 'When Nijinsky danced, they didn't care who the ballerina was.' He cited a knight move in Game 15 (21 Nf4), which Kasparov had identified as the key moment, but which the boys at the round table hadn't heeded. As general corroboration of this British insularity, Divinsky pointed out a news story in that morning's *Times*. An Englishman had just been awarded the Nobel Prize jointly with an American. The paper had printed the Englishman's photo, described his career, interviewed his gerbil—and not even mentioned the American's name.

The charge sticks (though British insularity is perhaps no stronger than, say, French chauvinism or American isolationism— each nation earns its own abstract noun). In defence, I could only plead the extreme rarity of a local challenge reaching this ultimate stage, and the deleterious effects of hype. Later, another explanation occurs. If you are a top player, one who in all likelihood has played against Short, it's probably not too difficult to imagine yourself in his position, challenging for the title, trying to assess the correct response to Kasparov's tormenting strategies. It's much harder—perhaps impossible—to put yourself into the champion's mind. The round table and the assembled commentators were frequently baffled by Gazza's ideas, awed by his chess brain. Two remarks from the Savoy Theatre commentary team that afternoon stressed the difference. The first was a reference to 'Nigel's habit of having big thinks and then playing the natural move' (which on this occasion he duly did). The second was an honest and exasperated complaint about Kasparov: 'It's depressing, he sees instantly more than we see in a quarter of an hour.'

However, Game 16, to everyone's great surprise, turned out to be the moment of cheer for the Nigel-this, Nigel-that brigade. For once the ballerina jumped higher than Nijinsky. Even more surprising were the circumstances of the leap. Short had white, and played one of his least attacking games against Kasparov's habitual Sicilian. (It later emerged that the challenger had a cold and didn't feel up to more than a *piano* approach.) After eighteen or twenty moves, the Analysis Room was calling it as dull as it was equal: Speelman wandered past the board I was sitting at with Colin Crouch, whacked a few pieces about and declared the position moribund. For a change of scenery in the most tedious game so far, I went off to the Savoy. As I settled in, Short was offering an exchange of queens, and the headphones were groaning: 'Oh, Nigel, that's *such* an unambitious move.'

In the commentators' box a bored, end-of-term facetiousness reigned. Cathy Forbes began speculating on Short's awkward body position, wondering if it was because no one had told him to pee before the game. We were all waiting for queens to come off and glutinous drawdom to arrive. Short later gave two slightly different explanations of why this didn't happen. At his press conference, he said, 'I was a little bit too ashamed to offer a draw and I think he was too ashamed, too.' Later, he suggested, 'I was too lazy to offer a draw and so was he.' Given that the match had virtually been decided, and the two players were now business partners popularizing a sport, shame was the likelier motive. And there was also perhaps a familiar unspoken sub-text as the rival queens stared at each other in a proposed suicide pact. Go on, *you* offer the draw. No, *you* offer it. After you, Claude. No, after you, Cecil. *I'm* not taking the blame. Well, you're six points down, it's up to you to do something. Kasparov appeared to be playing simply to stay equal, at one point rather futilely retreating his bishop rather than proffer a whisper of an attack. The commentary team interpreted the retreat like this: '"I'm not going to offer a draw, English swine"—that's what that move says.'

One leading tournament director seeks to discourage quick, crowd-displeasing draws by making contestants play at least as far as the forty-move time control. One effect of this is that seemingly drawn positions may come to life again, like some bonfire you think you have terminally tamped down by piling on a mound of sodden leaves. All of a sudden there is a thin spiral of smoke, and then, before you know it, a warning crackle. This is what happened in Game 16. Short called off the queen swap and fiddled around with a queenside knight, while Kasparov put his own queen imperiously in the centre of the board. The position began to stir, not just on the queenside but also on the kingside *and* in the centre. In just a few moves, a great woof of flame went through Kasparov's position, leaving it gutted. The champion shook hands, declined any on-board post mortem and stalked off. It was his first defeat in eighteen months. Short acknowledged applause fit for a diva with an unoperatic, soft, semi-clenched fist, then disappeared. This being a theatre, the audience worked to exact a second curtain call; but chess has not yet gone that thespian.

Afterwards, at his victory press conference, Short was engagingly modest and thoughtful, keeping his result in perspective. What had been his strongest move? 'I thought I played the middle game quite well.' He admitted to having been 'rather shaken' by his loss in the previous game and so 'didn't want to do anything drastic.' He acknowledged that after a seven-year gap he had almost 'forgotten what it was like to beat Kasparov,' and gently contrasted his own style with that of Karpov, who tended to play 'like a vegetarian against the Sicilian.' The visceral response to victory was time-delayed. Dominic Lawson described Nigel's touching behaviour over the dinner table that night: 'He jumped up repeatedly from the table, almost between mouthfuls, and clenched his fists together in front of his chest, like a footballer after scoring a goal. "Wurgh! Wurgh!"'

When I asked Professor Divinsky for his analysis of Game 16, the reply was straightforward: 'Kasparov blew his brains out.' With two bullets: 'Ba8 and g5.' Kasparov rather agreed, putting his errors down to the fact that he was 'tired and emotionally exhausted.' This was a prime example of post-game psychology from the Russian, and not surprisingly it infuriated Short. 'He can't really tolerate the fact that I have been playing on equal terms with him . . . He's used to me collapsing, as I used to do before this match. Now something has happened. So he thinks it has to be something wrong with him, because it *can't* be something right with me. He likes to think that if only he didn't have these worries—personal, political, whatever—he would win every game. It's not modesty at all—quite the reverse.' Asked whether winning Game 16 had changed his attitude, Short replied, 'It does make a difference. This was the last thing I really had to prove.'

After this brief interruption to normal service, Kasparov drew the next four games without much inconvenience, to come out the winner by twelve-and-a-half points to seven-and-a-half. The players relaxed with speed chess (for television viewers) and themed-opening games (for theatre-goers). In the first of the four speed games, Short finally deployed the French defence—which experts, including Viktor Korchnoi, had been urging on him for the previous three months—and duly lost with it. He lost the next speed game, too. And the third. And the fourth. Kasparov, who won the last two games with exactly the sort of glamorous, pouncing attacks that draw new recruits to the sport, confessed that though he was very tired, he had been 'irritated' by the fact that Short and not he had been the last to win a game in the match proper. Memo to the world: never irritate Kasparov.

Short trousered 637,500 pounds and was hailed by Kasparov as 'a partner who kept his word' (a pleasant contrast with Short's pre-PCA claim that the champion 'cannot do business with human beings'). Kasparov won 1,062,500 pounds and an enormous Waterford crystal knight. What else he won is rather unclear, since the world of chess is now as fissured as that of boxing: Kasparov gained the PCA/*Times* title in London, Karpov regained the 'official' title in a rival match organized by FIDE, and, just for good measure, Bobby Fischer still insists that *he* is the true world champion, since no one has ever beaten him. A Kasparov–Karpov match to unify the titles is about as probable as a grandmaster falling for fool's mate.

Asked which was his favourite game of the London match, Kasparov replied, 'I don't know, because unfortunately I made mistakes in every game.' This may be read as an indication either of modesty or of arrogance, or as an early strike at whomever emerges as his next contender. But, beyond this, it reminds us that the best chess contains a striving not just for victory but for something beyond: for an ideal, harmonious state that produces a perfect mixture of creativity, beauty and power. So it's not surprising if God comes into the chess player's equation at some point, even if only as a linguistic reference. 'I'm looking for the best move. I'm not playing against Karpov, I'm playing against God,' Kasparov said during his 1990 world-title match. Nigel Short, after winning *his* eighth game against Karpov, was even more hubristic: 'I played like God.'

However the Englishman's relationship to the Almighty is not just one of emulation but also (as befits a prospective Tory MP) one of negotiation. Cathy Forbes has revealed that part of Short's build-up to important games was 'to visit churches, even though he is an atheist.' An odd habit, which seemed even odder when Short explained it during his match against Karpov in Linares: 'At first I said, "Please God let me win this game," but I realized this was asking too much. So instead I asked, "Please God give me the strength to beat this shithead."' In the course of his subsequent match with Timman, Short elaborated on his atheistic prayers. Yes, he was an unbeliever, he admitted, but 'I am also an opportunist.' We shouldn't perhaps be too hard on him for this— it is only a rougher version of the Pascalian bet as to God's existence. After his sole and splendid victory in Game 16, amid a flurry of proper questions ('But what if f5 b6 cxd4 Nd8 Bc2 then can't he get a draw by perpetual check?' and the like), I asked Short if he had continued his churchgoing habit during the final. He gave the sort of strangulated, glottal pause that tends to precede his answers to non-chess questions, and replied, 'No.' But he had done so in earlier rounds? Short looked a little puzzled, as if some nutter had infiltrated the press corps and in his moment of incandescence was calling him a traitor to the Almighty. 'Perhaps I should,' he added politely.

Perhaps he should. Losing at sport releases a swarm of if-onlys, among which God is (as always) the most elusive. If only Short had saved a few more seconds on his clock in the opening game and/or accepted Kasparov's offer of a draw. If only there hadn't been that upsetting ruckus with his coach which also led to the loss of his database. If only he'd clinched Game 10 when even a blindfold patzer might have secured it. If only he'd been able to hold his score with black to a reasonable percentage. If only he'd had a cold more often, as he did when winning Game 16. All of which boils down to the main, the cruellest if-only: if only he hadn't been playing the strongest, the most competitive, the most undermining, the most carnivorous chess player in the world.

EUGENE RICHARDS
IN THE BEGINNING

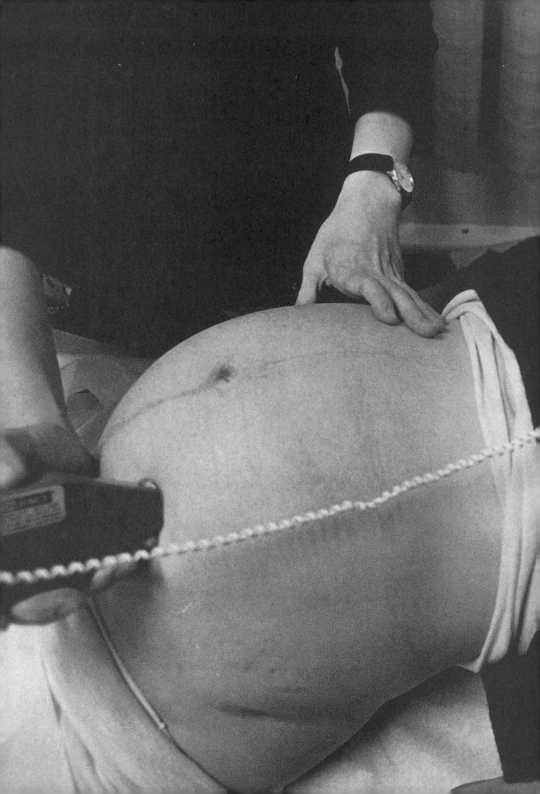

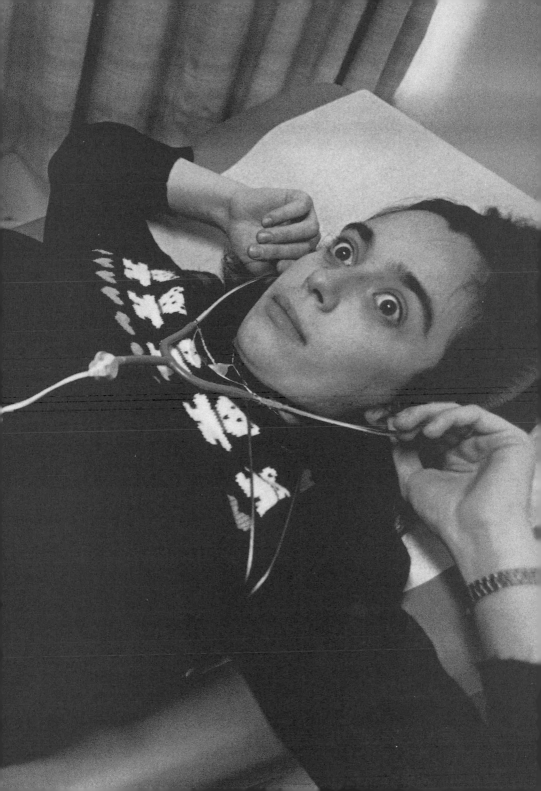

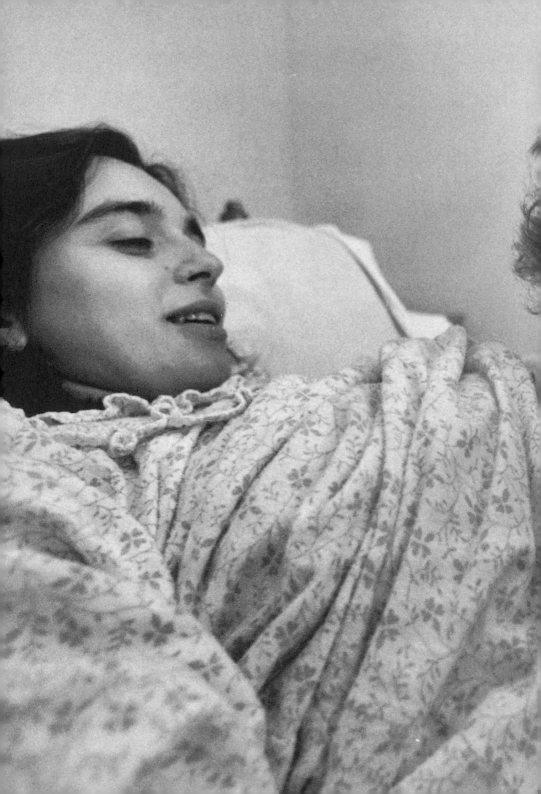

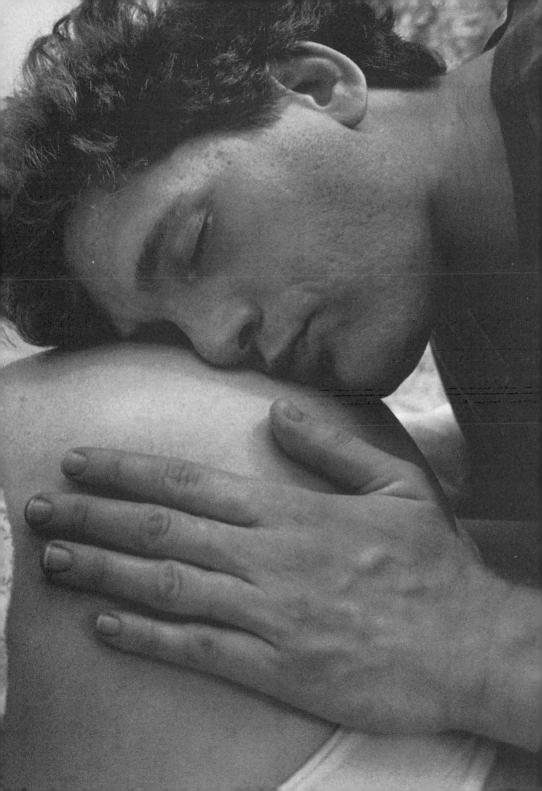

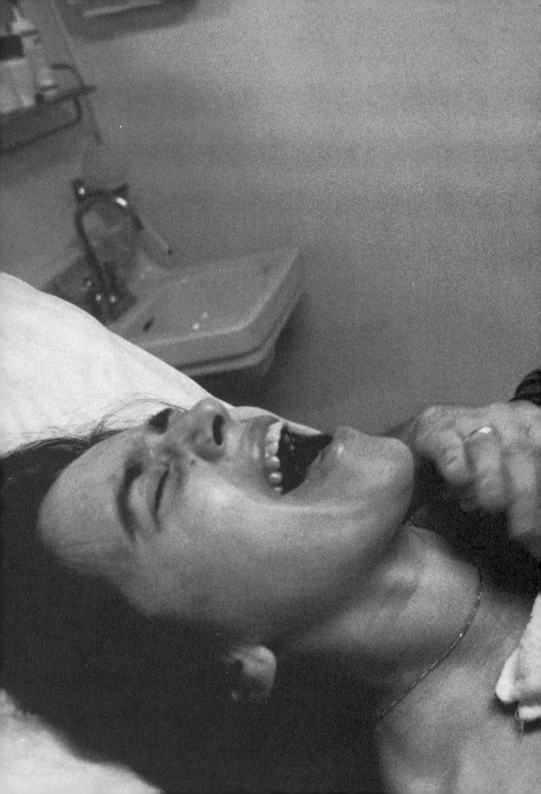

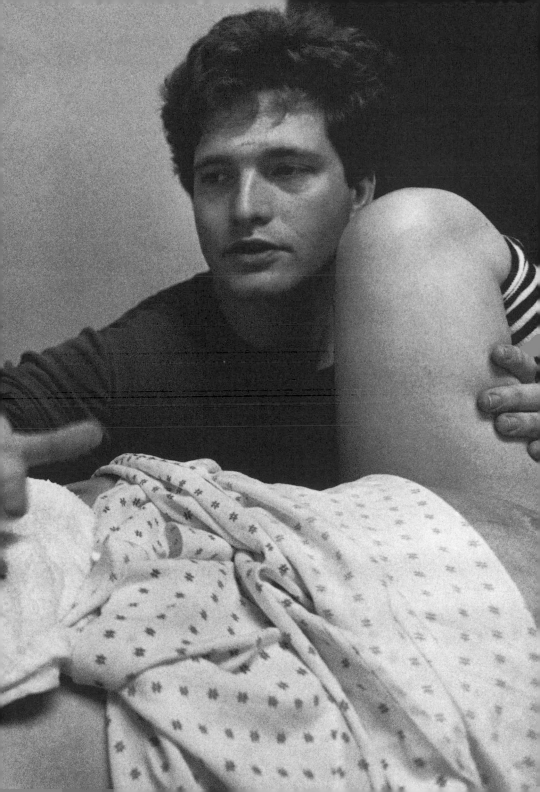

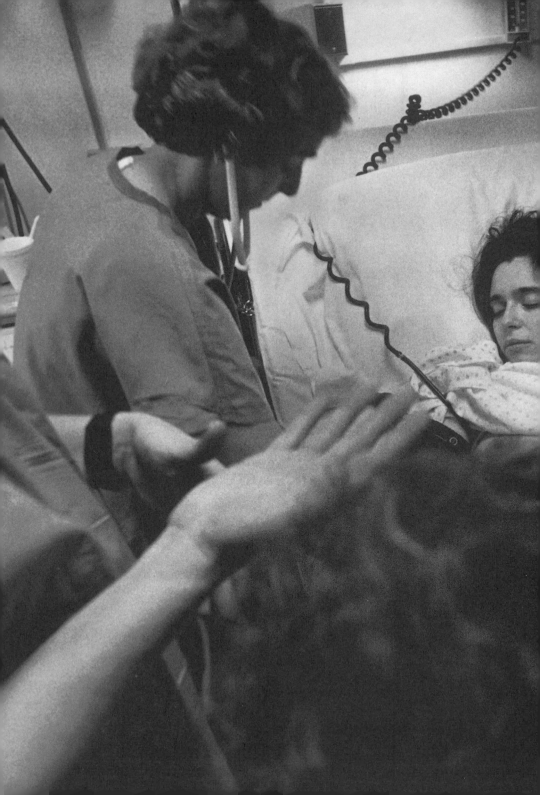

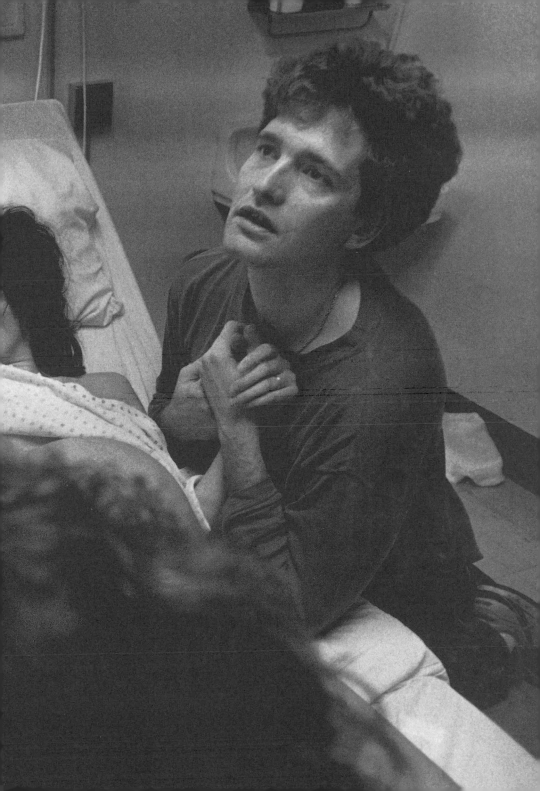

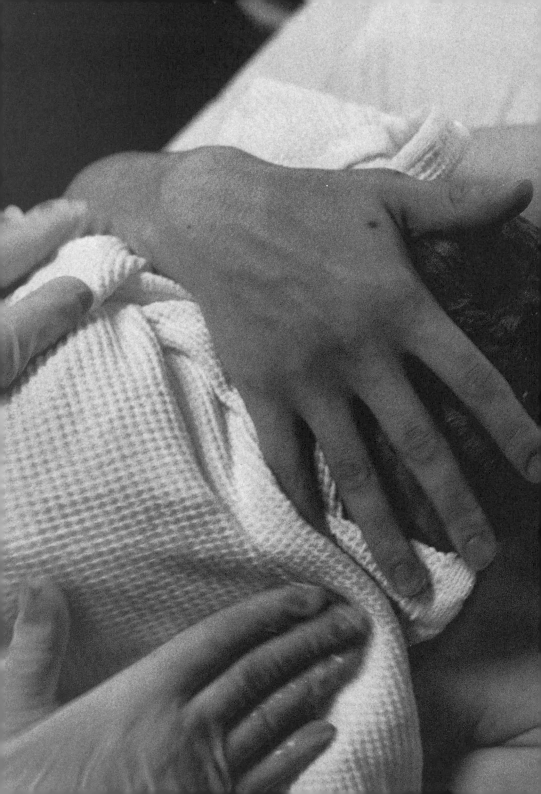

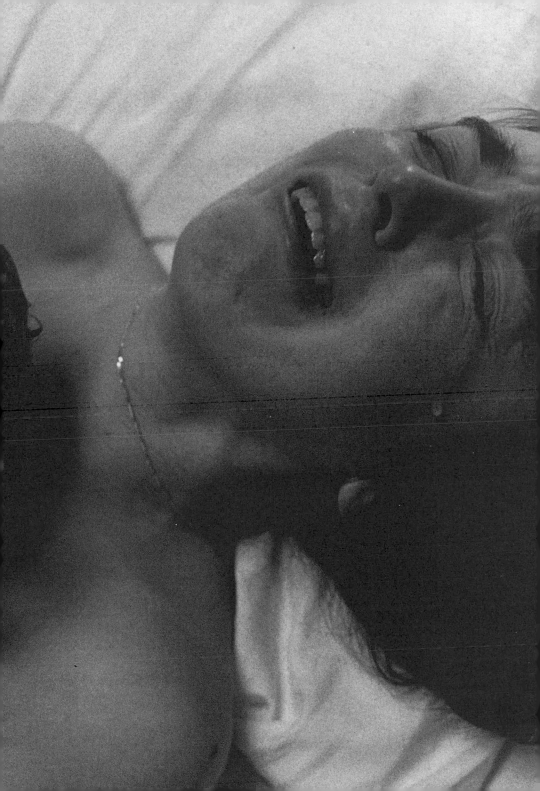

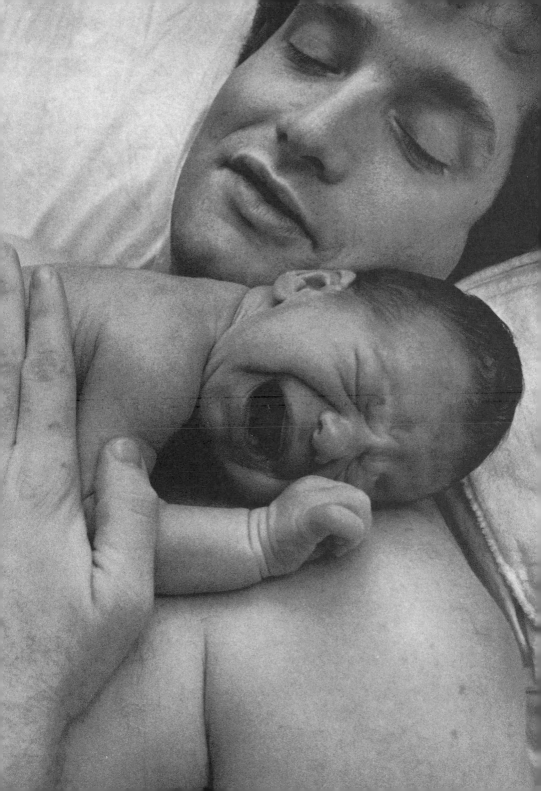

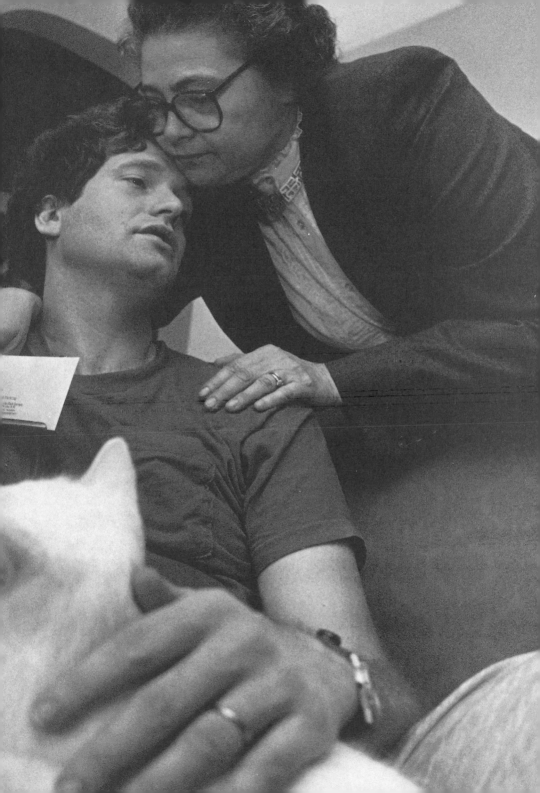

GRANTA

SUSAN J. MILLER
NEVER LET ME DOWN

One night, at an hour that was normally my bedtime, I got all dressed up, and my mother and father and I drove into New York, down to the Half Note, the jazz club on Hudson Street. I was thirteen, maybe fourteen, just beginning teenagehood, and had never gone anywhere that was 'nightlife'. I had heard jazz all my life, on records or the radio, my father beating out time on the kitchen table, the steering-wheel, letting out a breathy 'Yeah' when the music soared and flew. When they were cooking, when they really swung, it transported him; he was gone, inside the music. I couldn't go on this trip with him, but I thought I could understand it. It seemed to me that anyone could, hearing that music. Bird, Diz, Pres, Sweets, Lester, Al, Zoot. It was my father's music, though he himself never played a note.

I knew the players, for about the only friends my parents had were musicians and their wives. When I was a little kid, I'd lie in bed listening to them talk their hip talk in the next room. I knew I was the only kid in Washington Heights to be overhearing words like 'man' and 'cat' and 'groove', and jokes that were this irreverent and black. I knew they were cool and I loved it.

At the Half Note that night, the three of us walked through the door, and the owner appeared, all excited to see my father, and, in the middle of this smoky nightlife room, he kissed my hand. This was real life, the centre of something. We sat down. In front of us, on a little stage, were Jimmy Rushing, a powerful singer, and two sax players, Al Cohn and Zoot Sims, whom I'd known all my life. And there was a whole *roomful* of people slapping the tables, beating out time, breathing 'Yeah' at the great moments, shaking their heads, sometimes snapping their fingers, now and then bursting out with, 'Play it, man,' or, 'Sing it.' When the break came, Zoot sat down with us and ate a plate of lasagne or something and didn't say much except for these dry asides that were so funny I couldn't bear it. Too funny to laugh at. And there was my dad: these men were his friends, his buddies. They liked the things about my father that I could like—how funny he was, uncorny, how unsentimental, unafraid to be different from anyone else in the world: how he was unafraid to be on the edge.

Opposite: Susan J. Miller's parents in 1953.

As a child, I didn't know that my father and many of the musicians who sat with their wives in our living-room, eating nuts and raisins out of cut-glass candy dishes, were junkies. It wasn't until I was twenty-one, a college senior, that my father told me that he had been a heroin addict, casually slipping it into some otherwise unremarkable conversation. The next day, my mother filled in the story. My father had begun shooting up in 1946, when my mother was pregnant with my brother, who is nineteen months older than me. He stopped when I was around thirteen and my brother was fifteen—the same age as my father's addiction.

I never suspected a thing. Nor did my brother. We never saw any drug paraphernalia. There was a mysterious purplish spot in the crook of my father's elbow, which he said had something to do with the army. His vague explanation was unsatisfactory, but even in my wildest imaginings I never came near the truth. In the fifties, in the white, middle- and working-class communities where we lived, no one discussed drugs, which were synonymous with the utmost degradation and depravity. My parents succeeded in hiding my father's addiction from us, but, as a result, we could never make sense of the strained atmosphere, our lack of money, our many moves. The addiction was the thread that tied everything together. We didn't know that such a thread existed, and so decisions seemed insanely arbitrary, my mother's emotions frighteningly hysterical. My father was often away, staying out late or not coming home at all. My brother and I fought often and violently. My mother was terribly depressed, sometimes desperate. I regularly found her sitting, eyes unfocused, collapsed amid the disorder of a household she was too overwhelmed to manage. She would beg my father not to go out at night. As I got older, I tried to figure out what was going on. An affair? This was a logical explanation, but it didn't fit.

My father was a man of socially unacceptable habits. He was fat, he picked his teeth, he burped, he farted, he blew his nose into the sink in the morning, he bit his nails until he had no nails and then he chewed his fingers, eating himself up. He was a high-octane monologuer, a self-taught high-school drop-out who constantly read, thought and talked politics and culture, gobbling up ideas, stuffing himself as fast as he could—with everything.

He was from Brighton Beach, Brooklyn, and earned his living

dressing windows in what were called 'ladies specialty shops'—independently-owned women's clothing stores in and around New York City. He went from store to store in his display-laden station wagon, visiting them every month or so when they changed their windows. Being a window-dresser was a touch creative, but most importantly it meant he didn't have to fit in; all he had to do was get the job done.

How did a bright Jewish boy from Brighton Beach become a junkie in the late forties? It was partly the crowd he hung out with: white musicians deeply under the influence of Charlie Parker—and Parker's drug, heroin. Stan Getz, Al Cohn, George Handy—all were junkies and all were my father's friends.

My father began with marijuana—at age fifteen. Although drafted during the Second World War, he never made it overseas; he was, I was told, 'honourably discharged' from boot camp in Georgia for health reasons: he was deemed too weak to fight, having lost weight because of the heat. I've always found the story rather odd, if only because, in the army pictures I've seen, he looks so happy and active, even if a little thin, clowning in front of the camera with his friends. Perhaps the story is true, but it seems unlikely. By his late twenties, he was a heroin addict. Ten years later, he was taking amphetamines as well. He occasionally gave me some when I was in college to help me stay up all night writing papers; they were very strong. When he was about fifty, he was taking LSD, mescaline, peyote, whatever he could get.

At college, I received long letters from him, written when he was coming down from an acid or mescaline trip. Often he tripped alone in the living-room of my parents' New Jersey apartment, awake all night, listening to records, writing and thinking while my mother slept. I read pages of his blocky, slanted printing, about how the world is a boat and we are all sinking. So many pages with so many words. Usually I threw them away without finishing them, scanning his stoned raps in front of the big, green, metal trash can in the college mail room, picturing him in the living-room with the sun rising, wired up, hunched over the paper, filling up the page, wanting me to know all the exciting things he had discovered. Part of me wanted to hear them and love him—and indeed did love him for taking the acid, for taking the chance. But another part shut down, unable to care. I would look out of the mail room window on to the college's perfect green lawn, scenic mountains in the distance, little white houses with green shutters, the place of my willed exile, my escape.

One day when I was home from college on vacation, my father and I went into New York together. He was going to retrieve his car from a garage in the West Forties, take me to a friend's downtown and then pick up my mother at her midtown office and drive her home. We took the bus across the bridge, then got on the subway at 178th Street. After the doors shut, my father edged close to me, putting his mouth up to my ear to make himself heard over the screech of the train. I took acid before we left the house this morning and I'm just starting to get off, he said. He was smiling; a naughty kid out in the big grown-up world. My heart sank. My father had swallowed a psychic explosive that might detonate him and then me, if his trip turned bad. The train rocked furiously back and forth, its lights flickering, racing at sixty miles an hour through its pitch-black tunnel on the longest non-stop run in the city, from 125th to 59th Street. At any moment, the subway car might turn into a sealed tomb on an endless nightmare ride. Acid makes you vulnerable, a sponge. It would take only seconds, a quick switch in his head, and he would be gripping my arm and saying, Susan, I've got to get out of here. Now, right now.

We reached our stop, and I stayed close, following him through the smelly, mobbed, low-ceilinged station where at every turn I saw something I feared might set him off: glistening hot dogs revolving under infra-red lights; a legless man on a wheeled board, selling pencils. But at the garage my father understood the Puerto Rican mechanic's broken English better than I did. He checked the bill and counted out cash and coins the right way the first time. Last time I took acid, I found myself in a little family grocery in Santa Fe, staring dumbfounded at the meaningless discs of silver in my hand, unable to buy an orange popsicle without help, thunderstruck by the very concept of money, its simultaneous brilliance and folly. My dad was having no such problems. He was energized; he was having fun. He got behind the wheel and headed out into the river of cars, the honking, swerving cabs, the sticky stop-and-go jams. He dropped me off, waved goodbye, headed back uptown to pick up my mother.

Watching him trip was like discovering that your father was an accomplished deep-sea diver or high-wire artist. Yet I knew that even the best tightrope walker slips. I limped up to my friend's, exhausted.

Never marry a musician, my mother admonished me when I was growing up, in the same way, I suppose, that other mothers warned their daughters off criminals or *schvartzehs* or Jews. I suspected she had a point; life married to a man always on the road would be no picnic. I had heard about the hotel rooms and buses and daytime sleeping. I also knew she meant something more complex; that these men were not to be trusted. She could say, don't marry one, because she had seen so many. What she didn't say, and what I didn't know, was that so many were junkies. Because I didn't know what lay behind her warnings, they seemed mysteriously exaggerated.

The musicians who came to our house fascinated me: their pants with black satin stripes down the sides, their hip talk, their battered horn cases. My father could hear anyone on the radio and know who was playing. He'd say, That's Pres, or, Listen to Diz swing. I loved the fame of these men, the fact that the world knew their names, their sounds, that there were pictures of them in *Down Beat*. I knew some, like Al and Zoot, but most of them I never met. They were part of the life my father lived apart from us children. To me, these were names, or sounds on records, or sometimes faces in our photo album; they belonged to men leaning against lampposts in the Village, or sitting with their arms around attractive women on rocks in Central Park. Allen Eager, Tiny Kahn, George Handy, Stan Getz, Johnny Mandel, Georgie Auld, these names resonate in my heart like the Yiddish that I heard so often then.

I don't know what went on between my father and these men. All I know is that for my father, his junkie years were the greatest of his life. He wanted to tell me about them, so I would understand why he wasn't sorry about what he did. He wanted me to know about the great and wild people he had met, the music he had heard, the crazy underworld places he had been to. He needed to explain that, while being a junkie sounded bad to other people, it had been really wonderful for him. But I couldn't listen. For me, those years of his heroin addiction had been a time of fearful poverty, violence at the hands of my brother and terror that my mother would cease to function. No, I said, I don't want to hear. Each of us was furious: my worst times were his best.

As a child, I was convinced that if my father saw me walking down the street in an unexpected place, away from the clues that linked me to him, such as our apartment or my mother or my school, he would not recognize me. He didn't know what I looked like. But I knew nothing about the drugs; lacking knowledge, I could not say, he is stoned, he is high.

He would not have been a good father even if he hadn't been an addict. By his own admission, he came to parenthood ignorant of love and acquainted only with hate.

My mother told me about my grandmother Esther, the wicked witch of Brighton Beach. According to my mother, my grandmother despised men. She lavished attention on her daughter, my father's only sibling. She dealt in machinations, lies and deceptions, feeding the fires of hate between father and son, sister and brother, so that for weeks this one wouldn't speak to that one, that one wouldn't speak to this one, everyone crushed together in the one basement room where they lived. When my father did well in school, his mother scorned him. She tore up a citation he'd won—and then spat on it. She never kissed him, except on the day he went off to boot camp. His mother and my mother, then his young wife, were standing on the platform, saying goodbye. Seeing the other mothers tearfully embracing their sons, his mother was shamed into touching hers: she pecked his cheek.

We sometimes took her to Ratner's for dinner. Ratner's was a kosher dairy restaurant on lower Second Avenue, where, twenty-four hours a day, an aged waiter with a heavy Yiddish accent brought you baked fish or *kasha varniskes* or blintzes or icy *schav*. Later, when the neighbourhood became the East Village, I would occasionally return to Ratner's for a plate of blintzes, after seeing the Grateful Dead at the Filmore East next door. But at the time, I was ten, eleven, twelve and trying to learn the rules of public behaviour. My grandmother, the urban peasant, did not give a shit about public behaviour. The peasant: belching, slurping, sucking the fishbones. Picking her teeth with the corner of a matchbook. Unbuttoning her blouse to adjust her straps. It was amazing to watch her, truly not giving a damn about anyone or anything except the food in front of her. Across her broad face, she wore a thick layer of dead-white powder and a bright red circle of rouge on each cheek. Her hair was so thin you could see her waxen scalp and the dark roots of each strand. It was dyed a shade that was probably meant to be auburn but was actually a bright, rusty orange.

When Esther belched, my mother said nothing. The daughter of immigrants herself, she was shy and scared inside, afraid to make a mistake. But I was ashamed, sitting there in silence, eating my baked fish and looking up at the huge ugly oil portrait of old Mr Ratner that hung over the cash register.

I really wanted to learn what to do, how to eat, talk, act, seeking self-confidence the only way I could, from the outside in. But I was tethered with doubt and embarrassment. I suffered bourgeois afflictions that must have come from my mother, *and* the desire not to be downtrodden by convention, which came from my father. My mother was a slave to rules she wasn't sure of; my father knew there were rules and he loved to break them; my grandmother didn't even know rules existed.

Occasionally Esther spoke to me, addressing me brusquely in rapid-fire Yiddish (she never learned English, even though she had come here at sixteen: a fuck-you to the New World). Was she really trying to communicate with me, forgetting I didn't know Yiddish? Or did she care so little that she had no memory of what I knew or didn't know? At my look of incomprehension, her expression would turn to disgust: what use is this child, if she can't even speak? And she would dismiss me with a wave of her hand. I felt as though I was nothing more to my grandmother than a body sitting in the aqua, padded chair, a body with no one inside, much as I felt with my father. And again, if I had appeared before her without my parents, without those usual clues to my identity, she would have been unable to place me.

Above: Susan J. Miller's parents with her grandmother at her brother's bar mitzvah in 1960.

I didn't trust grown-ups. They didn't protect me; they didn't see me. To Esther, I was a speck, a smudge.

My father only once told me a story about himself and his mother. I was a college student at the time. The two of us were driving on the highway on a beautiful, clear, cold winter day. My father was behind the wheel. Fourteen years earlier, in 1956, when he was thirty-eight, his father, who had been very sick, died in the hospital while my father and Esther were visiting him. My father took Esther home to Brooklyn, where she asked him for a favour. There were some terms in her will she wanted to review. Would he read it out loud to her? (Even in Yiddish my grandmother was illiterate.) My father was tired and upset and somewhat puzzled that his mother wished to go over her will on the night of her husband's death, but he agreed. (As my father talked, I pictured Esther unlocking the black metal strongbox with the key she wore around her neck and handing him the will. They would have been in her tiny living-room, sitting on her overstuffed flowered chairs, knees almost touching, her heavy-featured face impassive, his eyes wary but hoping to please.) The will turned out to be simple: Esther's house and savings were to go to Sarah, her daughter. Then he heard himself, the fly in the web, reading: And to my son Sidney, I leave nothing, because he is no good.

My father stared at the road ahead.

Why, I cried, would she have you read that to her? What did you do?

My father's voice was tired and bitter. She wanted to see what I would do, he said; she wanted to watch my reaction. Ma, I said, I gotta go home now. I'm tired and it's late. I didn't want to show her how bad I felt, I didn't want to give her the satisfaction. It wasn't the money. I didn't care about that. Let my fucking sister have the money. But why did she have to write that sentence? Why did she have me read it?

My father started to cry. He had never cried in front of me. His hands loosened their grip on the wheel. The car began to drift into the opposite lane, across the white unbroken line.

Look out, I yelled. He grabbed the wheel and turned us towards safety. Look out, I had yelled, and he did. Look out, I had yelled, for what else could I have said?

In 1973, two years after my father told me about his addiction, he stopped in to visit me at my apartment on Charlton Street. He was distraught, not an unusual state for him. Damaged merchandise, he said, are the words that I see in front of me when things get bad, and when I see those words I know it's all over. Do you understand that? He fixed me with his wild, wide-open, hazel eyes. Do you understand what I am trying to say?

Yes, I said, over and over. Yes, I understand what you are trying to say, but I knew he could scarcely see or hear me through the haze and buzz of electric cloud around his head.

Damaged merchandise. He was a window-dresser; he spent

hours making signs on thick, white rectangular cards with a creamy, smooth surface, writing them out in front of the television the night before the job. SALE, they said, HANES HOSIERY, $1.99 A PAIR, or whatever. Next day he propped them up in front of the displays, a bra folded carefully, skilfully, and laid out on the floor, cups pointing up and out. Stockings draped over the Lucite stand, the card tipped in front. At Christmas, he piled mounds of fake snow, hung tinsel, attached big red bows, positioned empty packages wrapped in foil paper, red and green and silver. In the summer there were palm trees and beach balls. He was the window-dresser, his station-wagon filled with displays and rolls of no-seam paper, sprays of stiff flowers, thick cotton sockettes over his shoes to protect the floor, eyes bugged out, seeing in his mind's eye *himself*, on sale, marked down, damaged merchandise, an item nobody, not even the most inveterate bargain hunter, would want.

And he told me this, he spelled it out for me, and I listened even though I didn't want to. I hadn't yet learned how to tell him no; I still thought it was my job to listen to what anyone in my family wanted to say to me: as I had when my brother told me the details of his sex life; or my mother told me how horrible she felt about herself and us. My father paced around my living-room, his voice ranting, careening, echoing in the big empty room that was his sad and lonely and frightened heart. It scared me to listen because I knew that I had been damaged, too: by his not seeing me, as he was not seeing me right then. The room was turning into a funnel, and I felt myself being sucked down into it. I acted very polite, trying to remain a whole person. I asked him some questions. I tried to change the subject. And then I don't remember what I did. Maybe I yelled at him, or maybe I just asked him to leave, telling him I had to go somewhere. Or maybe I said, Oh Daddy, it's awful you feel that way. I was trying to hold on to myself, and no response I could choose would have been any better than any other. Nothing woke him up to me.

In August 1988, my father was diagnosed with liver cancer, the result of chronic hepatitis, a disease associated with heroin addiction. The doctors correctly predicted he would live for five months. He tried chemotherapy, ate a macrobiotic diet, enrolled in an experimental holistic treatment programme. When I visited him in November, it was clear that things would not turn around.

Al Cohn had died of liver cancer as well—that same year. Zoot Sims had been done in by alcohol in 1985. In the weeks before my father died, he played their records, and only theirs, as if they were calling to him and he could hear them.

My mother, who had stuck by him through everything, was still by his side. He was eager to share his latest revelation. A social worker in the treatment programme had asked him what he would miss most when he died. It was an interesting question, and I was interested to hear his answer. He said: I told her that, yeah, sure, I'll miss my wife and my kids, but what I'll miss most is the music. The music is the only thing that's never let me down.

That the revelation would hurt us—my mother especially—never occurred to him. He never kept his thoughts to himself, even if it was cruel to express them. Neither my mother nor I said a word. The statement was the truth of him—not only what he said, but also the fact that he would say it to us, and say it without guilt, without apology, without regret.

 **BARCLAYS**
New Stages

festival of independent theatre

 ROYAL COURT THEATRE

Sloane Square
London SW1

6 MAY - 5 JUNE

Box Office: 071 730 1745

WORKSHOPS

There are four series of workshops. The ticket price includes entry to all sessions on the dates indicated. Each session begins at 10am and ends at 6pm.

April 23 and 24
Holborn Centre for Performing Arts at Kingsway College
3 Cups Yard, Sandland Street,
London WC1

This year, prior to the Barclays New Stages Festival, we are offering a full weekend of activity with the opportunity for you to undertake a "dip your toe in" session with an individual company or group, or a total immersion throughout the two days. With....

LAURIE BOOTH, GABRIEL GAWIN (NEW BREED), PETE BROOKS (INSOMNIAC), EDWARD LAM, MARK WHITELAW AND EDDIE AYLWARD (THE GLEE CLUB), BARNABY STONE (RALF RALF), BOBBY BAKER, NENAGH WATSON & RACHAEL FIELD (DOO COT).

£45 (£40 - usual reductions)

May 14 and 15
Royal Court Young People's Theatre
309 Portobello Road, London W9
DOO COT - In Search of a Character
£35 (£30 - usual reductions)

May 21, 22, 23
Royal Court Theatre
PETE BROOKS - Falling
£45 (£40 - usual reductions)

June 4, 5
RALF RALF- Behaviour in Public £35
(£30 - usual reductions)

OTHER EVENTS

26 May at 6.15pm
Royal Court Theatre
AUTHORS ON STAGE
Alan Hollinghurst and Edmund White presented in association with Random House and Waterstone Books, Charing Cross Road.

Registered Charity No. 231242

TALKS

THE SEVEN AGES OF THEATRE
A series of symposia organised by ICA Talks in collaboration with the Barclays New Stages Festival and the Royal Court Theatre. These talks are available as a series or individually.

Friday 6 May - 6pm
STAGE(1) *THE EMPTY SPACE AND AFTER*
at The Cottesloe Theatre
in association with the Royal National Theatre and the ICA

Saturday 7 May 2pm - 6pm
STAGE(2) *The Place of Performance*
in association with LIFT at the ICA

Saturday 14 May
10.30am 3.30pm
RAGE *Issues beyond the Pole*
in association with Marginalia
and
4pm - 6pm
SAGE
Thinking New Theatres in association with Routledge at the ICA

Sunday 15 May 10.30am - 6pm PAGE
New Performance Publishing
in association with Marginalia at the ICA

Wednesday 25 May - 6pm
NEW OLD AGE
Avant Garding the 90s
at Turtle Key Arts Centre

Saturday 28 May
10.30am - 1.30pm
ENGAGE
A European Agenda in association with Routledge at Royal Court Theatre

Thursday 2 June 7.30pm - 9.30pm
WAGE
New money for New Performance at the ICA.

Full details are contained in a seperate leaflet obtainable from the Royal Court Theatre and ICA.

Royal National Theatre
(071) 928 2522
ICA (071) 930 3947

 ROUTLEDGE

Arts Council Funded

GRANTA

Bret Easton Ellis
The Up Escalator

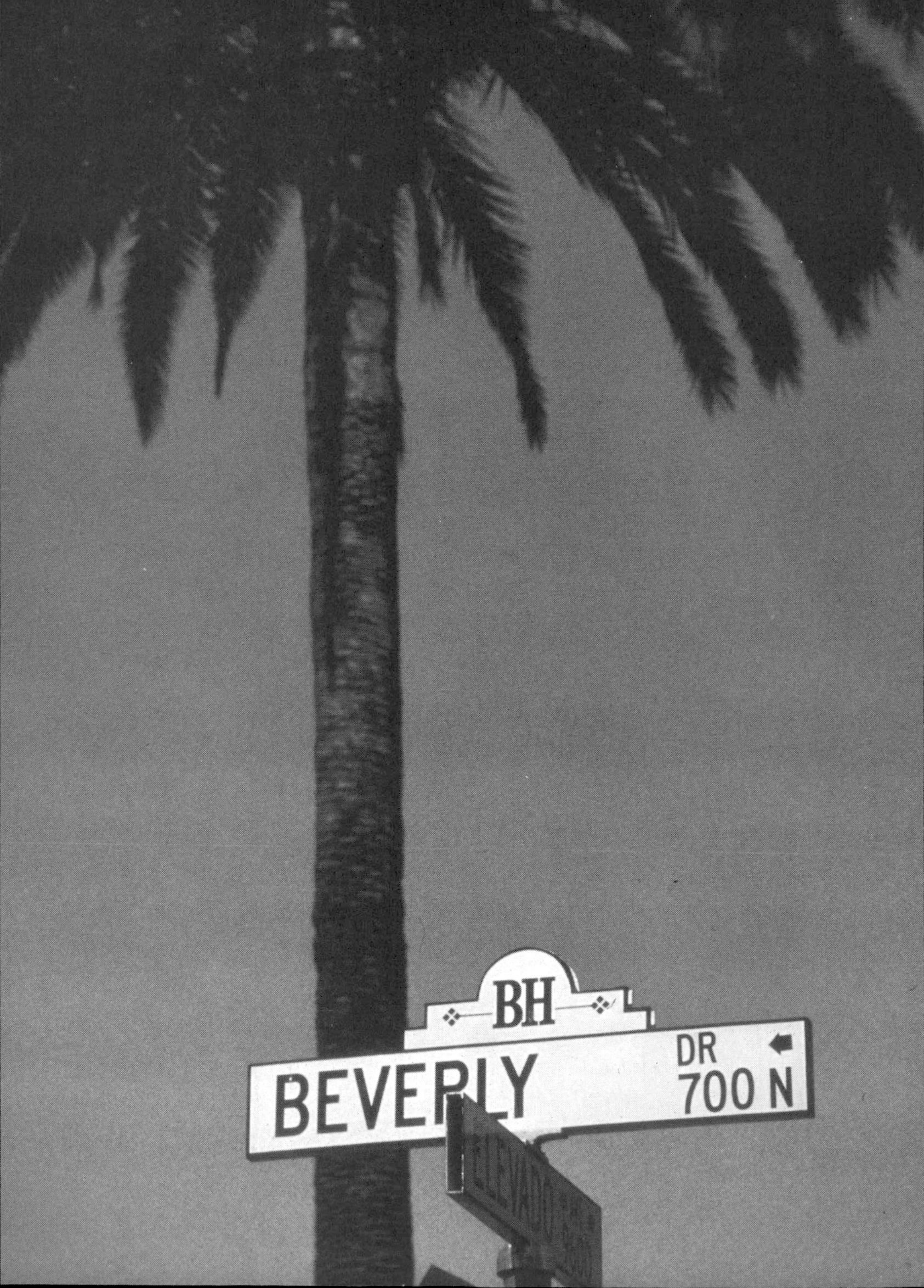
BH
BEVERLY
DR
700 N

I'm standing on the balcony of Martin's apartment in Westwood, holding a drink in one hand and a cigarette in the other, and Martin comes towards me, rushes at me, and with both hands pushes me off the balcony. Martin's apartment in Westwood is only two storeys high, and so the fall is not that long. As I'm falling I hope I will wake up before I hit the ground. I hit the asphalt, hard, and lying there, on my stomach, my neck twisted completely around, I look up and focus on Martin's handsome face staring down at me with a benign smile. It's the serenity in that smile—not the fall really, or the imagined image of my cracked, bleeding body, that wakes me up.

I stare at the ceiling, then over at the digital alarm clock on the nightstand next to the bed, and it tells me that it is almost noon, and I uselessly hope that I have misread the time by shutting my eyes tightly, but when I open them again, the clock still reads that it is almost noon. I raise my head slightly and look over at the small, flickering red numbers glowing from the Betamax, and they tell me the same thing the hands on the melon-colored alarm do: almost noon. I try to fall back asleep, but the Librium I took at dawn has worn off, and my mouth feels thick and dry, and I am thirsty. I get up, slowly, and walk into the bathroom, and as I turn on the faucet I look into the mirror for a long time until I am forced to notice the new lines beginning around the eyes. I avert my gaze and concentrate on the cold water rushing out of the faucet and filling the cup my hands have made.

I open a mirrored cabinet and take out a bottle. I take its top off and count only four Librium left. I pour one green and black capsule into my hand, staring at it, then place it carefully next to the sink and close the bottle and put it back into the medicine cabinet, and take out another bottle and place two Valium from it on the counter next to the green and black capsule. I put the bottle back and take out another. I open it, looking in cautiously. I notice there is not too much Thorazine left and I make a mental note to refill the prescription of Librium and Valium, and I take a Librium and one of the two Valium, and turn the shower on.

I step into the big white and black tiled shower stall and stand there. The water, cool at first, then warmer, hits me in the

137

face hard and it weakens me, and as I slowly drop to my knees, the black and green capsule somehow lodged in the back of my throat, I imagine, for an instant, that the water is a deep and cool aquamarine, and I'm parting my lips, tilting my head to get some water down my throat to help swallow the pill. When I open my eyes I start moaning when I see that the water coming down at me is not blue but clear and light and warm and making the skin on my breasts and stomach red.

After dressing I walk downstairs, and it distresses me to think of how long it takes to get ready for a day: of how many minutes pass as I wander listlessly through a large walk-in closet, of how long it seems to take to find the shoes I want, of the effort it takes to lift myself from the shower. You can forget this if you walk downstairs carefully, methodically, concentrating on each footstep. I reach the bottom landing and I can hear voices coming from the kitchen and I move towards them. From where I'm standing I can see my son and another boy in the kitchen looking for something to eat, and the maid sitting at the large, wood-block table staring at photographs in yesterday's *Herald Examiner*, her sandals kicked off, blue nail polish on her toenails. The stereo in the den is on and someone, a woman, is singing, 'I found a picture of you.' I walk into the kitchen. Graham looks up from the refrigerator and says, unsmiling, 'Up early?'

'Why aren't you at school?' I ask, trying to sound like I care, reaching past him into the refrigerator for a Tab.

'Seniors get out early on Mondays.'

'Oh.' I believe him but don't know why. I open the Tab and take a swallow. I have a feeling that the pill I took earlier is still lodged in my throat, stuck, melting. I take another swallow.

Graham reaches past me and pulls an orange out of the refrigerator. The other boy, tall and blond, like Graham, stands by the sink and stares out the window and into the pool. Graham and the other boy both have their school uniforms on and they look very much alike: Graham peeling an orange, the other boy staring out at the water. I'm having a hard time not finding either one of their stances unnerving so I turn away, but the sight of the maid sitting at the table, sandals by her feet, the unmistakable

138

smell of marijuana coming from her purse and sweater, somehow seems worse, and I take another swallow of Tab, then pour the rest of it down the sink. I begin to leave the kitchen.

Graham turns to the boy. 'Do you want to watch MTV?'

'I don't . . . think so,' the boy says, staring into the pool.

I pick up my purse which is sitting in an alcove next to the refrigerator and make sure my wallet is in it because the last time I was in Robinson's, it was not. I am about to walk out the door. The maid folds the paper. Graham takes off his burgundy letterman's sweater. The other boy wants to know if Graham has *Alien* on video. From the den, the woman is singing, 'Circumstance beyond our control.' I find myself staring at my son, blond and tall and tanned, with blank, green eyes, opening the refrigerator, taking out another orange. He studies it, then lifts his head when he notices me standing by the door.

'Are you going somewhere?' he asks.

'Yes.'

He waits for a moment, and when I don't say anything, he shrugs and turns away and begins to peel the orange, and somewhere on the way to Le Dôme to meet Martin for lunch, I realize that Graham is only one year younger than Martin, and I have to pull the Jaguar over to a curb on Sunset and turn the volume down and unroll a window, then the sunroof, and let the heat from today's sun warm the inside of the car, concentrating on a tumbleweed that the wind is pushing slowly across an empty boulevard.

Martin is sitting at the round bar in Le Dôme. He is wearing a suit and a tie, and he is tapping his foot impatiently to the music that is playing through the restaurant's sound system. He watches me as I make my way over to him.

'You're late,' he says, showing me the time on a gold Rolex.

'Yes, I am,' I say, and then, 'Let's sit down.'

Martin looks at his watch and then at his empty glass and then back at me, and I am clutching my purse tightly against my side. Martin sighs, then nods. The maître d' shows us to a table and we sit down, and Martin starts to talk about his classes at UCLA and then about how his parents are irritating him, about how they came over to his apartment in Westwood unannounced, about how his stepfather wanted him to come to a dinner party he was throwing at Chasen's, about how Martin did not want to go to a dinner party his stepfather was throwing at Chasen's, about how tiredly words were exchanged.

I'm looking out the window at a Spanish valet standing in front of a Rolls-Royce, staring into it, muttering. When Martin begins to complain about his BMW and how much the insurance is, I interrupt.

'Why did you call the house?'

'I wanted to talk to you,' he says. 'I was going to cancel.'

'Don't call the house.'

'Why?' he asks. 'There's someone there who cares?'

I light a cigarette.

He puts his fork down next to his plate and then looks away. 'We're eating at Le Dôme,' Martin says. 'I mean, Jesus.'

'OK?' I ask.

'Yeah. OK.'

I ask for the check and pay it and follow Martin back to his apartment in Westwood where we have sex, and I give Martin a pith helmet as a gift.

I am lying on a chaise-longue by the pool. Issues of *Vogue* and *Los Angeles* magazine and the Calendar section of the *Times* are stacked next to where I am lying, but I can't read them because the color of the pool takes my eyes away from the words, and I stare longingly into the thin aquamarine water. I want to go swimming, but the heat of the sun has made the water too warm, and Dr Nova has warned about the dangers of taking Librium and swimming laps.

A poolboy is cleaning the pool. The poolboy is very young and tanned and has blond hair; he is not wearing a shirt but he is wearing very tight, white jeans, and when he leans down to check the temperature of the water, muscles in his back ripple gently beneath smooth, clean, brown skin. The poolboy has brought a portable cassette player that sits by the edge of the Jacuzzi, and someone is singing, 'Our love's in jeopardy,' and I'm hoping the sound of the palm fronds moving in the warm wind will carry the music into the Suttons's yard. I'm intrigued by how deep the poolboy's concentration seems to be, at how gently the water moves when he skims a net across it, at how he empties the net that catches leaves and multicolored dragonflies that seem to litter the water's gleaming surface. He opens a drain, the muscles in his arm flexing lightly, only for a moment. And I keep watching, transfixed, as he reaches into the round hole, and his arm begins to lift something out of the hole, muscles momentarily flexing again, and his hair is blond and wind-blown, streaked by sun, and I shift my body in the lounge chair, not moving my eyes.

The poolboy begins to raise his arm out of the drain and he lifts two large gray rags up and drops them, dripping, on to the concrete, and stares at them. He stares at the rags for a long time. And then he makes his way towards me. I panic for a moment, adjusting my sun-glasses, reaching for the tanning oil. The poolboy is walking towards me slowly, and the sun is beating down, and I'm spreading my legs and rubbing oil on the inside of my thighs and then across my knees and ankles. He is standing over me; Valium, taken earlier, disorients everything, makes backgrounds move in wavy, slow motion. A shadow covers my face and it allows me to look up at the poolboy, and I can hear from the portable stereo, 'Our love's in jeopardy,' and the poolboy opens his mouth, the lips full, the teeth white and clean and even, and I overwhelmingly need him to ask me to get into the white pick-up truck parked at the bottom of the driveway and have him instruct me to go out to the desert with him. His hands, perfumed by chlorine, would rub oil over my back, across my stomach, my neck. As he looks down at me, with the rock music coming from the cassette deck and the palm trees shifting in a hot desert wind and the glare of the sun shining up off the surface of the blue water in the pool, I tense up and wait for him to say something, anything, a sigh, a moan. I breathe in, stare up into the poolboy's eyes, through my sun-glasses, trembling.

'You have two dead rats in your drain.'

I don't say anything.

'Rats. Two dead ones. They got caught in the drain or maybe they fell in, who knows.' He looks at me blankly.

141

'Why . . . are you . . . telling me this?' I ask.

He stands there, expecting me to say something else. I lower my sun-glasses and look over at the gray bundle near the Jacuzzi.

'Take . . . them, away,' I manage to say, looking down.

'Yeah. OK,' the poolboy says, hands in his pockets. 'I just don't know how they got trapped in there?'

The statement, really a question, is phrased in such a languid way that though it doesn't warrant an answer, I tell him, 'I guess . . . we'll never know.'

I am looking at the cover of an issue of *Los Angeles* magazine. A huge arc of water reaches for the sky, a fountain, blue and green and white, spraying upward.

'Rats are afraid of water,' the poolboy is telling me.

'Yes,' I say. 'I've heard. I know.'

The poolboy walks back to the two drowned rats and picks them up by their tails which should be pink but even from where I'm sitting I can see are now pale blue, and he puts them into what I thought was his toolbox, and then to erase the notion of the poolboy keeping the rats, I open the *Los Angeles* magazine and search for the article about the fountain on the cover.

I am sitting in a restaurant on Melrose with Anne and Eve and Faith. I am drinking my second Bloody Mary, and Anne and Eve have had too many kirs, and Faith orders what I believe to be a fourth vodka gimlet. I light a cigarette. Faith is talking about how her son, Dirk, had his driver's license revoked for speeding down Pacific Coast Highway, drunk. Faith is driving his Porsche now. I wonder if Faith knows that Dirk sells cocaine to tenth-graders at Beverly Hills High. Graham told me this one afternoon last week in the kitchen, even though I had asked for no information about Dirk. Faith's Audi is in the shop for the third time this year. She wants to sell it but she's confused about which kind of car to buy. Anne tells her that ever since the new engine replaced the old engine in the XJ6, it has been running well. Anne turns to me and asks me about my car, about William's. On the verge of weeping, I tell her that it is running smoothly.

Eve does not say too much. Her daughter is in a psychiatric

hospital in Camarillo. Eve's daughter tried to kill herself with a gun by shooting herself in the stomach. I cannot understand why Eve's daughter did not shoot herself in the head. I cannot understand why she lay down on the floor of her mother's walk-in closet and pointed her stepfather's gun at her stomach. I try to imagine the sequence of events that afternoon leading up to the shooting. But Faith begins to talk about how her daughter's therapy is progressing. Sheila is an anorexic. My own daughter has met Sheila and may also be anorexic.

Finally, an uneasy silence falls across the table in the restaurant on Melrose, and I stare at Anne who has forgotten to cover the outline of scars from the face-lift she had in Palm Springs three months ago by the same surgeon as did mine and William's. I consider telling them about the rats in the drain, or the way the poolboy floated into my eyes before turning away, but instead I light another cigarette, and the sound of Anne's voice breaking the silence startles me and I burn a finger.

On Wednesday morning, after William gets out of bed and asks where the Valium is, and after I stumble out of bed to retrieve it from my purse, and after he reminds me that the family has reservations at Spago at eight, and after I hear the wheels on the Mercedes screech out of the driveway, and after Susan tells me that she is going to Westwood with Alana and Blair after school and will meet us at Spago, and after I fall back asleep and dream of rats drowning, crawling desperately over each other in a steaming, bubbling Jacuzzi, and dozens of poolboys, nude, standing over the Jacuzzi, laughing, pointing at the drowning rats, their heads nodding in unison to the beat of the music coming from the portable stereos they hold in their golden arms, I wake up and walk downstairs and take a Tab out of the refrigerator and find twenty milligrams of Valium in a pillbox in another purse in the alcove by the refrigerator, and take two milligrams. From the kitchen I can hear the maid vacuuming in the living-room and it moves me to get dressed, and I drive to a Thrifty drugstore in Beverly Hills and walk towards the pharmacy, the empty bottle that used to be filled with black and green capsules clenched tightly in my fist. But the store is air-conditioned and cool, and the glare from the fluorescent lighting and the Muzak playing somewhere above me as background noise have a pronounced anaesthetic effect, and my grip on the brown plastic bottle relaxes, loosens.

At the counter I hand the empty bottle to the pharmacist. He puts glasses on and looks at the plastic container. I study my fingernails and uselessly try to remember the name of the song that is floating through the store's sound system.

'Miss?' the pharmacist begins awkwardly.

'Yes?' I lower my sun-glasses.

'It says here "no refills".'

'What?' I ask, startled. 'Where?'

The pharmacist points to two typed words at the bottom of the piece of paper taped to the bottle next to my psychiatrist's name and next to that, the date, 10/10/83.

'I think Dr Nova made some kind of . . . mistake,' I say slowly, lamely, glancing at the bottle again.

'Well.' The pharmacist sighs. 'There's nothing I can do.'

I look at my fingernails again and try to think of something to say, which, finally, is, 'But I . . . need it refilled.'

'I'm sorry,' the pharmacist says, clearly embarrassed, shifting from one foot to the other, nervously. He hands me back the bottle, and when I try to hand it back to him, he shrugs.

'There are reasons why your doctor did not want the prescription refilled,' he offers kindly, as if speaking to a child.

I try to laugh, wiping my face, and gaily say, 'Oh, he's always playing jokes on me.'

I think about the way the pharmacist looked at me after I said this as I drive home.

I walk past the maid, the smell of marijuana drifting past me for an instant. Up in the bedroom I lock the door and close the shades and take off my clothes and put a tape of a movie in the Betamax and get under washed, cool sheets and cry for an hour and try to watch the movie. I take some more Valium and then I ransack the bathroom looking for an old prescription of Nembutal and then I rearrange my shoes in the closet and then I put another movie in the Betamax and then I open the windows, and the smell of bougainvillaea drifts through the partially closed shades, and I smoke a cigarette and wash my face.

I call Martin.

'Hello?' Another boy answers.

'Martin?' I ask anyway.

'Uh, no.'

I pause. 'Is Martin there?'

'Uh, let me check.'

I can hear the phone being set down and I want to laugh at the idea of someone, some boy, probably tanned, young, blond, like Martin, standing in Martin's apartment, putting the phone down and going to look for him, for anyone, in the small three-room studio, but it does not seem funny after a while. The boy comes back on the line.

'I think he's at the, um, beach.' The boy doesn't seem too sure.

I say nothing.

'Would you like to leave a message?' he asks, slyly for some reason, and then, after a pause, 'Wait a minute, is this Julie? The girl Mike and I met at 385 North? With the Rabbit?'

I don't say anything.

'You guys had about three grams on you and a white VW Rabbit.'

I do not say anything.

'Like, hello?'

'No.'

'You don't have a VW Rabbit?'

'I'll call back.'

'Whatever.'

I hang up, wondering who the boy is, if he knows about me and Martin, and I wonder if Martin is lying on the sand, drinking a beer, smoking a clove cigarette beneath a striped umbrella at the beach club, wearing Wayfarer sun-glasses, his hair slicked back, staring out to where the land ends and merges with water, or if instead he is actually on his bed in his room, lying beneath a poster of the Go-Gos, studying for a chemistry exam and at the same time looking through car advertisements for a new BMW. I'm sleeping until the tape in the Betamax ends and there's static.

I am sitting with my son and daughter at a table in a restaurant on Sunset. Susan is wearing a miniskirt that she bought at a store called Flip on Melrose, a store situated not too far from where I burned my finger at lunch with Eve and Faith and Anne. Susan is also wearing a white T-shirt with the words LOS ANGELES written on it in red handwriting that looks like blood that hasn't quite dried, dripping. Susan is also wearing an old Levi's jacket with a Stray Cats button pinned to one of the faded lapels, and Wayfarer sun-glasses. She takes the slice of lemon from her glass of water and chews on it, biting at the rind. I cannot even remember if we have ordered or not. I wonder what a Stray Cat is.

Graham is sitting next to Susan, and I am fairly sure that he is stoned. He gazes out past the windows and into the headlights of passing cars. William is making a phone call to the studio. He is in the process of tying up a deal which is not a bad thing. William has not been specific about the movie or the people in it or who is financing it. In the trades I have read rumors that it is a sequel to a very successful movie that came out during the summer of 1982, about a wisecracking Martian who looks like a big, sad grape. William has been to the phone in the back of the restaurant four times since we arrived; I have the feeling that he leaves the table and just stands in the back of the restaurant because at the table next to ours is an actress who is sitting with a very young surfer, and the actress keeps glaring at William whenever he is at the table, and I know that she has slept with him, and she knows I know, and when our eyes meet for a moment, by accident, we both turn away abruptly.

Susan begins to hum some song to herself as she drums her fingers on the table. Graham lights a cigarette, not caring if we say anything about it, and his eyes, red and half closed, water for a moment.

'There's this, like, funny sound in my car,' Susan says. 'I think I better take it in.' She fingers the rim of her sun-glasses.

'If it's making a funny noise, you should,' I say.

'Well, like, I need it. I'm seeing the Psychedelic Furs at the Civic on Friday and I totally have to take my car.' Susan looks at Graham. 'That's if Graham got my tickets.'

'Yeah, I got your tickets,' Graham says with what sounds

like great effort. 'And stop saying totally.'

'Who did you get them from?' Susan asks, fingers drumming.

'Julian.'

'Not Julian.'

'Yeah. Why?' Graham tries to sound annoyed but seems tired.

'He's such a stoner. Probably got crappy seats. He's such a stoner,' Susan says again. She stops drumming, looks at Graham straight on. 'Just like you.'

Graham nods his head slowly and does not say anything. Before I can ask him to dispute his sister, he says, 'Yeah, just like me.'

'He sells heroin,' Susan says casually.

I glance over at the actress whose hand is gripping the surfer's thigh while he eats pizza.

'He's also a male prostitute,' Susan adds.

A long pause. 'Was that . . . statement directed at me?' I ask softly.

'That is, like, such a total lie,' Graham manages to say. 'Who told you that? That Valley bitch Sharon Wheeler?'

'Not quite. I know that the owner of the Seven Seas slept with him, and now Julian has a free pass and all the coke he wants.' Susan sighs, mock wearily. 'Besides, it's just too ironic that they both have herpes.'

This makes Graham laugh for some reason and he takes a drag from his cigarette and says, 'Julian does not have herpes and he did not get it from the owner of the Seven Seas.' Pause, exhale, then, 'He got VD from Dominique Dentrel.'

William sits down. 'Christ, my own kids are talking about Quaaludes and faggots, Jesus—oh take your goddamned sunglasses off, Susan. We're at Spago, not the goddamned beach club.' William gulps down half a white-wine spritzer that I watched go flat twenty minutes ago. He glances over at the actress and then at me, and says, 'We're going to the Schrawtzes' party Friday night.'

I finger my napkin, then I light a cigarette. 'I don't want to go to the Schrawtzes' party Friday night,' I say softly, exhaling.

William looks at me and lights a cigarette and says, just as softly, looking directly at me, 'What do you want to do instead?

147

Sleep? Lie out by the pool? Count your shoes?'

Graham looks down, giggling.

Susan sips her water, glances at the surfer.

After a while, I ask Susan and Graham how school is.

Graham doesn't answer.

Susan says, 'OK. Belinda Laurel has herpes.'

I'm wondering if Belinda Laurel got it from Julian or the owner of the Seven Seas. I am also having a hard time restraining myself from asking Susan what a Stray Cat is.

Graham speaks up, barely, 'She got it from Vince Parker whose parents bought him a 928 even though they know he is completely into animal tranquillizers.'

'That is really . . . ' Susan pauses, searching for the right word.

I close my eyes and think about the boy who answered the phone at Martin's apartment.

'Grody . . . ' Susan finishes.

Graham says, 'Yeah, totally grody.'

William looks over at the actress groping the surfer and, grimacing, says, 'Jesus, you kids are sick. I've gotta make another call.'

Graham, looking wary and hungover, stares out the windows and over at Tower Records across the street with a longing that surprises me, and then I close my eyes and think about the color of water, a lemon tree, a scar.

On Thursday morning my mother calls. The maid comes into my room at eleven and wakes me by saying, 'Telephone, *su madre, su madre, señora,*' and I say, '*No estoy aquí,* Rosa, *no estoy aquí . . .* ' and drift back to sleep. After I wake up at one and wander out by the pool, smoking a cigarette and drinking a Perrier, the phone rings in the pool house and I realize that I will have to talk to my mother in order to get it over with. Rosa answers the phone, which is my cue to move back up to the main house.

'Yes, it's me.' My mother sounds lonely, irritated. 'Were you out? I called earlier.'

'Yes.' I sigh. 'Shopping.'

'Oh.' Pause. 'For what?'

'Well, for . . . dogs,' I say, then, 'shopping,' and then, 'for dogs.' And then, 'How do you feel?'

'How do you think?'

I sigh, lie back on the bed. 'I don't know. The same?' And then, after a minute, 'Don't cry,' I'm saying. 'Please, please, don't cry.'

'It's all so useless. I still see Dr Scott every day and there's the therapy, and he keeps saying, "It's coming along, it's coming along," and I keep asking, "*What's* coming along, *what* is coming along?" and then . . . ' My mother stops, out of breath.

'Does he still have you on the Demerol?'

'Yes.' She sighs. 'I'm still on the Demerol.'

'Well, this is . . . good.'

My mother's voice breaks again. 'I don't know if I can take this anymore. My skin, it's all . . . my skin . . . '

'Please.'

' . . . is yellow. It's all yellow.'

I light a cigarette.

'Please.' I close my eyes. 'Everything is all right.'

'Where are Susan and Graham?'

'They're at . . . school,' I say, trying not to sound too doubtful.

'I would have liked to talk to them,' she says. 'I miss them sometimes, you know.'

I put the cigarette out. 'Yes. Well. They . . . miss you too, you know. Yes . . . '

'I know.'

Trying to make conversation, I ask, 'So, what have you been doing with yourself?'

'I just got back from the clinic and I'm in the process of cleaning out the attic and I found those photographs we took that Christmas in New York. The ones I've been looking for. When you were twelve. When we stayed at the Carlyle.'

For the past two weeks now my mother always seems to be cleaning out the attic and finding the same photographs from that Christmas in New York. I remember the Christmas vaguely. The hours that passed as she chose a dress for me on

Christmas Eve, then brushing my hair in long, light strokes. A Christmas show at Radio City Music Hall, and the candy cane I ate during the show which resembled a thin, scared-looking Santa Claus. There was the night my father got drunk at the Plaza, and the fight between my parents in the taxi on the way back to the Carlyle, and later that night I could hear them arguing, the predictable sound of glass breaking in the room next to mine. A Christmas dinner at La Grenouille where my father tried to kiss my mother and she turned away. But the thing I remember most, the thing I remember with a clarity that makes me cringe, is that there were no photographs taken on that trip.

'How's William?' my mother asks when she gets no reply from me about the pictures.

'What?' I ask, startled, slipping back into the conversation.

'William. Your husband,' and then, with an edge, 'my son-in-law. William.'

'He's fine. Fine. He's fine.' The actress at the table next to ours last night in Spago kissed the surfer on the mouth as he scraped caviar off a pizza, and when I got up to leave, she smiled at me. My mother, her skin yellow, her body thin and frail from lack of food, is dying in a large, empty house that overlooks a bay in San Francisco. The poolboy has set traps smudged with peanut butter around the edges of the pool. Randomness, surrender.

'That's good.'

Nothing is said for close to two minutes. I keep count and I can hear a clock ticking and the maid humming to herself while cleaning the windows in Susan's room down the hall, and I light another cigarette and hope that my mother will hang up soon. My mother finally clears her throat and says something.

'My hair is falling out.'

I have to hang up.

The psychiatrist I see, Dr Nova, is young and tanned and drives a Peugeot and wears Giorgio Armani suits and has a house in Malibu and often complains about the service at Trumps. His practice lies off Wilshire and it's in a large white stucco complex across from Neiman Marcus, and on the days I see him I usually park my car at Neiman Marcus and wander around the store until I buy something and then walk across the street. Today, high in his office on the tenth floor, Dr Nova is telling me that at a party out in the Colony last night someone 'tried to drown'. I ask him if it was one of his patients. Dr Nova says it was the wife of a rock star whose single has been number two on the *Billboard* charts for the past three weeks. He begins to tell me who else was at the party when I have to interrupt him.

'I need the Librium refilled.'

He lights a thin, Italian cigarette and asks, 'Why?'

'Don't ask me why.' I yawn. 'Just do it.'

Dr Nova exhales, then asks, 'Why shouldn't I ask you?'

I'm looking out the window. 'Because I asked you not to?' I say softly. 'Because I pay you one hundred and thirty-five dollars an hour?'

Dr Nova takes a drag from his cigarette, then looks out the window. After a while, he asks, tiredly, 'What are you thinking?'

I keep staring out the window, stupefied, transfixed by palm trees swaying in a hot wind, highlighted against an orange sky, and, below that, a billboard for Forest Lawn.

Dr Nova is clearing his throat.

Slightly irritated, I say, 'Just refill the prescription and . . .' I sigh. 'All right?'

'I'm only looking out for your best interests.'

I smile gratefully, incredulous. He looks at the smile weirdly, uncertain, not understanding where it comes from.

I spot Graham's small, old Porsche on Wilshire Boulevard and follow him, surprised at how careful a driver he seems to be, at how he flashes his signals when he wants to change lanes, at how he slows and begins to brake at yellow lights and then comes to a complete stop at red lights, at how cautiously he seems to move the car across the road. I assume that Graham is driving home, but when he passes Robertson, I follow him.

Graham drives along Wilshire until he makes a right on to a side street, after crossing Santa Monica. I pull into a Mobil station and watch as he pulls into the driveway of a large, white apartment complex. He parks the Porsche behind a red Ferrari and then gets out, looks around. I put on my sun-glasses, roll up my window. Graham knocks on the door of one of the apartments facing the street, and the boy who was over earlier in the week, in the kitchen, staring out into the pool, opens the door, and Graham walks in, and the door closes. Graham walks out of the house twenty minutes later with the boy, who is only wearing shorts, and they shake hands. Graham stumbles back to his car, dropping his keys. He stoops down to pick them up and after three tries, finally grabs them. He gets into the Porsche, closes the door and looks down at his lap. Then he brings his finger to his mouth and tastes it, lightly. Satisfied, he looks back down in his lap, puts something in the glove compartment and pulls out from behind the red Ferrari and drives back on to Wilshire.

There is a sudden rapping on the passenger window, and I look up, startled. It's a handsome gas-station attendant who asks me to move my car, and as I start the engine an image that I'm uneasy about the validity of comes into my line of vision: Graham at his sixth birthday party, wearing gray shorts, an expensive tie-dyed shirt, penny loafers, blowing out all the candles on a Flintstones birthday cake, and William bringing a Big Wheel tricycle out of the trunk of a silver Cadillac, and a photographer taking pictures of Graham riding the Big Wheel around the driveway, on the lawn and eventually into the pool. Driving on to Wilshire, I lose track of the memory, and when I get back home, Graham's car is not there.

I am lying in bed in Martin's apartment in Westwood. Martin has turned on MTV and he is lip-synching to Prince and he has his sun-glasses on and is nude and pretends to be playing the guitar. The air-conditioner is on and I can almost hear its hum which I try to focus on instead of Martin who begins to dance in front of the bed, an unlit cigarette hanging from his mouth. I turn over on my side. Martin turns the sound on the television off and puts on an old Beach Boys album. He lights the cigarette. I pull the covers up over my body. Martin jumps on the bed, lies next to me, doing leg lifts. I can feel him raising his legs slowly.

He stops doing this and then looks at me. He reaches down below the covers and grins.

'Your legs are really smooth.'

'I had them waxed.'

'Awesome.'

'I had to drink a small bottle of Absolut to endure the process.'

Martin jumps up suddenly, straddling me, growling, imitating a tiger or a lion or actually just a very large cat. The Beach Boys are singing 'Wouldn't it be nice'. I take a drag from Martin's cigarette and look up at him. He is very tanned and strong and young, with blue eyes that are so vague and blank they are impossible not to fall into. On the television screen there is a piece of popcorn in black and white and beneath the popcorn are the words: VERY IMPORTANT.

'Were you at the beach yesterday?' I ask.

'No.' He grins. 'Why? Thought you saw me there?'

'No. Just wondered.'

'I'm the tannest one in my family.'

He has half an erection and he takes my hand and places it around the shaft, winking at me sarcastically. I take my hand from it and run my fingers up his stomach and chest, and then touch his lips, and he flinches.

'I wonder what your parents would think if they knew a friend of theirs was sleeping with their son,' I murmur.

'You're not friends with my parents,' Martin says, his grin faltering slightly.

'No, I only play tennis with your mother twice a week.'

'Boy, I wonder who wins those matches.' He rolls his eyes. 'I don't want to talk about my mother.' He tries to kiss me. I push him off and he lies there and touches himself and mumbles the lyrics to another Beach Boys song. I interrupt him.

'Do you know that I have a hairdresser named Lance, and Lance is a homosexual. I believe you would use the term "a total homosexual". He wears make-up and jewellery, and has a very bad, affected lisp and he is constantly telling me about his young boyfriends and he is just extremely effeminate. Anyway, I went to his salon today because I have to go to the Schrawtzes' party tonight, and so I walked into the salon and I told Lillian, the woman who takes the appointments down, that I had an appointment with Lance, and Lillian said that Lance had had to take a week off, and I was very upset, and I said, "Where is he? On a cruise somewhere?" and Lillian looked at me and said, "No, he's not on a cruise somewhere. His son died in a car accident near Las Vegas last night," and I rescheduled my appointment and walked out of the salon.' I look over at Martin. 'Don't you find that remarkable?'

Martin is looking up at the ceiling and then he looks over at me and says, 'Yeah, totally remarkable.' He gets up off the bed.

'Where are you going?' I ask.

He pulls on his underwear. 'I have a class at four.'

'One you actually go to?'

Martin pulls on faded jeans and a Polo pullover, and slips his Topsiders on, and as I sit on the edge of the bed, brushing my hair, he sits next to me and, with a boyish smile spread wide across his face, asks, 'Baby, could I please borrow sixty bucks? I gotta pay this guy for these Billy Idol tickets and I forgot to go to the Instateller and it's just really a hassle . . . ' His voice trails off.

'Yeah.' I reach into my purse and hand Martin four twenties, and he kisses my neck and says perfunctorily, 'Thanks baby, I'll pay you back.'

'Yes you will. Don't call me baby.'

'You can let yourself out,' he calls as he walks out the door.

The Jaguar breaks down on Wilshire. I am driving and the sunroof is open and the radio is on and suddenly the car jerks and begins to pull to the right. I step on the gas pedal and press it to the floor and the car jerks again and pulls to the right. I park the car, crookedly, next to the curb, near the corner of Wilshire and Le Cienega, and after a couple of minutes of trying to start it again, I pull the keys out of the ignition and sit in the stalled Jaguar with the sunroof open and listen to the traffic passing. I finally get out of the car and find a phone booth at the Mobil station on the corner of La Cienega, and I call Martin, but another voice, this time a girl's, answers and tells me that Martin is at the beach, and I hang up and call the studio but I am told by an assistant that William is at the Polo Lounge with the director of his next film, and even though I know the number of the Polo Lounge I don't call. I try the house, but Graham and Susan are not there either, and the maid doesn't even seem to recognize my voice when I ask her where they are, and I hang up the phone before Rosa can say anything else. I stand in the phone booth for close to twenty minutes and think about Martin pushing me off the balcony of his apartment in Westwood. I finally leave the phone booth and I have someone at the gas station call the auto club, and they arrive and tow the Jaguar to a dealership in Santa Monica where I have a humbling conversation with a Persian named Normandie, and they drive me back to my house where I lie on the bed and try to sleep, but William comes home and wakes me up, and I tell him what happened, and he mutters 'typical' and says that we have a party to go to and that things will get bad if I don't start getting ready.

I am brushing my hair. William is standing at the sink, shaving. He has only a pair of white slacks on, unzipped. I am wearing a skirt and a bra, and I stop brushing my hair out and put on a blouse, and then resume brushing my hair. William washes his face, then towels it dry.

'I got a call at the studio yesterday,' he says. 'A very interesting call.' Pause. 'It was from your mother, which is a strange thing. First of all because your mother has never called the studio before, and second of all because your mother doesn't particularly like me.'

'That's not true,' I say, realizing it's better to pretend not to listen.

'You know what she told me?'

I don't say anything.

'Oh come on, guess,' he says, smiling. 'Can't you guess?'

I do not say anything.

'She told me that you hung up on her.' William pauses. 'Could this be true?'

'What if it could?' I put the brush down and put more lipstick on, but my hands are shaking and I stop trying and then I pick the brush up and begin brushing my hair again. Finally, I

155

look up at William, who is staring at me in the mirror across from mine, and say, simply, 'Yes.'

William walks to the closet and picks out a shirt. 'I really thought you hadn't. I thought maybe the Demerol was getting to her or something,' he says drily. I start to brush my hair in fast short strokes.

'Why?' he asks, curious.

'I don't know,' I say. 'I don't think I can talk about that.'

'You hung up on your own fucking mother?' He laughs.

'Yes.' I put the brush down. 'Why are you concerned?' I ask, suddenly depressed by the fact that the Jaguar might be in the shop for close to a week. William just stands there.

'Don't you love your mother?' he asks, zipping his pants, then buckling a Gucci belt. 'I mean, my God, she's dying of cancer for Christ's sake.'

'I'm tired. Please. William. Don't,' I say.

'What about me?' he asks.

He moves to the closet again and finds a jacket.

'No. I don't think so.' These words come out clearly and I shrug. 'Not any more.'

'What about your goddamned children?' He sighs.

'Our goddamned children.'

'Our goddamned children. Don't be so boring.'

'I don't think so,' I say.

'Why not?' he asks, sitting on the bed, slipping on loafers.

'Because I . . . ' I look over at William. 'I don't know . . . them.'

'Come on baby, that's a cop-out,' he says derisively. 'I thought you were the one who said strangers are too easy to like.'

'No,' I say. 'You were, and it was in reference to fucking.'

'Well, since you don't seem to be too attached to anyone you're not fucking, I'd think we'd be in accordance on that score.' He knots a tie.

'I'm shaking,' I say, confused by William's last comment, wondering if I missed a phrase, part of a sentence.

'Oh Christ, I need a shot,' he says. 'Could you get the syringe—the insulin's over there.' He sighs, pointing. He removes his jacket, unbuttons his shirt.

As I fill a plastic syringe with insulin, I have to fight off the impulse to fill it with air and then plunge it into a vein and watch his face contort, his body fall to the floor. He bares his upper arm. As I stick the needle in, I say, 'You fucker,' and William looks at the floor and says, 'I don't want to talk any more,' and we finish dressing, in silence, then leave for the party.

And driving on Sunset with William at the wheel, a glass of vodka nestled between his legs, and the top down, and a warm wind blowing, and an orange sun setting in the distance, I touch his hand that is on the wheel, and he moves it to lift the glass of vodka up to his mouth, and as I turn away and we pass Westwood, up, above it, I can actually see Martin's apartment flash by.

After we drive up through the hills and find the house, and after William gives the car to the valet, and before we walk towards the front entrance, a crowded bank of photographers lined up behind a rope, William tells me to smile.

'Smile,' he hisses. 'Or at least try to. I don't want another picture like that last one in the *Hollywood Reporter* where you just stared off somewhere else with this moronic gaze on your face.'

'I'm tired, William. I'm tired of you. I'm tired of these parties. I'm tired.'

'The tone of your voice could have fooled me,' he says, taking my arm roughly. 'Just smile, OK? Just until we get past the photographers, then I don't give a fuck what you do.'

'You . . . are . . . awful,' I say.

'You're not much better,' he says, pulling me along.

William talks to an actor who has a new movie opening next week and we are standing next to a pool, and there is a very young, tanned boy with the actor, who is not listening to the conversation. He stares into the pool, his hands in his pockets. A warm wind comes down through the canyons, and the blond boy's hair stays perfectly still. From where I'm standing I can see the billboards, tiny lit rectangles, on Sunset, illuminated by neon streetlights. I sip my drink and look back at the boy, who is still

157

staring into the lit water. There is a band playing, and the soft, lilting music and the light coming from the pool, tendrils of steam rising from it, and the beautiful blond boy and the yellow-and-white striped tents that stand on a long, spacious lawn, and the warm winds cooling the palm trees, the moon outlining their fronds, act as an anaesthetic. William and the actor are talking about the rock star's wife who tried to drown herself in Malibu, and the blond boy I'm staring at turns his head away from the pool and finally begins to listen.

GRANTA

JAYNE ANNE PHILLIPS
BUDDY CARMODY

Shelter County, West Virginia. Late July 1963.

No one was safe walking to church in the dark, but Buddy knew better than to beg not to go. While Dad was away in Carolina in prison, Buddy and Mam had walked down the road to the clapboard building maybe three nights a week, winter and summer, and every Sunday. Then home was like it used to be. He and Mam would play crazy eights and slapjack at the table, and pop corn on the stove in the covered skillet. Now they went to church only if Dad was asleep, and lately he drank himself into a stupor most nights.

Buddy hated going to church when it was already dark, pulling on his long pants and a button-collar shirt in the heat. The clothes stuck to his sweat. At least now he didn't have to take a bath first, or Dad might wake up and get to swearing. Mam wiped Buddy across the face with a cold cloth and made him scrub his hands, then shoved him gently towards the sink, whispering at him to hurry up. He squeezed the yellow soap, a slippery rectangular hunk of Fels Naptha she'd brought home from the camp kitchen. The strong-smelling lather stung his scratches.

Buddy didn't think he remembered Dad from before the prison visits, not really. He remembered someone, but Dad had gone away. Five years he was gone, and now Buddy wondered why he'd come back. It was like Dad didn't know he'd left jail, the way he woke up in the dark, not knowing where he was, and then went after Mam like a dog that was near starved and loony. When he was like that, she did what he wanted, and he was so loud he woke Buddy up. Fighting sleep to listen, Buddy got nervous and drowsy like he used to sometimes at school; he'd hear things, and then hear the shivery echo of each word or sound, the echoes coming faster and closer until he couldn't keep his eyes open. Sometimes in the morning Buddy didn't know what he'd really heard or what was animals fighting in his dreams, big animals with vast, muffled forms, making sounds that shook the room.

'Buddy? You ready?' Mam nodded towards the door. She had on her church clothes that fast.

He put the soap back on the drainboard and held his hands in cold water, splashed his face. He smelled wild onions on his fingers and wished it were afternoon. During the summers when Mam cooked at Camp Shelter, Buddy was on his own between meals in the big camp kitchen, wandering back and forth through the woods and along the road, using the house as an outpost he owned in Mam's absence. Now Dad was home, Buddy stayed in the woods and the fields, and walked back with Mam from Camp Shelter after supper. Once they rounded the bend she'd take off her crêpe-soled shoes and Buddy would carry them. She'd roll down her nylons that came only to her knees, like socks, and put them in her pocket. My God, she'd tell Buddy, them girls throw away enough food every day to feed us for a month. But she brought supper home to Dad, and she'd found an extra freezer at camp that worked once she plugged it in. Mrs Thompson-Warner, the directress, had already told her she could buy it cheap, since it looked like the camp might shut down when the girls left. Mam was not going to steal food, no, stealing was a sin, but it was all right to freeze leftovers, and when camp closed she hoped she'd get one of the pipe crew to move that big freezer in their truck. Hadn't they said how they liked the lemonade she sent out to them?

'Come on out here on the porch and dress. Ain't a soul going to see you, it's full dark, and he's not sleeping sound.' She leaned towards Buddy, her bulky shape vanilla-scented, her big arms filmy in her white blouse. Then she turned, her broad skirt preceding him out the door like a dark wall. They huddled down, her knees cracking as she knelt to hold his pants, and she pulled on the shirt and buttoned him in before he'd even got his hands through the cuffs.

'Mam, this shirt is hot. I'm sweating to pieces.'

'Now, I had to iron it, didn't I? We just get to walking, you'll cool down on the road.'

She was talking and they were down the rickety steps and the house was behind them with Dad in it, asleep like a bomb could sleep, Buddy thought, and the moon was up so bright he could see the shoulders of the road looking blond against dark brush. After the dew came up, the road didn't smell dusty, didn't smoke up a tawny veil that could drift and follow him. Now the road lay still, glowy and damp. It was the same road they walked to Camp Shelter, but church was farther on. The stone pillars of the camp entrance were dark shapes all grown over with vines. Honeysuckle licked up and down their height, countless sprays of blossoms emerging luminously ivory and gold against the dark, stacked rocks. The camp was all hidden, Buddy thought: some drunk going along at night, a drunk on foot, a drunk in a car, might not even find it. Tonight Dad had cursed how he couldn't drive out of this place, had to walk two miles even to get to a paved road. Maybe he knew a little lady who would lend him a car that worked. You get yourself a car from some girly trash, better you just keep driving, Mam had told him. I'll drive, he'd said. But how could he, he'd only wreck himself. Maybe he'd get a car and not drink so he could drive.

'Mam, is our road two miles out to the highway?'

'No, course not. It's barely a mile. Don't we walk it every day, all winter? We dress warm, why, we're all right.' Her breath came in soft, wuffling huffs, a kind of music. 'That's why I buy us the best boots I can get, and gloves for inside our mittens, and you got that fur hat I made you.'

Buddy wanted her to stay quiet so he could hear her beside him, the sound coming from above and just ahead of him, a sound familiar as his own heartbeat. Sometimes when he was by himself, he'd open his mouth a little and pant slowly, softly, trying to sound like her. In the winter her breath came out of her like furled clouds. Now she went on like a chant or a song.

'Wasn't enough for you to get a whole coat from that fur. Just pieces of an old muskrat jacket I got at Goodwill. Had I found more, I would have lined your coat . . .'

He stopped listening, aware of sounds beyond her voice. Just here the road was a space with tall, dense walls of foliage on either side. Honeysuckle trailers moved, slight and wafting. The same trembly flowers grew like a tangled webbing all around the frame church, and Buddy thought he could smell them too, like the heady perfume and the church itself and all the voices singing in it creeping back along the road. Spirit could creep that way. He smelled it coming towards them.

163

'Listen to me, Buddy.' Mam was talking still. 'Don't you pay Dad any mind when he rails on like he does. He rants out his head.'

'Out his head.' Buddy paused. 'Why is he like that?'

'Oh, he didn't used to drink so bad. But he never could stand being cooped up. Jail scared him, I reckon, reminded him of things he tries not to think about.' She felt for Buddy behind her, and took his hand. 'I know it's scary, but maybe the Lord means you to see what drink does to men. Then you know never to put that poison in yourself.'

Buddy wanted to say Dad was poison. Instead he asked, 'Will we ever get us a car?'

'Couldn't get a car moving on this road in much snow, and takes money to fix cars. They're always breaking down. And it don't hurt people to walk, whatever weather. You know my uncle gave me this house, and we own it free and clear.' She laughed. 'When you were little and starting school, I thought of finding something in town. But those rents were so high! So what I did was get one of those plastic saucer sleds, and I'd pull you all the way down the road to the bus. You had the best time!'

During the school year, she worked in the kitchen at Buddy's school. She was the biggest of all the big women in white uniforms. It was mostly country kids who ate hot lunch, and Mam who stood behind the counter, spooning red beans on to plastic rectangular plates. Town kids got mad if their beans touched their cornbread. Mam shoved the dense yellow wedges to the side, her hand in a see-through glove the kids called monster hand. When she began working at the sink instead, Buddy could eat better, but he wanted her near him; he'd never ridden the bus without her. Last winter, he'd made her stop pulling him on the sled. It started to scare him, how hard she'd be wheezing by the time they got to the bus stop. If she fell down in the snow, he wouldn't be able to move her.

'You think you're too grown up for that stuff now?' she said. 'Remember how we'd hide that saucer in the pine trees and get on the bus, then pull it out in the afternoon and go on back home?'

'Yeah.' Buddy peered up the road. Sometimes he was scared at church with Mam. Sitting in the long pews, she was like all the rest, saying amen, nodding, agreeing in a voice Buddy didn't recognize, a voice that was broken, gone soft. He was even scared of the road when they walked to church. It was his road, but at night it led to the church with the round windows that were like eyes. He wanted the sanctuary of the trees, their darkened leaves and layered pewter depths, and he longed to run into the woods where Mam wouldn't follow. He could imagine her standing in the road, looking at the border of the trees as at a surface of unmoving water, shouting his name, but he would have disappeared, vanished. Mam could never track him, no one could, not even Dad. A long time ago he'd learned how to run and move, cleaving sideways and upwards, using roots and vines, using stones in the stream to leave no trail at all. He could be running the stream now, hearing the rattle of the water, flying across and over it, but he was here with Mam.

'Will you look at this?' She pulled his hand for him to stop, and they stood seeing the thickly grown trees, how they were all tangled up with glossy piles of rhododendron. The moon shone bright and just here the honeysuckle had broken out in a long gash of whitey yellow that spilled like a waterfall down a length of green. The smell of it washed over them. 'Smells like honey cooked to a boil and cooling in the air. No wonder the bees go wild. But we got it to ourselves now the dew is up.'

'I figure all that's on this road is ours,' Buddy said.

'You do, do you? Even the bees that's thick in the daytime, even that camp where I'm working?'

'We're the only house on the road, and there ain't nobody at the camp all winter, all fall, even all spring.'

She laughed a warm, pleased laugh and moved her fleshy hand to the back of his neck. 'That how it seems to you, why that's fine with me. Used to be a couple more families, back before you remember, but they moved out. Reckon they did better in life.'

'Well,' Buddy said fiercely, 'them old broken houses of theirs don't count. This here is our road.'

'And this is our honeysuckle?'

'Sure it is.' And he grasped a leggy branch within his reach, bending it to break it off and make her take it.

'Hold on there. You don't pick honeysuckle, why it wilts right off if you pick it. Wilder than you are, and that's saying something.' She took the blossoming branch from his fingers and bent to look at the lacy flowers, holding them so they were just near Buddy's face. 'You know "honeysuckle" was one of your first words? Nearly three before you talked, and you come out with a big word like that. I figured you was going to be a late-blooming genius.'

'What's a genius?' He ran a finger along a flower, parts so small he couldn't feel them—small like a hair, like an insect's leg.

'Oh, someone who's different from other folks.' She straightened up and let go of the flower. 'And I reckon you are different, ain't you?'

Sometimes she said a question but it wasn't a question. He made the branch nod like a leafy wand. 'Is Dad a genius?'

'What? Not likely. No, genius means you know more, out of nowhere, but you might only know about a certain thing.' She paused. 'Like you know about this road and the woods around here.'

Buddy snapped the end off the long spray he held. 'Look, you can wear it to church. It'll last that long, I know it will. I'll fix it on you.'

'All right then, Buddy.' She bent down till she was his height, and he fixed the flower to the top buttonhole of her white blouse, her good one she always ironed for church, and the pale spray curled up around her collar.

'You know there's a Jesus story about honeysuckle?' She pulled off one of the flowers and touched its parts. 'These three long petals at the top, they're Jesus's head and arms spread on the cross, and this one petal going down, that's His legs bound together and nailed to the wood. And this long, thin neck of the flower, that's because He was so far from God in His agony.'

Buddy pointed to the delicate threads outflung from the centre of the bloom.

'That's the spirit flowing from Him when His soul went up to Heaven.' She touched the flower to Buddy's mouth.

He tasted an orange dust. Now she was funning with him a little, and he wiped his lips and spat the dust away, relieved. He looked into her eyes that were so known to him, her flat hazel eyes with their green flecks like lights shot through them from behind. Like she was hiding in her narrow eyes, behind her white face that was round and smooth as a big, bald moon. 'Was Dad there when I said that word "honeysuckle"?'

She kissed his lips a quick hard kiss and turned to keep walking. 'No, he wasn't there.'

'Was he in jail then too?'

'No, he just wasn't there. He didn't come to be your dad till after that.'

'Well, who was my dad back then?'

'Nobody. Was just you and me then. You and me playing on the road and back of the house and in the stream . . . ' She was walking away from him. 'Step it up now, we'll be late for service.'

But they wouldn't be late. Even this far away, he could hear the singing, the night was so quiet. And the singing always kept on until the preaching started. The songs were mournful from far off, but stronger and scarier as Mam and Buddy got closer. They could see the church in the clearing; like a dead thing come alive, the church could wear different faces. In summer dusk, a yellowy, jack-o'-lantern light crept across it, and the white building with its whitewashed steps looked illumined against greeny brush and bushes and honeysuckle bloom. By day, the windows with their little square panes looked blind and blackened. But inside, light fell among the singers like blue smoke, a smoke with no smell, a smoke like the dead would make if they were burning.

The different preachers talked about the dead, and how to be safe from burning. Buddy thought the dead would burn in the river, where no one but the dead could catch on fire. They would burn in Mud River, under the same rattling silver bridge the school bus crossed on the way to Gaither, and Buddy thought they started to burn as Mam walked up the steps to the double doors of the church. Mam's skirt was orange and her haunches moved the whole broad surface of the silky cloth. Black leaves on the cloth moved too, and her feet in their white sandals trod the steps so heavily that Buddy felt the wood shake as he made his own reluctant ascent behind her.

Seemed like they were singing from church still, all night they'd kept on. Buddy wanted to hear reveille from inside the camp kitchen with Mam, but he slept so hard he couldn't move. There were words in his mind: Mam had sayings she'd taught him if his prayers were said and he still couldn't sleep. Singsongs, she called them, and he liked the ones about the woods that had trees. He thought the words at night when he was safe, or he was safe when Mam told him the words: *Up the airy mountain, down the rushy glen.* Rushy glen was like the name of a town or a road, a fork of some road that twisted back through the county, and Arey's Feed Store was the big wooden store near the train tracks in Gaither, but no train stopped there any more. Mam and Buddy had to take the bus through Gaither and Bellington clear to Winfield to get on the train, and the train was like sleeping too, the way it rattled and swayed him in the dark. He remembered when they were going to the jail, how the train rattled through the night and the sound made him sleep but he knew Mam was awake, reading the palm-sized Bible she took travelling. She didn't like Buddy to ask her why Dad got sent to jail, just that he went. Later, once, when they were walking from the motel to the dead stone face of the prison, she said Dad had done a bad wrong and was waiting here to be forgiven. Buddy knew then that Mam was mistaken, that she knew even less than Buddy knew, because Dad would not wait to be forgiven. He was only waiting for them to open all the doors and gates, and that would take a long time. The first door didn't want to open at all, and Mam had a hard time pulling it while Buddy dragged through the paper sacks of fruitcake and baked chicken and new long underwear. Then they were inside where it was no longer cold but it was like night again, with the lights on overhead, and men in uniforms like mail clerks all had circular metal rings of keys. And all the time Buddy walked, burdened with sacks and parcels, he heard the jingling of the keys, their chiming, desolate sound. Before him Mam moved on silently in her long grey coat, the broad rounded wall of her backside wider than any two of the men.

He was safe with Mam, her tilting, gentle lurch the only indication he was where he should be. She walked her slow, considered, heavy walk, and he moved in her wake where there was no resistance, just a cleared path whose view was blocked by her bulk. He didn't need to see, it was all like blind man's buff, walking down the road to the school bus, fall, winter, spring, sucked into a tumult of voices as the bus wheezed and clamped shut its shuddered doors. Mam rode, too, sitting always behind the driver, a woman she knew, and the kids on the bus first taunted him, your mother is fat, big as an elephant, a house, and he spat back threats, challenges, shut up or she'll sit on your belly and crush you dead, she's done it, I've seen her. What's the ruckus back there? the driver yelled. You kids sit down, and Mam would turn and fix them all with a silencing look. When she worked in the lunchroom she wore her hair in a net. If they went to the grocery or the welfare or the welfare clinic they walked home or caught a ride with someone who let them off at their road. Behind her, Buddy didn't care whether he saw where they were going, he could feel by the air and the weighty sound of densely leaved branches above them that they were on their road. He knew the ruts and turns and the narrow, broken bridge where the stream ran under, the stream that bled its sound behind his house, through Camp Shelter, the stream that went underground in the cave and fed Turtle Hole. Behind the big rock near the water, a slanted hole opened like a hideout. Buddy didn't go in the cave; it was too low and still, and water rattled inside like something in a drawer. At the prison there'd been no sound but footsteps on cement, the buzzing of the lights overhead a low drone like insects trapped in glass tubes. In the prison he'd been glad he couldn't see. He'd wished he didn't have to see Dad, look across the counter and through the window. Dad wore pajama clothes, and his eyes were burnt.

Stand him up right there beside you, let me see if the wise guy has growed, eh? You still a wise guy?

Mam lifted Buddy before he could run, and Buddy was higher than the half walls of the cubicles. Clusters of huddled visitors looked up, dark rumpled men opposite them looked up, a guard started over and Buddy jumped down. He hid then under the counter. Jesus! Dad was laughing. You think he's gonna storm the gates? After an instant Mam laughed, too polite and quiet, the guard sat down again but Buddy stayed hidden. Mam's black

boots were wet and the white flesh above her rolled woollen socks
was veined with blue, like she was too big for her skin. At night in
the cold Buddy slept with her and dreamed he was running, higher
and higher, cleaving sideways and upwards on a loose dirt bank,
moving on all fours to grasp roots and vines under the canopy of
trees. *Airy mountain, rushy glen*. Buddy wanted to move now but
the words came again in their singsong to say he was still asleep,
he was hungry and asleep and he should already be awake. *We
dare not go a-hunting, for fear of little men*. Far off, he could hear
Mam talking on to keep him sleeping. *Down along the rocky
shore, some make their home. They live on crispy pancakes, of
yellow tide foam*—that sounded so good, like sweet cracker, Mam,
wouldn't it be? Where was she? In his sleep, he listened for
sounds, the rattle of the kettle, her footsteps on a floor. Buddy
heard the radio coming from the porch, but Mam never played
the radio, they left so early for camp. Something was wrong. He
opened his eyes and lay still.

There was the chair and the footstool Mam propped her feet
on at night. Down the room a way he couldn't see into the bigger
bed. The dark green blanket Mam had hung for a divider was
still; no one moved behind it. The woolly cloth was nailed right
on to the ceiling but had pulled free in one corner and drooped.
The same sunlight that fell almost direct into Buddy's eyes played
in panels across it. Mam had left him, gone to cook and left him
here asleep. She'd left him to sleep because he hadn't waked up in
time, and now he'd have to get away without Dad seeing him.

She didn't know about Dad. She didn't know.

He found his clothes at the foot of the bed where Mam
always put them, and he got out of his pajamas noiselessly. His
bed was a metal cot just like the girls slept in at Camp Shelter; it
squeaked something awful every time he moved. Mam had
brought it home just before camp started. Borrowed it, she said.
Before that, in the first week Dad was back, Buddy had slept on
an air mattress on the floor, softer and better; it was like since
the bed came, Dad could hear Buddy's every turn or twitch all
night, and started to notice him in the days.

Naked, he crouched on the floor beside his cot, got into his
pants and shirt. The radio was playing so clear, no static. No

other sound, like there were tiny girls singing out there about a boyfriend. *Hey la, hey la, wait and see!* Boom boom! Drums in the plastic box of the transistor. Dad might be in the back and Buddy should go out the front. Or he might be on the porch, just waiting, and Buddy should go out the kitchen door and around by the woods.

He was halfway across the kitchen linoleum. The red and white diamonds were flecked with yellow and Buddy had a charm about keeping his feet exactly within their dimensions and making it out the door.

'Hey there, boy,' said a voice. 'What about breakfast?'

Dad stood behind the porch screen door, a shape, tensed on the balls of his feet. He was fast, a fast runner, long and skinny. Buddy was nearly as fast. But he didn't want to run into the woods, lead Dad into the trees. He stood still, feeling the cool of the floor move up through his feet, into him.

'Come on out here,' Dad said. 'Come see what I got parked down here in front of the house.' He held the door open.

Buddy moved through it, past him. He went to the far side of the porch, by the railing, and looked down at the car. It was a red car with a dented fender. All the windows were rolled down.

'I got you something too,' Dad said.

He held out a blue leather bag in one hand, a pull-string bag open at the mouth. Buddy leaned to look inside and saw marbles, cat's-eyes and a big shooter. He reached out but Dad pulled the bag away, then jumped back on his toes and made as if to throw it. Buddy was supposed to catch, and the leather pouch landed in his cupped hands.

'You know how to shoot? I can teach you. After breakfast.' He eased himself into his chair, watching Buddy.

'I figured you two were at church last night,' he said.

Buddy nodded.

'While you were gone I took me a little walk out to the road. Got a ride into town. Damn if I didn't meet up with a nice little lady, wants me to take care of her car for a while.' He tilted back in the chair and propped his feet across the railing. Buddy couldn't get through to the steps unless he ducked under, and if Dad wasn't drunk, his arm could shoot out and grab whatever moved, quick as the flicked tongue of a lizard.

'I don't mind doing a favor,' he said now, and cocked an eyebrow at Buddy. 'You mind?'

'What's that?'

'You mind doing a favor?'

Buddy shook his head.

'Then put that bag of marbles in your pocket. Go in there and get the tomato juice out of the refrigerator, and my pint of vodka. I'll eat light.'

Buddy went back inside. He could get out the back door now, but Dad would only catch up later. He opened the squat icebox and stood staring. For a crazy instant he thought of getting inside, fitting right between the nearly empty metal racks. 'Well?' he heard from the porch. 'And bring some ice.'

The tray was so cold it stuck to Buddy's hand. He had the six-pack of V-8 in one hand and the pint bottle of vodka under his arm and the cold ice tray burning into his fingers; the screen banged as he went out. He wished he had a gun. Beyond the porch there were butterflies, six or seven bright yellow ones, dropping and starting like some little whirlwind had them in a swirl. But the morning was still and hot.

Dad had his shirt off already and he took the ice tray and whammed it against the porch rail near his chair. Splinters of ice flew everywhere and a couple of big chunks skidded along the board floor. 'She goes off to cook for a hundred girls and leaves us here to shift for ourselves. You believe 'at?' He smiled up at Buddy, waiting. Then he said softly, 'You forgot the glasses, Miss.'

But he had them sitting on the floor, under his chair, two plastic tumblers. Buddy leaned over and picked them up.

'Now you got the glasses,' Dad said. He put ice into both of them and poured Buddy some juice and himself, a pale red mixture. 'I been waiting for you to wake up,' he told Buddy. 'My God, all that religion must have tired you out. Couldn't skittle out the door with her this morning.' He drank down the glass and poured another. There were flecks of moisture on his lips. 'Bud-eee, Bud-eee,' he said, mimicking Mam, saying the name in the drawn-out way she pronounced it when she called Buddy in from the road or the woods. He shook the ice in his glass, and the liquid moved, and he drank it then, fast, his Adam's apple moving in his throat.

'Chugalug,' he said, watching Buddy.

Buddy picked up his own cup and began to drink. He had just to keep drinking the cold, thick juice. He had to drink without stopping.

Dad was drinking too, another glass. Then he put in more ice and poured the rest of the pint in, only faintly pink, and he drank it, blinking, and his eyes got wet. He pointed at Buddy. 'I'm going to be taking a ride, now I got me a car. Just need me a stake.' He laughed. 'Maybe I'll take you with me. That would get her goat, wouldn't it.'

Buddy stepped back, drinking.

Dad leaned forward, like a bird arching its long neck. 'You don't want to come, though, do you? Nah.' He took a deep breath, then, in one long motion, heaved the empty bottle into the air, out from the porch. It tumbled end over end, twinkling a little, and fell soundlessly into the brush down the bank, on the other side of the road.

Buddy could hear himself breathing. In. Out.

'You and your Mam,' Dad said. 'You a couple of girls, ain't you?'

Buddy knew not to answer yet. Not to move.

'Well, ain't you? Couple of girls? Or not. Yes or no?'

Buddy nodded. He held out his glass.

Dad put an ice cube in it. 'Two girls,' he said. 'Then do what a girl does.'

Buddy put the ice cube in his mouth and held it.

Dad took hold of Buddy's wrist and turned away in his chair, so Buddy stood just behind him. Maybe he would leave the radio on this time. But he turned it off. He breathed a few times, jerked his head hard like he was shaking water off, settled in, opened his fly. 'All right then,' he said.

Buddy took the big ice cube from his mouth, his jaws aching. He held it in his free hand and moved it over Dad's head, in his hair, around and around, then down on to Dad's neck. Dad began to breathe like he did, his feet down off the rail, his legs

spread out in front of him. He would have hold of himself by
now, but Buddy kept watch on the solid bank of trees across the
road, their foliage level with the porch. Their leaves moved;
Buddy strained to hear them, heard them, made the sound big in
his ears. A saying in the air, a singsong that stayed awake. He
could see the air whisper through the leaves, track its movement,
like some form made of air was in the trees, and he kept his eyes
on the shape that rippled there. He moved the ice along Dad's
white, freckled shoulders but he didn't look at them any more; he
had to move the ice down Dad's chest, on to Dad's flat brown
nipples, into the hollow between, exactly right, to get it over with.
He had to do just this, the same each time, exactly the same.
Buddy could hear Dad slapping, straining, but Dad couldn't
make Buddy look; he couldn't see Buddy's eyes. Even someone
walking right below couldn't see up on the porch, and there was
no one to hear. The trees rustled, their layered foliage ruffling
out towards Buddy, then moving backwards, pulled in as though
what was far behind the trees beckoned, nodding. Buddy had to
lean over Dad's shoulder to reach down his belly with the ice,
and Dad began to whimper. He tensed until his whole body
seemed to vibrate and his grip on Buddy's wrist squeezed like a
vice. When he started to talk it was almost over. 'Don't do that
to me,' he would say, the words all run together and his voice
high-pitched, shrunken. 'Don't do that to me, don't do that to
me.' But he wasn't talking to Buddy. Buddy was supposed to
move the ice, not stop. And there was a pent-up squealing, and
Dad was finished, and Dad was crying. He let go of Buddy then
and Buddy could run, he was supposed to, if he was still there
Dad would yell at him, 'What are you looking at? You get away
from me, you leave me alone!'

The first time, Buddy had watched, he had looked, but now
he never looked. He ran down the porch steps, across the road
and down the bank into the trees. He ran yelling, pouring it all
out of himself into the wide woods. Today he threw down the
stub of ice and jammed his wet hand in his pocket. The leather
bag of marbles clanked into his palm as he ran towards the camp
to Mam.

GRANTA

BEVERLY LOWRY
PATRICIDE

By now, the shooting is old news, and Rush Springs, Oklahoma, has had its five minutes of notoriety. The story has been all over national magazines and newspapers and featured on prime-time television news—how, on a blistering day last July, Lonnie Dutton's two elder children, Herman, fifteen, and Druie, twelve, took a .243 deer rifle into the living-room of the trailerhouse where they lived, set the barrel of the gun against their sleeping daddy's head, just below his right ear, and blew him away, right there on the couch, a can of beer on the table beside him. How they killed him together, Herman steadying the gun while Druie pulled the trigger. How they had decided to do it—'kill Daddy'—that afternoon, when their sister, Alesha, who is ten, came out of the house crying and told them that their daddy had molested her. How the two boys were working in the field next to the trailerhouse that day—105 degrees and they'd been sent to chop and hoe—and decided that while they'd been putting up with their daddy's cruel mistreatment for years, this was different.

By mid-afternoon, all hush-hush to keep it secret from Alesha and their baby brother, Jake, eight, Herman and Druie Dutton had figured out what they had to do: their daddy had always told them that, if they ever discovered anyone fooling with their sister, they should pick up the .243 and shoot the son of a bitch in either the head, just below the ear, or the heart. Their daddy then poked the side of his head, to show where the bullet should go, then slapped the left side of his chest, to show them the heart, and then poked both boys in the side of the head, repeatedly and hard, and then slapped their chests. He wanted to be sure they understood. Herman and Druie were good children; they did what they could to keep their daddy calm, including stealing, calling their mother names, biting her and throwing darts at her. And so they waited until they were sure that their daddy was good and asleep, so that he wouldn't draw out the nine-millimetre from underneath his overalls bib and shoot them first. Then they went inside the trailerhouse and killed him with the .243, which had been stolen from somebody in Lawton, Oklahoma, some eight years earlier.

Opposite: the Dutton family.

In October, three months after the shooting, the Oklahoma sun still beats down like emergency floodlights. People in Grady County are used to it. The ones I've met are friendly, plain and very white, with flat, twangy accents. The women grow their hair long and leave it; the men drive pick-ups. The economy is down the tubes, politics what you would expect. On the turnpike between Oklahoma City and Chickasha, I pass a billboard saying SOCIALISM IS WRONG.

In Grady County, a woman on her own gets company fast. While driving, I watch as car after car pulls alongside, slows down, revs up; the drivers look over, I go on. It's a world in which bars are windowless and dark, their parking lots filled with pick-ups and the occasional Ranchero. My first night in Rush Springs, I stepped outside my motel to go for a short run. It was early evening, the sun was low, but there was plenty of light. A pick-up came by, slowed down; there were three men inside, raising cans to their lips. A couple of minutes later, a woman and a young girl in a brand-new, extended-cab pick-up stopped, and the woman asked where I lived and if I had seen the three men who were parked at the top of the road, waiting for me. She offered to take me back to the motel.

Eighteen miles south of Chickasha, at a yellow blinking caution light, I turn right off US 81, away from downtown Rush Springs. The telephone book gives 'N of city' and 'SW of city' as addresses. The house I am heading towards, the home of Luther Dutton, the dead man's father, is on a road with no name, 'W of city'.

When I spoke to Luther Dutton on the phone, he said he had no problem talking to me or anybody else. He wanted the story told right, and for that to happen, 'There's only one way.' Just so long as it wasn't for a book. He didn't go for that book stuff. 'We're the only ones who know,' he assured me. And he told me how to get to his house.

Southwest Oklahoma is farming country, watermelons and peanuts mostly—Rush Springs calls itself Watermelon Capital of the World. There are cattle, some sheep, some goats. The rolling countryside lies between mountains to the east and dry plains not that far to the west; and it is lush, green and wet, with heavy-headed oak and pecan trees and thick, webby undergrowth.

Scrub oaks line the road to the Dutton house. Mustang

grapevines grow over the tops of the stunted trees like a shroud. Beyond them, all you can see is more scrub, denser brush. Just before the Dutton mailbox, there is a beat-up locked gate with a rusted sign hanging on it saying PRIVATE PROPERTY. Over the gate, five huge, dark, withering catfish heads swing in the breeze.

Luther Dutton's new mailbox is shaped like a barn. It is festooned with blue bows. There are bows on the fence and across the top of the gate.

The red clay road leading to the house slants down a little in a tunnel of overhanging trees, then curves to the right. The landscape opens up and there is a big house with a wide front porch set on a cleared, very pretty rise in the land. There is a refrigerator on the porch and a couple of nonfunctioning cars out front, but it isn't trashy. The trees are big, and the grass a deep green. Lonnie Dutton and his children lived on this same piece of land, back in the scrub oaks and underbrush, with nothing but a rutted cowpath for a way in or out. Nobody lives in the trailerhouse now.

It is six o'clock on a Friday evening. The season's first crop of peanuts has come in. The governor of Oklahoma is under investigation for illegal campaign funding. At seven o'clock that night, the unbeaten Rush Springs Redskins will take on the Hinton Comets in a Homecoming football game.

When I ring the doorbell, Luther Dutton answers. He is wearing jeans and a saggy white T-shirt. He has a kind of potato face, lumpy and uneven, a droopy lower lip and a bulbous nose. His hair is grey and thinning, uncombed. He is in his sixties, but he looks a good ten years older.

He invites me in, and we go through to a large room, kitchen, dining-room and living-room all in one. The room is clean and plain with fake wood panelling. There are little pictures on the wall, including a child's 'I-Love-You-Daddy' drawing which Luther says one of the kids made for Lonnie. A flyer is tacked on the refrigerator, announcing the town meeting in support of Herman and Druie held three months earlier, at which blue bows were sold to help pay legal expenses. The house is easy to keep and serviceable, with built-ins and new appliances.

We sit at a round table. Luther spits tobacco into a styrofoam cup, staring off in the general direction of the opposite wall and

179

meeting my eyes only when it suits him.

He introduces me to his wife, Nancy. In rural areas, middle-aged women tend to fall into one of two categories: the chunk and the rail. The chunk puts on weight and acquires a bosom, hips, dimples, a double chin, a rolling gait; she has a girlish look and loves her food. The rail shrinks, her skin clings to her bones, her behind flattens, her neck turns into a column of folds. The rail usually chain-smokes, preferring cigarettes to food. A rail still in the ball game may cover up the damage with ice-blue eyeshadow and frosted pink lipstick; her hair will be dyed: black, yellow or red.

Nancy Dutton is a rail and has not been in the ball game for years. She could be eighty; it turns out she's sixty-one. In her thirties, she was institutionalized for mental and emotional problems and had shock treatments for more than a year; her daughter, Linda Munn, says that's why Nancy has a hard time remembering and sometimes seems so . . . flat. She sits on a bar stool next to the breakfast bar, smoking steadily, and lets Luther do most of the talking.

Lonnie Dutton lived on his father's property for nine years. Records list him as an unemployed roofer, but no one can remember him ever doing a day's work for wages. He lived on the dole, getting food stamps and money from government programmes and making his kids steal. When social services people came out for a home study, Lonnie pretended to live in Luther's house, and Luther and Nancy covered for him. The electricity in his trailer was illegally tapped from his father's line. His water supply came from his father's well. He would neither allow his parents to enter his trailerhouse, nor leave his own children with them when he went out. Wherever Lonnie Dutton went, his children went too. When he went to bars, they stayed in the truck until he was ready to go, no matter the temperature or the hour. If Lonnie came out drunk at two or three in the morning, fifteen-year-old Herman drove home.

Lonnie graduated from high school in Sterling, Oklahoma, one of only three boys in a class of thirty, and so he was elected Class Favorite, Most Handsome and Best Dancer, the other two boys being pretty squirrelly-looking. He had two elder sisters,

Linda, now forty-three, and Dina, who is forty-one. Lonnie died four days short of his fortieth birthday. Nancy says his kids were planning a surprise party for him, and that Druie had asked her to make a cake with candles.

'He was a hard-working boy,' Luther says of his son. 'All his life he worked hard. He had a deformed heart you know . . . He raised registered hogs.'

Luther makes statements like this, statements that clearly—to him—have some kind of resonance. And then he will pause, waiting for a response, I can't tell to what. After a beat, he goes on.

'Won nearly every prize in the county.'

And he describes his son, the hard-working, all-American farm boy, and Nancy tells me about Lonnie's deformed heart with the oversized valve and his high blood pressure.

As for school, 'He didn't do no good. But he was a damned fine carpenter.'

Luther Dutton backtracks, rethinks his story, checks himself. Nancy Dutton adds details, corrects small errors and contributes to Luther's main thrust, which is to let the world know that nobody understands what it has been like for him all these years, nobody. He is cagey, deft, sly, and thinks he can put one over on anybody. Luther and Nancy rarely use their son's name, but when they say 'he', I always know who they mean.

Yes, Luther will admit, he did thrash his son with a belt from time to time, but that's what people did in those days, striped their sons' backsides. He was trying to straighten him out, that was all; of course it didn't do any good.

I go over some of the stories I have heard: how Lonnie made his wife, Marie, stand against the wall, then told his kids to throw darts at her; how he poured jalapeno pepper juice in her eyes; how he chased Herman with a two-by-four and kicked him between the legs with a steel-toed boot; how he used to shoot at the chicken coop while Herman and Druie were inside; and how he played William Tell with Druie by making him stand against a wall, then shooting bullets in a circle around his head. I ask him, have any of these stories been exaggerated?

Luther thinks a long time. When he shakes his head and says simply no, there is no knowing what his attitude is. When cornered, he has a mantra which goes: 'I loved my son. I love my grandkids. My grandkids killed my son. And I have mixed emotions about that.' At first, I thought by mixed emotions he meant he was confused, then later on I decided he meant exactly what he said.

Luther has been interviewed a lot. He often asks and answers his own questions.

'Were those children abused? I'd have to say, yes. Those children were belittled, berated, beat on, abused, called everything in the book. But you know, I never heard those boys use a cuss word.'

Nancy shakes her head.

'They killed their daddy, yes. But they never used foul language.'

And he waits a beat or two and then restates his theme: 'Nobody knows what it was like, being a prisoner in your own home for years, nobody. But he was my son and I loved him. When you love somebody, you love them. Don't make no difference what they do.'

Luther pulls up his shirt sleeve. 'He cut me. Here.' Traces a scar on his bicep. 'Here.' Touches his arm close to the wrist. 'He shot me once—just birdshot, but I would have gone after him with my gun if my wife hadn't stopped me.'

Luther says Lonnie never should have got married, and that on his wedding night he said he'd rather go coon hunting. 'He hated women. He used to say, there's only one good woman in the world and that's her'—nods in Nancy's direction—'and all the rest are whores and liars.' Thinking about why Lonnie believed this, Luther goes to the sink, paces, starts to say something, then stops, mentions family secrets, things he can't talk about. 'But I'll tell you this,' he finally says. 'He was jilted and that's all I'll say. It was when he was a senior. He was always a man to hold a grudge, and that did it.' As for his sisters, he probably hated them most of all. 'But then,' Luther says darkly, 'he knew the things they did.'

And so, at twenty-two, Lonnie married Rosemarie Standford, even though he didn't want to—'It was her wanted to,' Nancy declares—and Luther says he would be the first to take the stand and say that, yes, Lonnie abused her and beat her up so bad you couldn't tell who she was. But as for the question of whether he molested Alesha, Luther Dutton says that's hard for him to know.

'I'll tell you this, Lonnie hated a pervert. He had no use for homos. He hated a queer. And I ask myself, would he molest his own child? I have a hard time with that, you see. I have mixed emotions about that. But to answer your question, I'd have to say I don't think he ever did. Or not that I ever knew of.'

At one point, Luther leaves the room and comes back in carrying a three-foot length of hard rubber tubing and a pistol in a holster. He puts them on the table.

'Now, ma'am,' he says, 'I don't meant to disrespect you, but you know what that is.' He nods at the tube. 'It's a tube from a pump to air up your tyres.' He pauses. 'That's what he used to beat them with.' He takes the pistol out of the holster. 'Ma'am. I don't mean to disrespect you.' The gun is an automatic. He takes the clip out. 'This was his gun. He was left-handed. A left-handed man.' He puts the nine-millimetre back in the holster. 'He wore it here.' He lays his hand across his heart. 'In the bib of his overalls. Always.'

Marie left Lonnie in 1989 and went to Texas to live with her mother. She took her children with her. A few months later, Lonnie went down there and made it up with Marie, saying he would change, they'd all move and make a life in Texas. Then things happened. Lonnie beat Marie up, Marie's mother called the police and Lonnie was thrown in jail. When he got out two weeks later, he went back home to Oklahoma. Soon afterwards, Herman and Druie asked to go back to live with their dad. This was before he started beating up on them, and anyway they didn't really trust their mother, especially after Lonnie had drilled certain facts into their heads and made them call her pig and whore dog. Lonnie filed a custody suit, which he won. Most people believe Luther helped his son pay for a good lawyer. Marie didn't have one.

Oklahoma has a law stating that, if a parent is absent from a child for twelve consecutive months and provides no support, then the parent's rights can be terminated without notice. As Marie Dutton has not seen her children in at least three years, she is no longer legally considered their parent. And one day recently, when the boys were in court, they were given the chance to see Marie. They refused. Druie eventually gave in and talked to her, but Herman stood firm.

Luther Dutton says he called the social services on 'this very phone—so many times,' and he gets out old telephone bills showing calls to a Chickasha number. As for the police, Luther says, 'The police are thirty-five miles away. You know what happens. Time they get here . . . And it's complicated. I mean, if you file charges, you have to stop and think, what's going to happen to the kids? We'd get into it over those kids. I'd see Herman with his head swollen up, Druie with a black eye, and we'd get into it. He'd tell me to mind my own damned business, those kids were his and he'd do what he damned pleased, and nobody better try to come between him and his kids. So . . . '

He shows me Lonnie's photograph album. There are diamond-shaped cuts in many of the snapshots, where Lonnie gouged out the face and body of Marie. One picture is of Lonnie on his wedding night, standing by a dog-pen, holding his arm over the coon hounds' heads to get them to jump up. He is trim, of medium build, a fairly good-looking young man. His smile is rascally, but not mean. In later photos, he is big and burly and will not look at the camera. In most of them, he is wearing a shapeless hat with a big brim, and you can see the gun holster sticking out of his overalls bib. I hold the pictures up in Nancy's direction. I would not have known, I say, that these were of the same person. She nods.

In one picture, it is Christmas, and Lonnie's four children and Nancy are lined up inside Luther and Nancy's house. Nancy is in the middle, looking pathetic in a droopy dress. The four children all hold rifles on their shoulders, like soldiers. Herman stands at one end, chin tucked in like a Marine, shoulders severely squared.

'See there,' Luther points at the right side of Herman's head. 'You can see how swollen up it is. And look at his mouth.'

Herman's head looks soft and melonish on one side, and his mouth is twisted and off-centre. Druie has a black eye.

'That's the gun they shot him with.' Luther taps the photo. 'Right there.' He points to the gun Herman has on his shoulder. 'That's the .243.'

Linda Munn, Lonnie's elder sister, has not lived in Rush Springs for ten years. But she has come back to Oklahoma to testify to her brother's brutality; there are pictures of her in the middle of the main street of Rush Springs, holding up a sign saying BRING OUR ANGELS HOME.

When I spoke to her later, her first words were, 'You didn't believe everything Daddy said, did you? That's what scares me. That people will go out there and take everything he says at face value.'

Linda Munn says her daddy beat up on her as far back as she can remember, once so badly she had blood streaks from the back of her neck to her ankles, and on Lonnie too—one time in the barn, so brutally that everybody went and hid so they couldn't hear. She also says that Lonnie didn't have a deformed heart or high blood pressure. 'That's bull poop. He was lazy. If those little boys are going to have to tell the truth about what went on, then we should too. That place he says Lonnie cut him? My brother didn't cut Daddy there. He did that himself, welding. I told him I knew that, but he just said, "Well, *they* don't."'

When Linda Munn was fourteen, she got pregnant, got married and came home to her parents' house to live with her new husband. Those were bad years. Nancy was in hospital getting shock treatments, and Luther was beating up on all of the kids.

Linda says that no girl was ever going to be good enough for Lonnie in her mother's eyes. 'If she didn't use the recipes my mom used or clean house the way my mom did, she was ridiculed. Marie never had a chance.'

Linda Munn says that she is prepared to believe just about anything that's said about her brother, and wonders about his sexual problems. She says he wouldn't let Marie change Alesha's diapers if anybody else was in the room, in case some man saw the baby's genitals and started getting ideas. When his daughter was a toddler, he used to introduce her as 'my nigger' and 'my little slut.' Once, when Alesha was about four, she fell off the porch and cracked her head. Linda's son Wayne picked her up and held her on his lap to see if she was badly hurt, and Lonnie came running up, waving his pistol, and told Wayne to take that child off his lap; he knew what Wayne was thinking—Linda says, because Lonnie was having those thoughts himself. And there is the story about Lonnie beating up Marie to make her have sex with another man, then, when she wouldn't, pouring alcohol down her throat until she did, then beating her up worse afterwards because she did it, and everybody blaming Marie because she didn't after all *have* to do it. Linda says she remembers her brother bragging that there was one thing he could say about Marie: she took an ass whipping better than any man he knew.

There are other houses on the road with no name, 'W of city'. Karen Caveny and her family live in a trailerhouse on the front part of their land, where they are building a home and share a fence line with the Dutton place. The living-room of the trailer is warm and comfortable, the walls covered with family portraits. Karen Caveny is a pleasant-faced woman in her mid-forties, smart and plain-spoken as a stop sign. She has a lot to say about what she heard out there. From 1984, when Lonnie moved his trailer on to his father's land and settled down with his pregnant wife and their three kids, she and her family never felt safe.

'Lonnie liked to shoot. My kids have dodged his bullets; we have bullet holes in the side of our house. When Lonnie and Marie first moved in, they had six white dogs. Those dogs were chasing livestock, and I sent my daughter Jodi to tell Herman to tell his daddy he had to do something about them. Next day, Herman told Jodi, "Daddy says you don't have to worry about those dogs any more. He stepped out on the front porch and shot them all."'

Karen Caveny caught Lonnie Dutton peering in her windows at least twice, and one time he stalked a neighbour who complained about goats in her yard, following her car in his pick-up and parking alongside it while she went to church.

'What you have to understand about Lonnie is, he liked intimidating people. And when you're doing the kinds of things he was doing and enjoying them, then I'd have to say that was evil.

'Marie?' Karen Caveny's eyes fill. 'Just after they moved in, we were in the house, the television was on, the washing machine was going, it was night, and on top of all that noise I heard screams. I thought it was one of the animals, but when I went outside, I knew it was a person. It went on for forty-five minutes. She was screaming his name out loud, begging him to stop.'

Karen Caveny eventually went back inside and turned up the

television so she couldn't hear any more. At a quarter to six the next morning, there was a knock at the door and there stood Marie, holding Druie by the hand with Alesha on her hip. She was pregnant with Jake. 'That child was so big she was waddling. Her face was out to here, her eyes were black, and there wasn't a part of the whites of her eyes that was white; they were completely red. The blood vessels had all burst, I guess. Her mouth was busted and one ear was torn. She had black-and-blue marks all over her. She needed a ride into town, and so we took them and put her and the children on a bus to Texas. Next thing I knew she was back. She came to us lots of times. Nancy would call me and I'd lie: Oh, I haven't seen Marie, haven't seen her in a long time. Marie would hide the children, lay them down under some bushes and wait for the right car to come along and she'd get up and put them in the car and get a ride where she needed to go.'

Karen Caveny says that she called the social services 'between thirty and fifty times' but that 'nobody came.' She made the reports anonymously because for a long time she and her family were Lonnie Dutton's only neighbours. 'He would know it was me turning him in. I had children of my own to think of. If he was doing the things he was doing to his own children, what would he do to mine?'

Lonnie liked to set fires on other people's land, and one time a dozen or so people who lived in the area got together and called the sheriff. Nobody came out until eventually someone from another county told a friend, who was a special investigator from yet another county, about what was going on, and that person roused some members of the Grady County Sheriff's Department. And when they arrived, Karen Caveny told them the whole story, about the screams and about Lonnie being a peeping Tom. 'They told us there was nothing they could do unless we caught him red-handed and held on to him until somebody came. Now can't you just see me saying, "Lonnie, will you wait right there while I call the sheriff?"' And while this was not said outright, the message Karen Caveny got from the Sheriff's Department was: be your own vigilante; do what you have to do.

People who live outside the city limits don't always live there from necessity or because they are farmers. They live there because they get a kick out of having their own way, by God; and living where they don't see, by God, anybody else; and having, by God, beaten the system. The Cavenys never thought of moving because of, 'Oh, the pioneer spirit. You don't let people run you off your property. You just don't.'

On 12 July, some time between four and five in the afternoon, Karen Caveny heard there had been a shooting on the Dutton place, and she was not surprised. But she thought Lonnie had shot his dad. Why? 'Because Lonnie was just that crazy and his dad was just that scared.' When she heard what had really happened, she says it was the last thing she would have imagined. 'I had a mental picture of those two little boys—you know, they're small; they look more like ten and twelve than twelve and fifteen—and I could see them holding that gun and praying to God that Lonnie wouldn't wake up before they pulled the trigger and I felt terrible for them. I wish they hadn't had to go through that. Nobody deserves to live the way they lived. They didn't just haul off and shoot their dad. He was a demon. He was living hell.'

There are constant and hurtful questions in Grady County these days: who saw the bruises or heard the screams; who called the social services or the child-abuse toll-free number to make reports; who was responsible for the fact that, while there were a lot of people who thought that Lonnie Dutton was a man in need of a good killing, his kids were the only ones up to doing it?

Employees of the Department of Human Services can't talk about individual cases. The Sheriff's Department will only say that, if a child won't talk, there's nothing they can do. A math teacher at Herman's school once took the boy aside and asked him about the bruises and abrasions on his face. Herman made up some tale about the limb of a tree hitting him and, even when the teacher said he didn't believe him, held fast to his story. And people in Rush Springs want to make it clear, they didn't know what was going on, they didn't even know Lonnie Dutton, he never came into town.

Everybody thinks something had to go wrong for those children to have fallen through the cracks of the system, but nobody knows exactly what. And I find myself wondering if *anything* could have been done to stop Lonnie Dutton's bullying, short of his children rising up and shooting him. The Dutton family was isolated and secretive. Nobody much knew where the trailer was, and Lonnie had installed motion detectors in his yard, connected to lights. He slept on the couch, surrounded by guns. If the lights came on in the night, he started shooting. It didn't matter what was out there. He didn't wait, he didn't aim. He just shot.

As I leave 'W of city', the sky is blood-red along the horizon. I keep thinking about Herman. Herman was the caretaker child, the one in charge; it was up to him to keep things on an even keel, take the hits for his brothers and sister, lie when anyone asked him about his bruises, run round at lunch-time to make sure the other kids were OK. Herman never quit trying to be the good child and please his dad. When Lonnie took them all shoplifting, Herman knew he would beat up on whoever didn't steal enough and so he cut back on his take. Last year, after Herman had failed to do a chore exactly right, Lonnie went after him with a two-by-four and knocked him out cold in the back yard; there is a declivity in Herman's skull now, big enough to lay your finger in.

Herman is the smallest boy in his class—I have seen his school group picture. He is in the front row, sparky-looking, perfectly proportioned, wiry. He is standing at an angle to the camera, one hand loosely curled on his thigh. His blond hair is in big waves, dramatically dipped to one side, and he is wearing a bright western shirt, a black belt, tight jeans and cowboy boots. He may be tiny, but his body is taking an adult shape, and he has a great sense of style.

That July afternoon, Herman told Druie he would be the one to shoot their daddy, but when they got in there, he couldn't do it. At fifteen, Herman was old enough to know the consequences, legal and otherwise. So the younger, more concrete-thinking Druie took the gun, but he couldn't do it either, although he said that if Herman could steady the rifle, he thought he could pull the trigger. Lonnie wore a droopy moustache, sometimes a forked beard and had had his head shaved to give him a meaner look. I imagine the two boys standing beside him, passing the rifle between them, keeping a careful eye on the bald head, the moustache, the chin, the bulked-up body of their two-hundred-plus pound dad in his overalls, the nine-millimetre automatic in a holster beneath the bib.

And so Herman aimed the .243 and put his finger on the trigger again, and just as he was about to lower the barrel once more, Druie pushed the trigger back. The bullet made a neat three-quarter-inch entry hole, then exploded inside Lonnie Dutton's skull. It did not exit. There was a lot of blood. Lonnie died instantly.

Herman and Druie ran out the front door. Alesha and Jake were playing in the back yard, Herman had made sure of that because he didn't mean for them to see; but Alesha heard the noise and ran in the back door, saw her daddy lying dead on the couch and started screaming.

Herman herded his brothers and sister together, and all four children ran down the rutted cow path to their daddy's pick-up, bawling. They were heading down to the main road, going God knows where, when their cousin, Linda Munn's son Wayne, who until a week before had been a Rush Springs policeman, drove in. Herman told him, 'I think Daddy's dead.' Wayne was not surprised; people had been expecting a shooting out there for years; they just didn't know who would end up dead. But he thought it would be Luther or one of the kids, not Lonnie.

The first police officer on the scene was Guy Huggins, the deputy Sheriff. He said that the trailerhouse was swept up and fairly clean, and that there were no illegal drugs on the premises. Later on, he went to pick up Herman and Druie at a relative's house, and all four kids were still bawling. Herman said that he was the one who shot his dad; then, when Huggins got the boys to the Sheriff's annexe in Chickasha, where they were questioned separately, Druie said that Herman held the gun but that he pulled the trigger. Both boys knew what they had done and said they loved their daddy. When was the funeral? Could they go?

It is dark now. In Rush Springs, the Homecoming game is in progress. The scoreboard lights say ten minutes left in the second quarter, the Redskins leading by two. I park on the highway. The stadium lights up the pitch-black night. Everybody's there: men with their feet up on a fence rail, smoking; women selling tickets, talking to their daughters. Let loose in the warm night air, kids run around like wild things.

At half-time, I drive into the parking lot and buy a ticket. The band—mostly white children in red and black uniforms—has marched out and plays 'Ebb Tide'. Convertibles circle the field, as Homecoming maids perched atop the back seats smile and wave. They have a lot of hair, frizzed up, fanned out, shiny with goo. Their cars stop at the fifty-yard line, where each maid is escorted through a flower-decked arbour. The queen and king are crowned, flashbulbs pop.

The Dutton compound is only five miles off, but it's a long way from there to here. As the band and the Homecoming court leave the field, and the Redskins roll back on, I think about the boys, what might have been happening to them, right now, this minute, if they hadn't killed their father.

All four Dutton children have been made wards of the court, a ruling that Marie Dutton is still fighting. Alesha and Jake have been put into the temporary care of a relative. Herman and Druie were sent to the Oklahoma Juvenile Diagnostic and Evaluation Center, which recommended unequivocally that they be put in therapeutic foster care with two adults as role models, and should receive long-term counselling and therapy with their siblings. It was strongly recommended that a court trial be avoided. If Herman and Druie stay out of trouble until April 1996, their records will be clear.

Nobody knows when the four children will be together again. The court has ruled that any member of the Dutton family seeking custody must first agree to therapy.

Back on US 81, heading north, I wonder what secrets are buried with Lonnie Dutton and what Luther Dutton was making up. I wonder how all four kids will turn out. I think about Herman. Herman has his own room now, his own things. I wonder what his nights are like, what he thinks about, what kind of plans he is making.

Later that night I wake up screaming. A rat is at me, biting and biting me, and I cannot move.

THE TRAGEDY OF VUKOVAR

The three month siege of Vukovar, in the autumn of 1991, when an average of 5,000 shells a day landed on the city, set a pattern for events in the former Yugoslavia. We are living with that pattern still. And yet, strangely, the world appears to have forgotten what occurred there. The heavy toll suffered by Sarajevo does not compare with the fate of this city. Only the siege of Mostar, two years later, comes close to reproducing the same total misery and destruction (although even there the world concentrated most of its attention on the collapse of Mostar's historic bridge). It is timely and salutary to recall the sheer horror of the underground existence endured by so many, while, above them, buildings were being pulverized.

A year after the fall of Vukovar, I saw the shattered remnants of the city from a helicopter. It was an awe-inspiring sight. I had not seen anything remotely like it since I returned to my home city of Plymouth at the age of six and walked amid the rubble of the Blitz. I will never forget Vukovar; I certainly could not forget it during the later discussions about the heavy artillery positions that ringed Sarajevo. As no military adviser ever believed that we could successfully take out the majority of these artillery positions from the air, the question remained: how would the Serbs respond if we went ahead with the air-strikes anyway? I used to invoke the famous saying of Aneurin Bevan: 'Why look in the crystal ball when you can read the book?' Vukovar had shown us how the Serbs would react: if there had been air-strikes, I never doubted that there would be a pounding of Sarajevo that would more than match anything we had seen.

Historians will long argue about the exact origins of the war between the Serbs and Croats that started the break-up of Yugoslavia. Unlike the war in Bosnia-Herzegovina, where the politicians had, and continue to have, a major role in the conflict that ensued, the Serbo-Croat war has been a peculiar one between generals of what was once the same army—the Federal Army of Yugoslavia. The siege of Vukovar became proxy for fighting for Zagreb and Belgrade. Within weeks, the people became engaged as their different television stations evoked all the hatreds of the civil war that had torn up Yugoslavia during the Second World War. The Croats, according to Serbian television, were fascist Ustashe; the Serbs, according to Croatian television, were royalist Chetniks.

So many terrible precedents were established here. The siege as a bargaining tool was one. This was the time when the various Federal Army barracks were surrounded by Croat forces. General Kadijevic, the defence minister of the Federal Army, made it clear that, if his soldiers were released, the siege of Vukovar would stop. Civilians, too, became bargaining tools, despite the protests of the International Red Cross. We also now know that the hospital patients at Vukovar were taken away when the siege ended and never seen alive again. A forensic investigation into a mass grave is being conducted as I write.

What would have happened had President Bush authorized the United States, as a member of NATO, to intervene to stop the bombardment of Vukovar? We will never know. But at the time, a critical military threshold was not crossed. It's possible that had that occurred, then the shelling of Vukovar would have been curtailed. There would never have been the same siege of Mostar. Or of Sarajevo.

David Owen

I was sitting on a pile of plaster and rubble on a street corner in front of one of the few apartment blocks—this part of Vukovar consisted mostly of the lime-green houses the town was so fond of—listening to an old man telling me stories about the Second World War. The clouds had rolled over and made the November afternoon a little more gloomy, as though their only intention was to take the edge off the light. The old man—someone's grandfather, muffled up in a frayed jacket of fleecy cotton, his forage cap square on his head—stirred a large can of cabbage leaves on a charcoal stove that he had made from a rusty drum. In front of us the bodies of several dogs with matted fur, and those of two disembowelled pigs, rotted in the channel that ran between the rubbish in the street and the debris covering the pavement. Mud and broken tiles lay so thick on the road that it was hard to believe it had ever possessed a Tarmac surface.

In the house opposite, some militia members had stretched out on mattresses covered with old-fashioned brown and grey ticking that they had unearthed from a cellar. They were waiting for food. The noise of the guns was deafening and relentless; shells whistled and whooshed over our heads, following the same trajectory, cracking and exploding in the same places.

Near the water-tanks, by the museum, over the town centre, scrolls of smoke eddied upwards, grey and then white and then grey again. If you crept up to the third floor of a nearby building, you could make out through a breach in the wall the area where the Dunav Hotel, the shopping centre and the bridge used to be. They were now draped in a blackish smoke.

I regretted not having stayed down in the centre of Vukovar. Not just for the people left there, even less for the pleasure of being able to write the account of the final hours, but for the town itself, for the sympathy and affection I felt for it. I wanted to share in the intimacy of its final moments.

Later on, I would spend time in many besieged towns, but no other place—not Osijek, or Srebenica or Goradze, not even Sarajevo a year later—would be squeezed by the kind of vice that destroyed Vukovar, or would suffer an artillery bombardment as shattering and as systematic. Shells came down without a minute's respite. The sheer weight of the lead which fell on the

Photo: Christopher Morris (Colorific)

197

town—its last lifeline through the maize fields already cut—
finally stopped its heart for good.

The tactic used by the Serbs was childishly simple; we were
able to watch it from the top of the building. (It was the same one
they would use throughout the conquest, first in Croatia, then in
Bosnia.) In August, the Federal Army flanked Vukovar and began
pounding its centre with shells. The inhabitants and defenders
entrenched themselves in their basements. Two months later, the
army was joined by Serbian militias, who were let loose to the
south and east of the city, suburbs with a Serb majority. They
pushed their way forward with Kalashnikovs, block by block—
each building fiercely defended by Croats armed with
Kalashnikovs. Each time the Croats retreated, the Serbian militias
cleared out the building that had been abandoned with grenades
and bazookas. When the dust settled, they emptied the cellars,
evacuated any survivors, took away the wounded and then
prepared to attack the next building.

The commissariat spread through the ruins behind the
militiamen. The soldiers—volunteers and conscripts, NCOs,
veterans from the Second World War who had dug their rifles out
of the attic—occupied the evacuated buildings, collecting television
sets and eiderdowns from the apartments and setting up kitchens.
House by house, junction by junction, they, too, advanced a step at
a time, just behind the militias.

The gunners often observed a truce at the end of the
morning. The people in the cellars took advantage of it to go up
into the street. They stretched their legs and went to inspect a
patch of garden or the state of their old workplace if it was not
too far away, or exchange a few words with a neighbour. The
young people left in town tried to renew their friendships. The
purpose of this truce was always a mystery to me. Why hold
back? Why postpone a carefully planned piece of destruction?
Was it a game of cat and mouse, to wear down the besieged
populace more easily, to break their personalities at the same time
as breaking down their walls? Or was it the opposite, a chance for
the inhabitants to get out in one piece before the town was razed
to the ground? I suspect that these truces, in Vukovar as in every
other town under siege, also served the aggressors: the truces were

a kind of injection of humanity, a momentary inoculation against the madness of the shelling, which threatened everyone.

As we were about to start on the food which had been heated up for us by the old man in the forage cap, astride his pile of rubble, peaceful in the way of a man whose life has been spent working the land, the bombardment began again, pounding the banks of the river, targeted on the hospital and the barracks adjacent to it. The previous day, our field kitchen had been located on a different corner, at the crossroads higher up, a little further from the town centre. Now, from our new position, we heard the patter of machine-gun fire in the intervals between the shelling. There were occasional shouts and the sound of running. When the gunfire died away, it was replaced by the periodic woof of bazookas. Tomorrow, the field kitchen would be re-erected at the new crossroads, just down the hill.

The Serbs happily invited us to share their food, as they were happy to offer us relics and souvenirs picked up here and there in the ruins. They radiated a sense of exhaustion from sleepless nights and fierce gun-battles, and a quality of cheerful anticipation of the day they would be demobbed. They were entirely absorbed in their own fantasies, grandiloquent and grotesque, of liberation.

The old man, a peasant from the village of Sotin ten kilometres from Vukovar, filled our plates and explained that each week he used to come here to sell his crop at the agricultural co-operative, Vupik, and then buy from the industrial wholesaler, Vutex, and then drink his bottles of Tramijac, the fresh wine from the slopes that faced the terrace of the Dunav Hotel. He was an ancient from ancient times, recounting memories that were less than six months old, talking as if everything was going to start up again tomorrow. He no longer saw the town in front of him.

I was reminded of an evening the month before. In Belgrade, after a difficult day around Vukovar, a friend and I returned to the run-down restaurant of the Moskva Hotel. A man and a woman at one of the tables nearby, hearing a conversation in French, asked if they could join us. The woman was the head of a humanitarian organization in Belgrade. She seemed lost. She was attempting, she said, to evaluate what supplies were needed by the inhabitants of

Vukovar, but was unable to set foot there. (To remedy her ignorance, she subsequently wrote down everything that was said over dinner in a spiral-bound notebook.) Her companion, a likeable Slav-speaking Serbophile, was a specialist on the former Yugoslavia at the French Ministry of Foreign Affairs. He had been seconded to prepare a report on the war in Slavonia. He was one of the closest advisers of the Foreign Minister and, therefore, of the French Ambassador in Belgrade as well.

My friend and I were soon expressing our indignation, protesting against the blindness—the word hypocrisy had not yet been uttered—of French and European policy. The diplomat's sense of humour began to fray and he cut our protest short. 'You shouldn't exaggerate everything, particularly the fate of Vukovar. One Timisoara is enough. Have no fear—the quai d'Orsay and the Elysée are following this war more closely than you seem to imagine. If the casualties ever exceed a thousand, or if the centre of Vukovar is threatened by an artillery attack, France and the European Community will not shirk their duty. We know the meaning of the word Europe!'

At the time of this absurd declaration, 15,000 people had already perished in Croatia during that summer alone—and at least 4,000 were from Vukovar. Vukovar itself was as good as destroyed. Vinkovci, a few kilometres away, was undergoing a similar fate in a similar climate of indifference. The diplomat, however, seemed genuinely to believe the rubbish he was coming out with.

Before we left the old man at the street kitchen, he slipped a silver coin into my hand in a gesture of friendship. The militiamen clapped us on the shoulder. One asked with faint embarrassment if we would mind giving him a lift to his mother's in Belgrade—she was a postwoman, worried that she had had no news from her son. He was lean and tall and had a sweet, almost simple look about him; in peacetime he would have shared Yugoslavia's national passion for basketball. Before the war he had worked in the railway workshops but had become fed up with his job as a mechanic. He had dreaded the vicissitudes of ordinary military service; he wanted to see action. So in the first days of September 1991 he had handed in his overalls and gone to join a special militia on the Vukovar front: his salary was to be maintained and he would be exempted from ordinary military service.

He told us about the nights spent drinking beer and talking under the blankets in abandoned apartment blocks on the outskirts of town, waiting to be called out for the house-to-house engagements. He talked cheerfully about the Croats they observed with field-glasses, then pulverized with bazookas. He described the bodies they went on to inspect and rob after the raids. He referred to the men who surrendered not as 'enemies' but 'ustaches': the men who were then shot or had their throats cut on the spot so the militia would not to have to hand them over to the army machinery, which would imprison or exchange them for prisoners on the other side. He showed emotion only once, when he mentioned the casualties among his comrades.

By now we were on the Sid road, but held up by the traffic. The youth carried on unselfconsciously. For torture they used a red-hot iron from the kitchen, he said, or a knife, to extract information about positions, or, sometimes, for no reason at all. We were moving again and it had got dark on the plain. I thought, either he hopes we will be shocked by his inventions, or he himself genuinely believes them. I asked for details of the prisoners. They were, he said, both Croat militiamen and civilians. He then described their terror when he and his friends pulled out their blades, the begging for mercy. He explained how in his section—the Lynxes of some mountain whose name I have forgotten—the initiation test consisted of forcing a prisoner to his knees and then slowly severing his jugular. A Lynx who went about it too hesitantly was forced to do it a second time; few refused and, if they did, they soon left the section. He said that of course the first time it felt pretty strange, but afterwards you went and got out of your head, and it was fine.

We had seen irrefutable acts of savagery here and there all through the summer, and they had hardened our reactions. In a war the phrase 'no smoke without fire' is truer than it is at other times. This time, though, I was too sceptical to hand the driving over to my friend Ivo and get out my notebook. I was, I thought, immunized against this sort of Yugoslav fantasy, and I noted almost nothing apart from his name, Jovica, and his age, twenty-two. Of his testimony, which lasted over more than two hours of country roads and then the motorway, I wrote only this phrase: 'He confirmed: "For a month my commando has taken no prisoners." With a gesture of his thumb below his throat he added with a strange expression, half-smiling, half-embarrassed, "It's a civil war . . . "'

But eight months later, dressing wounds and visiting hospital beds, listening to Bosnian prisoners who had escaped from Serb militias, or the Serbs who had escaped Bosnian or Croatian prisons, I remembered Jovica: his gangling walk and his stories, his naïvety. I am convinced now, for the most part, that the killings he told us about actually happened. My scepticism, I think, derived from my belief that concocting stories belongs to Yugoslav culture as much as the fiddle belongs to the Russian or the sun-dance to the Incas. Popular memory had been traumatized by the Second World War, but I had not suspected that the trauma would be actively expressing its consequences, in this way, today.

Later on that winter, when the siege was over and Vukovar had fallen, we wandered—my friend Patrick and I and Arsa, the interpreter—around its icy ruins. As we reached the doors of the Gradski museum, a commotion from a group of young people caught our attention. The museum, a building of butter-coloured stone that dates from the eighteenth century, stood in a magnificent park, full of sweet chestnuts and long grass. The museum's façade and the torn trees around it testified to the ferocity to which this peaceful place had been subjected by the federal howitzers. Museums and churches (and later, in Bosnia-Herzegovina, mosques), factories and water-towers seemed to inflame the Serbs' passion for destruction.

One young man, a Serb student in a long parka that he wore over a rollneck pullover sprinkled with dandruff, invited us inside the museum. It was the familiar spectacle of demolition: fallen plaster, glass splinters, gaping windows. But there were other elements: fragments from gilt frames, torn canvases, thousands of crumpled pages torn from old books, broken femurs from neolithic skeletons, here and there a greave from a broken suit of armour, the base of a vase. The local Serbs were accusing the Croat militiamen of sacking the building before they ran away. It was impossible to say. The bulk of the task had been accomplished by the shells that had destroyed the walls and roof.

The students took us down to the cellars. At the base of a staircase carpeted with torn-up books was a scene that somehow rang false. The ground was littered with debris from an advance medical unit and an arsenal of Croat weapons. The students gleefully brandished syringes, grenades and Kalashnikovs. The very presence of this equipment seemed to justify, in their eyes, the systematic destruction of the museum by the guns of the Serbian tanks.

The young man and his friends were from the Belgrade Art School. A professor was supervising them, a man with a bland face and carefully combed thick white hair. He wore a pair of delicate spectacles with round lenses and metal frames; his chin was extended by a longish grey beard which he stroked voluptuously as he spoke. He and his students had come to sort through the pieces and take to Belgrade those which were still transportable. While the rescuers carefully carried the objects out, the professor compiled a meticulous inventory, patting and toying with each object as it passed, sometimes with a word of comfort for a scarred icon or a ragged piece of parchment. He explained in mannered French that he awaited the release of Unesco funds to initiate the reconstruction of the museum and its collections—so that the cultural cosmopolitanism of the town (which dated from the dawn of history) should be preserved. The discussion was about to take a depressing turn, I knew. This professor, in some other time, might have been an interesting representative of the Serbian intelligentsia to which Belgrade had owed its charm for more than two centuries. Not any longer. We promised to resume the conversation the following day in Belgrade, and I fled, in an atmosphere made even more cheerless by the winter twilight.

On the way out of town, we stopped at a two-storey villa, the home of the recently set-up Radio Vukovar. In this heated and lit house, journalists, militants and organizers from a stream of associations—all of them Serbian—met and debated the future of the town. A member of an ecological movement—a Green Serb, recognizable by the yellow badge of the anti-nuclear lobby—stood in the middle of the smoke-filled room. (His curly hair was tied back in a pony-tail; he wore purple trousers and an elephant-hide bracelet on his wrist.) According to him, now was the time to set in train truly visionary ecological experiments. The resurrection of Vukovar should be based on a more natural, ecologically friendly lifestyle. Nature would resuscitate the town. I mischievously asked him about the resurrecting of the tens of thousands of Croats who had formerly peopled the place. Without waiting to translate his response—in which I could make out the words 'fascists' and 'terrorists'—Arsa hustled us out of the room and pushed us into the white Opel Kadett under the protection of an embarrassed militiaman who kept repeating his apologies as he stood on the steps.

In May 1992, six months after the battle for Vukovar, Belgrade's central office of tourism was offering excursions to the martyred town. In the bus that bumped through the ruins, a guide with a microphone recounted the bloody epic and the genocide committed by the 'Ustache' forces.

One evening I met a Serb friend for dinner in what had been one of Belgrade's most cosmopolitan restaurants. He was accompanied by his wife, a woman of a distinctive and charming Slav type, baby-faced, with a gaze marked by an attractive astigmatism. The restaurant was empty apart from the Swiss delegation of the Red Cross, who had been joined by a forlorn nurse from another humanitarian organization.

The maîtresse d'hôtel in her navy blue uniform spoke five languages. Her maternal smile could not quite mask her concern at the sorry state of the dining-room. The forsaken air of the place didn't matter to us; we were there to talk and to celebrate a success. My friend and his wife, a town planner in a community organization in the distant suburbs, had recently managed to enrol their children in the French school in Belgrade, removing them from the bellicose, patriotic atmosphere of the city schools. In their pleasure and relief, they decided to honour the famous steak tartare (the one dish which had resisted the recession) with one of the last bottles of Zilavka, a heavy red wine from Mostar. To entertain them, I told them stories, including my account of the surreal day-trip to Vukovar. My friend's wife asked for some practical details about the trip and then announced to her husband that she intended to take the children so they could learn about the genocide committed by the 'Ustaches'. She proceeded to recite a jumble of 'facts' about the bloodthirsty and perverted habits of her former Croat compatriots. She had a steady voice and spoke excellent English.

I swallowed my first glass of wine and cast embarrassed glances at her husband. He had already visited the ruins, and was nodding in approval, supplementing her account with his own litany of horrors. I emptied a second glass of wine in one gulp.

For three months, without interruption, hundreds of Serbian guns had pounded Vukovar with up to 5,000 shells a day. Since the bombardment, I had found history-of-art students, a renowned archaeologist, a militant ecologist and a tourist office perpetuating the same, paranoid, Serb delusion, and here were two friends happily going along with it. The Serbs are curious people: friendly, hospitable, brave—but brave in the sense of stupid and dogged too. Their folly, matched by their blindness, drives them straight into the realms of fantastic illusion. At the mere mention of the Croats, the Muslims or the Albanians they lose themselves in a bloodthirsty, suicidal, barbaric downward spiral.

F rom my notebook:

> On the eighty-eighth day of the siege, an architectural apocalypse rises from the dawn: its reflection lies flat on the undisturbed surface of the Danube. Dresden, Beirut, the visions intermingle. Mournful ruins. Vukovar, still smoking at its heart, without question worse than both . . .

Nothing had prepared my imagination for what we found on 18 November 1991.

Dawn brought with it a pallid autumn sun as we approached Vukovar by the Negoslavci road. The day before, we had witnessed the surrender of thousands of prisoners: they were loaded on to unending convoys that disappeared into the night. We had passed the first processions of ambulances taking away the dead and wounded whom the first-aid workers previously hadn't been able to reach because of the fighting. The town had fallen, the guns which had thundered on the horizon for so long were silent.

At sunrise on this clear, still day it was the lull that was the most striking thing of all.

The crowds on the Sid road that led into Vukovar were jubilant. On their tractors, farm-workers waved their trilbies at the Serbian soldiers riding the bonnets of armoured vehicles and at the militiamen in Golfs that sagged on their springs. Horns and bottles and the wild semaphoring of arms produced a ragged guard of honour. The celebration of the Serbian conquest, all the way to the far suburbs of the town by the bank of the river, lasted until evening. The new arrivals, the Red Cross delegates and the European observers in their white tunics, were diverted one after another from the line moving into the town, away to the yard of the Velepronet warehouse, where they were to be received by the victorious officers. Presentations and speeches were to be made, and refreshments offered—one could not help thinking there would also be congratulations.

A small street opened up to us, half-hidden by two trucks into which scavenged furniture was being piled as quickly as possible. Aided by a piece of paper that had been stamped by a former footballer from Lille—now the chief commando in Sid—we passed the militiamen and slipped into a narrow street strewn with debris. We drove slowly across the rubble of the quarter—it was full of federal soldiers with Kalashnikovs and ammunition-belts, spades in hand, dragging their feet in boots too big for them—until the rubble forced us to abandon the car and follow the soldiers on foot into town. All around stood shattered tree trunks, trunks which had been flayed and burned, their roots torn up and their branches smashed. Not one tree was intact in the small park that used to welcome visitors as they entered the town. Not a single shrub. A cross was held on to the spire of a nearby church with a length of twisted metal, but it hung upside down, beating time against chipped white stone. When the photographers came the next day, they would not miss this: a handy and ironic symbol for the martyrdom of the city.

By the church, the street turned and took us into the town,

into a place too surreal to be called a nightmare. There were three road signs nailed together: one warning that the road narrowed, one indicating roadworks ahead and one calling for a reduced speed limit. Two metres away, the torso of a corpse in a reflective jacket lay by a pile of wood, pointing the way ahead with a stiff finger. A row of bombed-out houses, their roofs caved in, their floors littered with mounds of rubble, continued to the end of the street. We looked up and saw the burnt spectres of the first tall blocks of the town centre, silhouetted against a periwinkle-blue sky; between the untouched piles of debris, which occasionally rose as high as the bonnets of the abandoned cars, we moved towards these masses of blackened concrete as if they held the key to the mystery of the siege of Vukovar.

Republic Square was at the end of this street. It was where the smartest shops of the port town had once been arrayed beneath the arcades of ochre and pistachio-green walls. Here people had made a start on clearing up. Some militiamen were laying the body of a bleeding woman on a trolley, her face disfigured with pain and whitened with plaster dust; they had just dragged her out of the mass of fallen rubble. Others, sitting on tanks parked side by side, sang and offered each other toasts with some slivovitz that looked far too green. Empty bottles of it littered the ground around the tracks of their machines; their hair slick with dirt, their clothes covered from head to foot with the insignia and badges of dozens of warring clans, their weapons next to them, the militiamen gave off the smell of exhaustion and drunkenness. They were curious about us and invited us to share their revelry with a childish gaiety.

Here and there I saw bodies that had been left behind. A young mother wearing short boots, her legs bare despite the season, still held her shopping bag under her arm, while her headscarf protected her head from the dirt of the street. Croat fighters lay scattered on the ground, dressed in the same uniforms as the victors, frequently in the same black woollen hats; in some cases a gold Catholic cross had been pulled out from inside a jacket to identify its wearer. Some seemed petrified, others only sleeping. A woman and her young son were lying at right angles to each other; their hands were stretched out, the tips of their fingers trying to touch. I wondered if one had seen the other die. A man whose forehead bore the white imprint left by a helmet had been killed not far away. The impassive dead seemed to be playing the part of extras, as if the square had been overtaken by some cinematic lethargy.

Further on, near the shopping mall, a man lay against his motorbike. The bike drew me to him. He was a fat man and wore a fur-lined jacket and an old leather flying-cap with ear-flaps. He rested against a two-stroke single-cylinder machine, rusted and muddy, which had once been black, with the maker's name—JAWA—in gold letters on the petrol tank.

I stayed crouching next to the motorcyclist for a long time, contemplating his features, trying to penetrate this minor enigma. Was he a Croat, a Serb, a Hungarian, a Romanian? Was he a native of Vukovar, or an immigrant? A worker in the Vupic factory, a retired teacher, a Serb under house arrest by the Croats or a defender of the town? An old man in retirement, or a liaison agent between two defence bunkers? What craziness had persuaded him, beneath a sky black with shell-bursts, so shortly before the end, to get on his motorbike? Had he taken advantage of the lunchtime lull in the bombardment to treat himself and his beloved machine to a spin? Had he been on duty? Had he had an accident in the rubble and lain there with no one to help him until an explosion did its fatal work? Had the enforced confinement of a cellar driven him a little mad, or had he wanted to put his motorbike somewhere safe? Had he been upset by a piece of bad news and tried to rejoin a relation—one of his children? Or did he belong to that impressive caste of old people who will always go where they please, as if nothing were happening? One meets them on every battlefield: indifferent to danger; too old, they say, to change their habits; too hardened by life to be afraid of accidental death; too philosophical to be taken in by a war. Scraps of daily life in this town, itself in tatters, kept coming to light, as a marsh-like smell, imperceptible to begin with, floated on the cold air.

We reached the flat concrete bridge that spanned the Vuka. Only the previous summer it had been the meeting-place for the town's youth before they headed for the café terraces and discothèques of the far bank, or for walks along the river as it traversed the town to pour into the Danube, in front of the Dunav Hotel.

The water no longer moved: it had been soaked up by the sponge of debris and filth flung into it by the tenants of the cellars close by, and blocked by the smashed river-craft and the twisted metal of unrecognizable equipment and the animal and human remains, swollen and decomposing bodies half-covered by the shrouds of leaves from the chestnut trees.

Later, on many occasions in the course of the war, I would congratulate myself on having been a witness to this morning. It was a privilege granted to me over my fellow-journalists who didn't get into the town that day. This un-ordinary visit was not an inoculation against horror; it was the opposite. Nor, despite its morbidity, was it a contamination. It was, instead, an initiation into the implausible quality of war. To see it enabled me to interpret the fantastic tales of the Balkans, to decipher testimonies that perpetually went beyond reality. Later it would encourage me to look for—and recognize—other Vukovars concealed in the Bosnian mountains or the forests of Slavonia. I had the authentic experience; I saw what was possible, which meant that now everything else could be, even the methodical massacre of every inhabitant of an ordinary village by the side of an ordinary country road.

On the far side of the bridge we skirted a vast graveyard of the cars that had been destroyed by shelling during the first two months of bombardment and piled up by the local council workers. I glimpsed shadows ransacking the engines for a starter motor or a carburettor. We left the centre of town by the street that led to the hospital. During the last weeks of the siege, the immense, windowless concrete building had seen an intense concentration of military activity and was now utterly ravaged. It was the one structure in the town that the occupying Serbs continued to defend *manu militari*, as if the battle could flare up there again at any moment. Access to it was denied by a cordon of tanks and armoured vehicles and a troop of soldiers. Red Cross delegates, encouraged by European observers, were protesting in several Swiss accents, to the ironic, surly and, as it turned out later, habitual indifference of the Serb officers.

The officers claimed that hundreds of wounded were being evacuated from the hospital basement, which necessitated tight military control. The explanation was, to my astonishment, accepted by the various foreign observers. It was obvious what was about to take place. The hospital adjoined the police barracks which had been the headquarters of the Croat militias during the siege. The proximity of the two buildings had led the Croat fighters to use the hospital as an annexe to the barracks—a long-standing wartime custom—not just to care for their wounded but also for protection from the guns. On occasion they put their mortar batteries there as well. This was sufficient reason for the Serb gunners to single it out as a privileged target.

Under the nose of everyone present, the victors continued to load into a fleet of ambulances everyone they could find in the building, including all the enemy fighters hidden below ground. These prisoners would not reappear until the discovery of mass graves.

On the other side of the wooded street, a small wild garden beckoned us into a museum of slaughter. Dozens of bodies were laid out in neat rows on the ground, occasionally cloaked by a sheet or a blanket. Often a jaw was tied shut with a handkerchief, the way characters with toothache are drawn in cartoons. Time and the cold had given the dead faces the appearance of wax: eyes closed, heads thrown back, indifferent, they seemed indolent. A woman was grimacing in a theatrical expression of disgust; a bearded man lolled with his mouth open. Were these the last expressions of the living or the first expressions of the dead? Some—identifiable by a numbered ticket pinned to their chest, '430', '678'—had come from the hospital. The others had been delivered here by their families or passers-by after they had died in the street: the shelling had prevented people even digging a hole in a patch of garden. The place had become a depot of sorts, in case it turned out to be possible—when the siege was over—to come back and bury the bodies properly. Now, before these bodies were carried to the communal graves, Serb militiamen had come to visit, filing down the rows with the walk of conquerors; they stared at the dead with scorn, dominated them like matadors. They turned away with quick movements of the head, as if they still wanted to prove something to the dead or to themselves. The dead lay in their thick woollen stockings: shoes were too precious to be left to them.

At the end of a line of sweet chestnuts, the street ran into what was left of the factories of Borovo Selo: an immense plain of rubble and broken walls and girders twisted by the flames. It was a vision I was to see again a fortnight later, on the edge of Vukovarska Boulevard in Osijek, where the name-plates of huge factories lay rusting in the ruins of the burnt-out buildings. And I would meet it several times more in the industrial suburbs of Vinkovci, Tuzla, Sisak and along the length of Radomira Avenue in Sarajevo.

On the flattened site of Borovo Selo—the lung and stomach of Vukovar that had drawn in more than 20,000 workers from the surrounding regions—a host of militiamen moved like ants over the destroyed warehouses, turning over the debris in search of booty. I thought at first that they were still hunting fugitives, but then saw one holding up a pair of boots in triumph. The Borovo Selo factories were well known for the shoes they produced; one, a model of boot which laced over the ankle in pale or tanned hide, hand-sewn and with notched crêpe soles, was said to be as waterproof and comfortable as a pair of Eagles or Timberlands. The boots were exported to Germany and Austria, to the frustration of the local people, to bring foreign currency to the town. In the rubble of the factory, the militiamen were hunting down the last pairs ever produced. At the end of the afternoon, the failing light made it impossible to differentiate the uniforms of the federal army from those of the militiamen; a pair of boots knotted around the neck was all one had to go on, the militiamen being the only combatants allowed to collect the spoils of war. I had had the idea of taking a pair myself as a souvenir. The triumphal coarseness of the militiamen dissuaded me.

The following April in Sarajevo, I came across the BOROVO SELO sign in a shoe shop. A pair of the boots stood in the window—one of the last two pairs in the country, the salesman said. I bought them and hid them under the mattress in the hotel. That afternoon the shop exploded in a rocket attack. The boots are one of the few souvenirs I have kept from the war. The others include a small framed portrait of Tito that my friend Jean picked off a pile of rubbish in Vukovar, three bullets preserved from two of the cars I drove in, a piece of shrapnel that landed between my legs and a bouquet of plastic flowers from a bloody wedding.

Beyond the shoe warehouses stood the first houses of the village of Borovo Nasselje, where the confrontation had germinated in the spring of 1991. Behind that lay fields and meadows. Standing there, I could hear the muffled echo of the obsessive bombardment of Vinkovci eighteen kilometres further on. Away to the right, the Danube curved and disappeared behind some motionless cranes.

Back in the town centre, I walked down to the river. To reach what was left of the Dunav Hotel, I had to scramble over a small mountain of rubbish; a pudgy cat rummaged on its summit, the first living animal I had set eyes on since I arrived. At the hotel, the soldiers were already setting up camp. (In subsequent days this would be where they served their thick potato soup to the groups of foreign visitors.) On the burnt-out terrace I walked into Zoran: a Belgrade journalist, a desperado and half-mad, always on the look-out for the wildest stories; in Gdańsk years before, in the early, euphoric Solidarity days, we had shared some epic times. Here he stood in a circle of Serbian officers, raising toasts to the victory. He broke off to introduce me to the famous Arkan, a tall heavily-built man of legendary vulgarity. He was surrounded by his inevitable band of over-excited thugs—the *Arkanovci*—who were like extras from a Rambo picture: boasting, arrogant, clumsy boors. Arkan stood out by his serene sense of irony. That day, he posed for photographs in his beret with a bazooka and a lynx kitten in his arms, beneath the gun-barrel of a tank covered with the crouching figures of his bodyguards in black balaclavas. The atmosphere was heavy, sinister in a banal way; I made an excuse and left. I met Arkan again in May at Ilidza, shortly before the siege of Sarajevo tipped over into a street-battle, and then again in June at Zvornik, when the massacres were coming thick and fast in the villages of eastern Bosnia.

Outside, the sun, paler and paler, coated the length of the Danube with a diaphanous light. In it were half-submerged barges, the twisted skeletons of hoists and the planks of black timber boats. No hooter on the horizon warned of any ship or barge approaching; there was nothing to disturb the peace of this corrupted shore. The path stank of rubbish. Bodies with greenish faces swollen with water rotted beneath the low branches that had snagged them. On a low hill near the river's edge, a water-tower stood out triumphantly like a lighthouse. Of course, it had been an irresistible target for the Serb gunners, who had struck at it obsessively, over and over again, with shells and rockets that had left it with a thousand scars: it was a miracle of the siege.

I asked myself what, out of this landscape of desolation, made the strongest impression on me: the unending ruins, the blackish colour of everything, the depth of the rubble, the corpses one stumbled over, the fairground atmosphere among the victorious militiamen, the petrification of the abandoned quarters of the town? No, it was the pockmarked surfaces of the buildings: the effects of the storm that had rained down, chipping, holing and disfiguring the smallest area of wall and roof and street. Covered in this raddled skin, the town seemed contaminated with a strain of pox.

As the time came to leave for Belgrade, a salvo of shell-bursts started up again in a neighbouring village. On the evening of the eighty-eighth day of the siege, wild-eyed Croat fighters were still selling their lives dearly to Serb fighters, who were no less crazed themselves.

Three days later in Vukovar, my friend Ivo and I came across a convoy of twelve orange coaches parked at the roadside. The doors and windows of the vehicles—abandoned by their drivers— were locked and bolted. Inside, the silhouettes of women and children and old people shivered with the cold beneath colourless blankets. Behind the dirt-covered windows, women with tears in their eyes held up empty bottles, pleading for water, parched despite the polar temperature. We had collected a few used bottles, intending to get them filled at the farm across the road, when five or six militiamen emerged from the house and ran in our direction, yelling threats. With their Kalashnikovs aimed at us, they ordered us to get back in the car and make ourselves scarce. Their jumpy manner, shocking in the frozen silence of the open country, made the convoy seem contaminated or cursed. Cautiously, we drove over the muddy road to the village. At the Café Sidro, the first place we came to, a group of men sat sipping Turkish coffee and brandy to warm themselves. They were the drivers of the convoy.

The passengers—women and children, and men aged over seventy—had once been Croat citizens of Vukovar. The Serbian army had pulled them out of their underground refuges as it advanced on the centre of the town and dispatched them to a Serbian village five kilometres away, where they were held in the grain stores. They were interrogated for two days and denounced by their Serb neighbours, who had been evacuated from their cellars at the same time—people in whose company they had lived through three months of siege, not to mention the years before the war. In the end they had not been found guilty of bearing arms or helping the Croat militia. The older people had been cleared of having a son in the Croatian officer corps and so were of no use as hostages. They were worthless, free to leave their detention area for whatever destination they chose. So these people, who had lost everything—husbands, houses, jobs, their most precious possessions, often their children—had asked to go to Croatia, in the direction of Zagreb, to find their relations, or some international aid, or just to begin their exile.

Thus the convoy had formed and started off two days earlier from the village, after four days of waiting. The passengers had been given water and meat paste and a crust of bread in the morning, and in the evening a bowl of soup. The buses, unescorted, had been sent in the direction of Sid, forty kilometres away, where the military administration had detained them for nearly twenty-four hours in order to exchange fruitless messages with the headquarters in Negoslavci and Belgrade. Then they had set off for Slavonski Brod, a Croatian town, where normally the local authority received and took charge of such refugees. They had been delayed another night at the frontier. At dawn the coaches had finally entered Croatian territory. And at that moment, when the passengers finally believed themselves to be delivered from their nightmare, the journey had suddenly taken a turn for the worse, the drivers said, accepting another round of brandy.

On the outskirts of Lipovac, the first Croatian village on the other side of the frontier, the buses had found themselves being shot at. The snipers stopped their fusillade as soon as the buses stopped. The Serb drivers thought they were the victims of their compatriots' mistake; they turned round and drove back to the frontier, where the Serb military assured them that the area had not been a firing-zone since the previous spring. The drivers, all disciplined men, returned, and again found themselves under fire, in the same place, from gunmen who still refused to show themselves. They turned back and returned to Serbia a second time; the officers in the village had given them permission to park their vehicles at the roadside, where we had come across them, on condition that none of the passengers got off—neither to refill their water bottles nor, with good Serb military logic, to use a lavatory. For two days and two nights they had not had a drop of water. Some of the faces at the windows looked as if they were made of clay.

It was Ivo who finally interpreted the surreal situation. Three days after losing Vukovar to federal troops and Serb militias, the Croatian government in Zagreb was still denying that the town had fallen. Since there had been no surrender, there could not be any refugees, nor buses full of desperately thirsty people on the road to Zagreb. As proof, that evening, the Zagreb Television news described the heroic, irreducible resistance of the Croat fighters of Vukovar, the commentary given against a montage of artillery salvoes filmed at least three weeks ago, before the journalists of Zagreb TV had packed up and left the town. I then flipped to Belgrade TV, which was broadcasting a sequence of images of children's mutilated bodies—mutilated, it was claimed, by Croatian forces. The bodies had been assembled and laid out in a cellar in the Serb district of Vukovar to simulate the wholesale massacre of Serb children. This was how the programme editors of two news programmes on rival channels, 350 kilometres apart, competed— one perpetrating the heroism of a battle which had already been lost, the other putting a faked collection of bodies on display. As the atrocities increased the sordid films of the beginning of the war would eventually be replaced by game-shows and sitcoms.

The wanderings of the thirsty convoy came to an end two hours later when the commander of the village, in a magnanimous gesture, sent the drivers back to their cabs (deeply frustrated not to be able to take a bottle with them). Behind a Red Cross LandCruiser which had suddenly appeared, they drove their passengers into the foggy night, along narrow country roads inaccessible to civilians and slippery with mud from trailers full of beets. In slow lines, barely visible in a darkness lit only by their weak headlights, they disappeared.

From the last days of the siege to the day after the capitulation, there was a clandestinely-run, human-rubbish clearing operation, a bulk transport of human beings. I thought about the mystery of it only when I got back to Paris, and friends asked me, perfectly reasonably, where the 60,000 inhabitants of Vukovar had gone. There were the 20,000 women and children who had fled in the summer of 1991 before the town was sealed off. Then there were the 7,000 or 8,000 people convoyed to Belgrade or Novi Sad or the towns of Montenegro. There were also the 3,000 or 4,000 who had been dispatched to the Croatian frontier. What of the others? Fifteen thousand at least, men for the most part, were missing from the count. How had the male population of this smart and prosperous town by the Danube vanished? Where had they gone? It was not possible to give a full answer, nor will it be for a long time. At the end of 1993, as I write, mass graves are still appearing in the countryside around Vukovar. Today I think to myself that the craziest part is not that the question can't be answered, but that everyone has ceased to ask it—as if the drama of the inhabitants of Sarajevo has erased from their memory the disappearance of the people of Vukovar.

How had people survived for three months living underground? To answer that question we were risking our necks on this road which took us through Sid. Jeeps and trucks careered towards us, their drivers soaked in the drunken haze of victory, forcing us to swerve to avoid them. The road finally took us past an unending stream of bulldozers and mechanical diggers: for several days they parked along the outskirts of Vukovar before they turned around and left. For their own reasons, Vukovar's military administrators had decided to keep the ruins as they were.

This did not prevent intense activity in the streets. Squads of soldiers continued to clear the pavements by shovelling the rubble into the destroyed houses and piling up the rotting rubbish in heaps which the cold would preserve during the winter months. The militiamen kept on with their task of mine-clearing, according to the rustic Balkan method, which favoured systematic use of the Kalashnikov. They emptied their magazines into suspect places— public buildings, strategic buildings, parks—and when the gunfire was interrupted by the explosion of a mine struck by a round, a general cheer went up, followed by laughter; the gunman was slapped on the back, the bottle was passed round and the militiamen returned to work.

Around them, small groups of civilians advanced with timid steps along the uneven streets. These were the first Serb exiles returning. The majority had left at the beginning of the summer after the first skirmishes between Croat militiamen and Serb police. Issued with a twenty-four-hour pass, families visited the ruins to see the extent of the damage. They inspected the rubble of their homes and tried to save a quilt here, a small table there; the luckier ones might salvage a television. The Dante-esque proportions of what surrounded them seemed to stifle all sorrow or surprise. Further on, dual commandos of soldiers and militia continued to search through basements, pipework and communal cellars to bring out docile stragglers, whom they marched off—sometimes with embarrassment—to the processing stations.

Three days after the surrender, some of Vukovar's inhabitants were still confined in their holes. Of these last spectral survivors, many were women. Their headscarves concealed slightly dirty hair, and they cradled babies and young children from whom they had not wanted to be separated in the summer, when it was still possible to get them out. Old people held each other by the arm. They people were not emaciated—their confinement showed in their extreme pallor and the beginnings of obesity. They had rings around their eyes, as though hollowed out by an etching tool and blackened with sticks of charcoal, emphasizing their haunted gaze. The survivors emerged from their basements in a stupor: they were close to collapse. Then, unexpectedly, they would tense up; in the open air these 'rats', as the soldiers affectionately called them, seemed reborn, like animals leaving a cage. They stretched their backs, shook themselves rather like dogs, straightened their jackets, turned their heads and looked around.

Two women, their arms tightly linked, came up the steps from the basement of a building in Amoriceva Street that afternoon; they were helped discreetly by two patient soldiers, whose consideration seemed to spring from their having divined a bond to be respected between the survivors. The women took three steps along the pavement and breathed in the dust-filled air. The soldiers allowed one of the the women to talk to us in English. They wore identical anoraks and looked about the same age. They smelt strongly, though not unpleasantly, of fatigue. Their nails were impeccably cared for. Jelena was a Croat gynaecologist, Mariana a Serb worker. Jelena wore her hair short and brushed back: the style refined her slender face and her straight nose. She was tall, though no taller than Mariana, who let her long blonde hair fall straight and tied it back with a scrap of cloth. Mariana's features were thick and heavy after her diet of meat paste but, paradoxically, soft and calm.

I was immediately taken by the tenderness which emanated from the two women. They had not known each other before the start of hostilities. One day the shelling had virtually blown Jelena—who was a long way from home, out looking for her three daughters who had been missing for several days—into the corridors of this building: the same building where Mariana had already taken refuge after her own house was destroyed. For two months they had peeled beets together, kneaded the dough for pancakes, shared the water from the tank and slept between a double thickness of blankets on the tiled floor of the hallway, better protected there than in the apartments.

They had listened as long as their batteries had lasted to Radio Belgrade, Radio Zagreb and Radio Novi Sad, and they had despaired of everything. When the transistor had given out they listened to the bombardment and to each other talking about their children and their husbands and their lives. Jelena said, 'We talked to each other every night, of everything and nothing.' Towards the end of the morning, if the artillery stopped, they went out into the street. They emptied their chamber-pots behind the silent hen-house in a neighbouring garden. They cleaned their saucepans with chestnut leaves and dug up cabbages wherever they found them. They kept up appearances as much as they could: one helped the other to wash her hair, as if on a camping holiday, with water collected in a bucket and a jug from a pipe at the crossroads. When it rained, the bowls in the garden filled with water, and if there was a lull in the shelling, they washed their underwear and stockings, which they wore only intermittently. At night they cleaned their skirts and sweaters as well as they could. If the sky permitted it, they also slipped out to a bread distribution point.

Jelena did not go back to her empty apartment, for fear that she would have to confront the fact that her three daughters had disappeared. Mariana's son and daughter had also vanished. That afternoon they asked for permission to visit the makeshift morgues in town, 'at least to be sure,' as Jelena explained. The permission was denied. Mariana wept as Jelena told us the story in English, though she understood none of it. Then she spoke. 'In the beginning the Croat militiamen behaved very well, but the atmosphere became terrible near the end. They were very nervous. They came in yelling that they were going to shoot all Serbs before the Serbian army got here. Three days ago a boy from round here came—before the war, an honest, good boy—he took an old couple whose son was fighting in the Serbian army and led them out to a pile of rubbish and shot them, shot them in the head with his revolver, one and then the other, in the middle of the rotting rubbish. In front of us.' They said nothing more, possibly because they couldn't express it.

The next day at the Velepronet processing centre I met Jelena and Mariana again: two women who had shared their nights in a corridor with the shells falling outside, telling each other about their lives, who had swapped their bras when they washed them to relieve the monotony. One was in the middle of a group waiting to be taken away, the other in another group a few metres away. They were no longer allowed to talk to each other; they were to be separated and put on convoys of orange buses going in opposite directions. They stared hard at each other, looked into the distance and turned back to stare at each other. In the end they broke away and ran to each other; one buried her hands in the folds of the other's sweater, and they hugged and kissed.

On the pavement of Nazozrac Street, a pretty road lined with rose bushes, a Serb woman employed by the military court came up and told us how she and her children had lived for four days with her husband's body on the kitchen table before they had dared go out and bury him, hastily, 'without a coat on his back,' in the common grave. She had known his killer well, a man named Goran Bogdanovic, who had shot him like a rabbit from the window of his sitting-room when he was drunk, as her husband was taking out the rubbish. The day of the surrender this Bogdanovic had himself been executed in his house with a bullet in the back of the head, by the victors acting on the evidence of one of the victim's brothers. The woman said only: 'A week before, I had been shopping with his wife Gabriella.' This very dignified woman, who dared not utter another word for fear of being unable to hold back her tears, grabbed my notebook and pen and wrote down in French: '*Radmila et Nicola Crevar. 32 ans. Fini.*'

A well-spoken Hungarian woman, on her way past on her bicycle, accosted us to tell us how she had been press-ganged as a cook and servant in a billet of Croat police. Every day from dawn until night she had been made to cook meals for them. Wherever we went, we collected scraps of extraordinary adventures. We found ourselves in a kind of ghetto, devastated by shellfire, made up of stories that faded as their narrators were led away to the camps.

As we wandered through the town, I watched intently at every encounter—every time we entered a bedroom or sitting-room, handled an ornament or a piece of household equipment—for signs that would help me reconstruct the daily life of Vukovar. In the ruins of this town by the Danube, with its mauve tiles and green arcades, this city of boots, this port of registry for the blue boats from Bulgaria, the emergence of its last people into the open air was unforgettable.

I couldn't conceive how these inhabitants of Vukovar—imprisoned in the rubble for three months; trapped in basements; scarcely knowing the reasons for their confinement, let alone how long that confinement would last; surviving on tins of mortadella; having lost family, relations, friends, houses and possessions—had survived, had endured the endless period of waiting without losing their minds. In the underground galleries of Osijek a month later, and then in the basements and cellars of Sarajevo the following spring, I began to understand the power of the present moment in the day-to-day life of a population under siege. I began to be able to measure the extraordinary energy such people bring to surviving during a war.

Postscript

With Vukovar flattened, the main force of the Serb artillery struck camp to continue its work elsewhere.

Thirty-seven kilometres to the north-west, it set out its tanks on the edge of Osijek; eighteen kilometres to the south-west it advanced on Vinkovci, where heavy artillery had been preparing the terrain since August. It was pointless to try to follow this lumbering migration. In any case, a plethora of military administrators had sprung up and stood between me and the battlefield, all obstructive. So I had to leave Ivo, who was a Serb, and skirt around the killing, by following a long diversion to the north and returning through the region of Vojvodina, where I took the ferry at Mohàcs across the Danube, which was dotted with crowds of grey geese. So close to the airport at Budapest, another diversion by way of Paris was too tempting.

The city sparkled at the end of November. On either side of a waterway free of bodies, the banks of the Seine were lit up. The cursive menus hung in the brasserie windows, and the season's novels were piled on the bookshop tables with the publishers' red bands around them. I cut through the streets on my motorbike. They were congested with Christmas shoppers, but after walking down so many dark and deserted streets in Vukovar I reflected that these bright yellow bulbs and the garlands that swung across the avenues were introducing an element of happiness to the inevitable melancholy of the end of the year.

Very quickly, though, the truce of Paris became irksome and painful. Everything was out of step: the contrast between there, grey Slavonia (the bombardments, the underground rooms that smelt of cabbage and dried urine), and here (the whirl of a snug world with its light-hearted dinners and its fun) was too great. An entire universe lay between the stuff drunk from an unlabelled bottle in a cellar with a meal of beets and fatty polenta, and the lamplight falling on the silky garnet of a Margaux in a glass against a white cloth. The first evening back, I confirmed the truth of the axiom that it is impossible for a man who has come back from a war to talk about it to his girlfriend. During dinner with friends, they talked a great deal—and with great sympathy—of Vukovar, but they doubted the truth of the war even if they didn't dare say so. They merely worried, which was not the same thing as understanding. I soon gave up trying to tell them anything other than what they had been able to read in the paper. I gave up trying to explain, for example, that I found it easier to love people in a war. The overturning of habits, the fear, courage, distress, uncertainty that make us more fragile or, conversely, strengthen us—they all permit encounters of a sincerity I have never found anywhere else.

In Paris, a feeling of boredom and loneliness grew day by day. Maybe it was simply the call of the forest.

Jean Hatzfeld returned to the former Yugoslavia and was severely wounded by gunfire in June 1992.

Translated from the French by Julian Evans

GRANTA

GILLES PERESS
COMPULSORY DEPARTURES

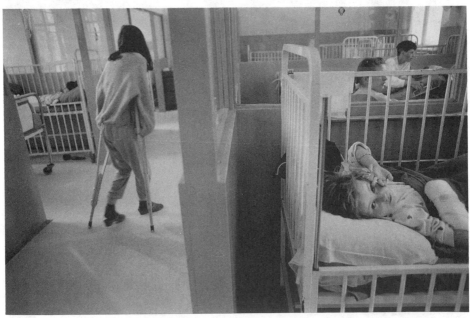

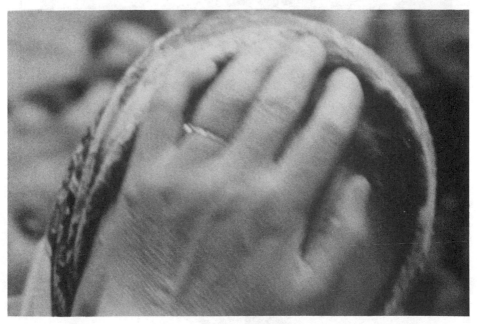

TRACY KIDDER

Old Friends

WHY DID Tracy Kidder (the robust, youthful Pulitzer Prize winner) voluntarily enter an old people's home, and live there for a year?

For the mystery of the old things he would find there: old memories, old lives – and old friends.

'A wonderful book, on the most unlikely
subject imaginable.'
CHICAGO TRIBUNE

Hardback   £14.99   31 March 1994

GRANTA BOOKS

GRANTA

ORVILLE SCHELL
HERO OF TIANANMEN SQUARE

To reach the Ranch House Restaurant, one exits from the Bayshore Freeway just past San Francisco International Airport at the Redwood City Putnam Lexus dealership, turns left near the Chef Peking Chinese Restaurant and then stops in a parking lot where the sound of traffic roaring down the freeway is as deafening as a jet plane taking off. As I walked past an outdoor illuminated sign proclaiming WE WELCOME LARGE PARTY FUNCTIONS and stepped inside the Ranch House, Frankie B. and the Wolfmen lit into Hank Williams's 'If You've Got the Money, Honey' from a small stage facing a bar overhung with Tiffany lamps. At the same time, a disco version of 'Joy to the World' poured out of a Muzak system in the dining-room.

Kevin, the friend I had come to meet, was the night manager of this northern California roadhouse. He was responsible for dealing with customer complaints, mediating disputes between employees, keeping track of receipts and closing the place down at night—in short, for dealing with all the problems that arise at a large restaurant where the public comes to eat, dance, drink and drown its sorrows. At two a.m. the night before, just as he was about to lock up, Kevin had discovered a woman passed out in the ladies' room. He revived her, phoned her home and then waited until her angry husband arrived in his pick-up truck to retrieve her. Kevin's authoritative manner and his experience dealing with large numbers of unruly people seemed to be standing him in good stead.

When I had first seen him, he had been wearing a headband, standing in front of the Monument to the Martyrs of the People in Tiananmen Square, a bullhorn raised to his lips. 'Kevin' was Wu'er Kaixi, a leader of the dissident students who began the Tiananmen Square protest movement in 1989.

Wu'er first became involved in the protest on the night of 19 April 1989, when some 20,000 demonstrators were massed outside the Chinese Communist Party's leadership compound in Peking at Zhongnanhai, near the Forbidden City, chanting for Premier Li Peng to come out and listen to their grievances. As the

Photo: Reuters/Bettmann Newsphotos

Opposite: Wu'er Kaixi shouting slogans through the gate of the headquarters of the *People's Daily* newspaper in Peking, 1989.

crowd's pushing and shoving against phalanxes of police threatened to get out of hand, Wu'er, who was studying education at Peking Normal University, happened to cycle past with a girl. Seeing the situation was heading towards violence, he got off his bicycle and began calling for the mob to sit down on the pavement. Within minutes, he had transformed the dangerous shoving match between demonstrators and police into an enthralled sit-in.

Nonetheless, around three a.m. that night, when only a few hundred demonstrators still remained outside the compound, Public Security Bureau loudspeakers suddenly crackled to life: 'A small number of people have been attacking and insulting Party and government leaders and poisoning minds, spreading rumours and shouting reactionary slogans calling for the overthrow of the Chinese Communist Party,' a voice ominously declared. A short while later, policemen waded into the remaining demonstrators with clubs flying. It was the first outbreak of violence that spring.

Wu'er's big moment came on the evening of 18 May, after his appointment as chairman of the Peking Autonomous Student Federation. Premier Li Peng had finally agreed to a televised face-to-face dialogue with the protesters. Throughout the meeting, Li Peng sat stony-faced in an overstuffed armchair adorned with lace antimacassars. His awkward posture, hands resting stiffly at his sides, and his Mao suit, accessorized with nerdish grey Hush Puppies, made him look deeply ill-at-ease—perhaps understandable given the circumstances, which were indeed strange. One student leader, Wang Dan, was wearing a leather jacket, a dirty blue T-shirt, cotton Chinese slippers and a headband; Wu'er Kaixi, who had come straight from the hospital where he had been convalescing from a hunger strike, wore a pair of striped pyjamas and clutched a khaki-coloured oxygen bag that trailed plastic tubes, which he stuck up his nose at intervals during the meeting in order to fortify himself against chronic fainting spells. The wearing of pyjamas during an audience with the Premier was unusual to say the least, and left some viewers aghast. Others, however, were left squirming with delight by this peculiar gesture that perfectly captured Wu'er's studied defiance of authority. In case viewers missed the message implicit in his fashion statement, Wu'er also refused to get up as the Premier began shaking hands with each of the students. Not until he was almost face to face with Li did Wu'er rise, and then only for a disdainful moment before irreverently slumping back in his chair.

'I am delighted to meet you all,' Li Peng began, as if greeting a group of model workers. But then he began laying down ground rules for the discussion. 'In today's conversation we are going to talk about only one subject, and that is, how to get the hunger strikers out of their present plight,' he said. 'The Party and the government are very concerned about this matter. We are deeply disturbed by the situation and concerned over the health of the students.' Li then surveyed the company slouched around him and incongruously declared, 'We look on you as if you were our own children.'

Wu'er, who was in no mood to be Li Peng's figurative child, interrupted the Premier with a dismissive wave of his hand. 'We don't have much time,' he said. 'While we are sitting comfortably here, students outside are suffering from hunger.' Without giving the Premier a chance to regain the initiative, Wu'er continued. 'Now, I would like to tell you what we have to say. You said that we were going to talk about only one subject. But the reality is not that you invited *us* to this discussion, but that *we*—all those people in the Square—asked *you* to come and talk.' He wagged an admonitory forefinger. 'How many topics will be discussed is up to us!'

With his jaw clenched, Li charged his young interlocutor with rudeness. 'Rude?' Wu'er shot back. 'You've got a million people on the streets, and you're calling me rude? Premier Li, I don't think we have time for this kind of talk!'

'In the past few days Peking has fallen into a state of anarchy,' countered Li. 'We must protect the safety of our students, protect our factories, protect the achievements of socialism and protect our capital. Creating turmoil may not have been the original intention of most people, but nevertheless, turmoil is what has occurred.'

'It seems that some of you leading comrades still don't understand me,' objected Wu'er, as it became clear that Li was going to make no major concessions. 'Let's avoid this endless quibbling. If this meeting leads nowhere, then we can only conclude that the government is not sincere—that it does not have the slightest interest in solving the problem. In that case, there is no point in us sitting here any longer.'

The tantalizing drama ended with Wu'er diving for his oxygen bag as five white-smocked medical personnel jumped to attend him.

On the night of 3 June, when People's Liberation Army troops began mustering for a final assault on Tiananmen Square, Wu'er was taken to safety in the back of an ambulance with several seriously wounded demonstrators. On its way out of the Square, the ambulance was flagged down by a group of hysterical students trying to get a wounded friend to the hospital. 'The ambulance was already carrying four people, but the doctors and nurses crammed someone else into the back with me,' Wu'er remembered. 'Brains and blood were coming out of his head. By the time we reached the hospital, two of the people in the ambulance had already died. I will never forget that I left Tiananmen Square holding a dead body.'

For several days after the massacre, Wu'er tried to hide out in a succession of friends' houses, but it soon became obvious that he would have to leave Peking. He and his nineteen-year-old girlfriend, Liu Yan, set off on a cross-country trek to Canton in the hope of escaping to Hong Kong. Since almost everyone in China had seen Wu'er during his televised contretemps with Li Peng, he was in constant danger of being recognized; to make matters even more dangerous, halfway through the trip south, the Public Security Bureau released a '21 Most Wanted' list of student protesters, and Wu'er's picture was again flashed across the country on television.

Despite the government dragnet and several close calls when police moved in on places that Wu'er and Liu had left only moments before, the couple finally reached the Zhuhai Special Economic Zone just across the border from the Portuguese territory of Macau. There they made contact with the 'underground railway'—an informal network of volunteers who were helping protesters flee the country. Wu'er and Liu were hidden in a safe-house while the arrangements for their escape were made. Since the government was well aware that many of those on its 'Most Wanted' list were in the Canton area, trying to make it across the frontier, border patrols had been stepped up on both land and sea, making it extremely difficult to remain undetected, much less to cross over into either Macau or Hong Kong.

Nonetheless, after almost a week of waiting, a contact finally appeared with a car and drove Wu'er and Liu to an isolated oyster farm on the coast. They were told that if things went according to plan, at 7.50 p.m. they could expect to see two long flashes of light out of the water. They were then to swim in the direction of the light, where a speedboat would pick them up. If no such signal appeared, then they were on their own.

By eight o'clock, they had seen no signal. Eight-thirty came and went. Wu'er knew that the boat's captain would only attempt one rendezvous, and he feared they had somehow already missed it.

At nine-thirty, just as Wu'er and Liu were on the verge of giving up, they saw two flashes of light. They waded out into the water. The shoreline was encrusted with sharp oyster shells which sliced at their legs as they stumbled through the shallows. 'But it didn't matter,' Wu'er told me later, 'because as we started swimming, I knew we would be saved.'

Wu'er and Liu had imagined that in Hong Kong they would be greeted as heroes by cheering crowds. Instead, they found themselves sequestered by British officials anxious about antagonizing Peking. Wu'er was allowed to make only one public statement, an impassioned address on Hong Kong television on 28 June. After denouncing the 'bestial fascists' who had fired upon the people of Peking, he said, 'As survivors, our lives no longer belong to us alone. Our lives must now embrace those of our fellow students and compatriots who died for democracy, freedom, our beautiful motherland and for her strength and prosperity. Their lives have now been melded together with ours.'

Wu'er was then put on a flight to France. It was not until he reached Paris and found himself in an alien world with no means of support and no permanent place to live that he began to appreciate the enormity of what had happened. Escape was the beginning not of a chapter of liberation but of a period of agonizing exile that would leave him exhausted, deeply confused and depressed.

In this disoriented state, Wu'er was drawn into plans to organize an overseas Chinese opposition movement. In Paris he was elected vice-president of the newly formed Federation for Democracy in China, and thrust into a new political maelstrom, this time a factional struggle among members of the defeated and exiled democracy movement.

That August, Wu'er went to the United States on behalf of the Federation where he soon found himself consumed in a cyclotron of media hype. His television appearances during the Peking demonstrations had made him a superstar, and everywhere he went he was besieged by pushing crowds of reporters, fawning well-wishers, frenzied autograph hounds and people eager to make contributions to the cause of Chinese democracy. At one banquet, he was able to auction off a handwritten note pledging his allegiance to the democracy movement in exchange for a $3,000 contribution to the Federation.

It is hard to imagine a place further removed from Tiananmen Square than Los Angeles's Federal Plaza. The Plaza surrounds an ivory high-rise office building festooned with American flags that looks out over a panorama of manicured lawns, palm trees and a cascade of gleaming cars speeding along Wilshire Boulevard. One August day in 1989, just two months after soldiers opened fire in Peking, a crowd of several thousand gathered in the Plaza. When walkie-talkie-toting security guards rounded the corner of the Federal Building, heads jerked around in anticipation and photographers and television crews jumped to their feet. As the entourage approached the podium, a hush fell over the crowd. There in its midst was Wu'er, his face puffy and contorted with pain, sourness and fatigue. He was almost doubled over, held up by two acolytes, like a wounded soldier. Whether his incapacity was due to exhaustion, psychological trauma, his mysterious heart condition that had caused fainting spells in the Square or his penchant for the dramatic was impossible to know, but here in LA Wu'er seemed spent and lost. It was not until he stepped up to the microphone and the cameras began rolling that he regained even a suggestion of his old Tiananmen Square swagger.

'We want to say that we Chinese have hope and a future,' he said through a grimace of apparent pain. 'Our wish is to allow people to have a choice.' He squinted out over the crowd into a haze of sun-infused smog. When a concerned adjutant offered him a straw hat to shield his eyes from the brightness, he looked at it for an instant and then rejected it. Even in this state of near collapse he had not lost his awareness of image and concern for appearances. He began speaking again, but after only a few minutes he clutched his midriff and had to be helped away by his retinue, leaving a stunned and alarmed crowd behind him.

The evening I met Wu'er (Kevin) at the Ranch House Restaurant in California four years later, he was resplendent in a pressed white shirt, a tie and a pair of stylish pants. Instead of the bullhorn, he had a ring of keys. Around his face and body there was more than a suggestion of corpulence— not surprising perhaps, given his stewardship over a chop house serving prime rib, steaks and roast chickens garnished with baked potatoes smothered in sour cream.

Although Wu'er looked more composed than I had ever seen him, he still flashed the same boyish grin and gave the same kinds of quick-witted answers that had made him such a favourite of the press. Now, however, there was less of the braggadocio about him. By day he was studying for his BA at the Dominican College of San Rafael, a small Catholic liberal arts school north of San Francisco. By night he oversaw his new dominion, not of student protesters and hunger strikers, but of busboys, waitresses, fry cooks, cashiers and bartenders. His no-nonsense manner suggested that he had lost none of the confidence that had made him such an effective student organizer. But he now spoke more quietly and gave orders in a far less peremptory and theatrical manner. Moreover, his attitude towards China had also undergone an unexpected change. Instead of railing against the government, Wu'er now readily acknowledged that the reforms of Deng and his allies were, in some respects, a real step forward.

'It's amazing, but people in China can actually change their jobs now!' he said with a grin. 'To be stuck with a lousy government-assigned job and not be able to do what we wanted used to be such a headache. So we exiles must admit that in certain areas the government is making progress. Sure, it is because of our pressure! And sure, the level of freedom is still not yet up to our standards! But it is still doing many of the things we demanded in the Square.'

The Muzak system had just started murdering 'O Little Town of Bethlehem' and the band had erupted into 'Good Golly Miss Molly' when Wu'er was paged over the restaurant's PA system to the cash register. When our waitress appeared with dessert in his absence, I could not resist asking her about 'Kevin'.

'Oh, Kevin's a real good guy,' she replied with a uniquely Californian cheerfulness.

'Isn't it strange to find someone with a background like his at a place like this?' I asked.

'What are you talking about?' she replied, looking at me strangely. 'I mean, he's just Kevin, right?'

When Wu'er returned, I asked him what other Ranch House employees thought of working with a person who had once been such a prominent political figure. 'Oh no!' he said, laughing. 'They don't know who I am! The owner is a Chinese friend, and I promised that if he gave me this job I'd keep quiet.'

When I asked if he sometimes found himself thinking back to Peking and 1989, he looked around the restaurant wistfully. The dining-room was almost empty; only a few stalwarts were slumped at the bar. 'Yeah,' Wu'er finally said, letting out a long sigh. 'Each spring I still become very depressed, and start calling friends who also escaped. And when June fourth actually rolls around, I can't help dreaming about Tiananmen Square.'

The spring of 1989 was so apocalyptic that at the time it had seemed unthinkable that the year's events would fade or that China would ever be able to forget them. But the Square had been returned to the Party, and China had undergone an extraordinary period of change as Deng Xiaoping rammed his economic reform programme into high gear. History had moved on. And now, here was Wu'er Kaixi, darling of that protest movement, sitting before me in a Californian roadhouse eating prime rib.

'Of course,' Wu'er exclaimed almost indignantly when I asked him if he still wanted to go back.

To do what?

'One of two things,' he replied. 'Either something really politically meaningful, or . . .' he hesitated for a moment, then he grinned and said: 'I want to be a billionaire.'

GRANTA

IVAN KLÍMA
PROGRESS IN PRAGUE

Ivan Klíma

Culture in a Totalitarian State

People in the West are aware of the hardship and bewilderment that accompanied the political and economic transformation of central and eastern Europe after 1989. They also believe that they understand the origins of the problem. But they do not realize that the events of 1989 completely altered central and eastern European culture, nor that it is this change which has actually had the greatest effect on people's lives.

People who have always lived in a free society cannot grasp the concept of culture in a totalitarian regime. They only know about the intellectual sterility, the dogmatism, the censorship, the centrally directed system of schooling and the state control of the arts: what room can this have left for culture? But our situation was not quite that simple. Books were published, television programmes were made, art was exhibited and the theatres were full. It is true that bookshops stocked a rather limited range of titles, and that the repertoire of the theatres and cinemas was a little thin. Television was often monotonous, with current affairs programmes tending towards the mendacious (mendacity, of course, infected many areas of life, from the school curriculum to the act of voting). On the other hand, books and tickets to cultural events of all kinds were cheap because the state subsidized all it permitted. While censorship denied everything that was new and disturbing, it also blocked the worst trash—for instance, the pornographic and violent videos and magazines that have swamped free countries had to be smuggled in small quantities across our borders and so never invaded the mass media. The idea that somebody slaughtering a sheep in front of an audience and then displaying its blood and entrails might constitute a work of art was incredible.

I have long tried to argue against the notion that change and newness are what most people want. The frantic pace of modern life actually encourages conservatism, manifested in the commonly held belief that it is the function of art to entertain rather than disturb and provoke. The cultural policy of totalitarianism dovetailed in this respect with the views of the majority. The problem for the state was one of taste: state-sponsored art was insufficiently populist because its function was primarily to 'educate'—i.e. to reinforce the values of the political system.

Lifestyle

The totalitarian system encouraged a lifestyle which in some ways resembled that of the West: it aimed at a limited consumerism, it encouraged hero-worship of record-breaking athletes, pop singers and champion hockey teams. It cultivated loyalty, obedience, a restrained optimism, discipline and egalitarianism, and fostered an aversion to enterprise, excessive wealth, criticism and creative, combative intellectualism. Jobs and wages were guaranteed (even for work that was more pretence than real), as was free schooling which, despite all efforts to the contrary, occasionally provided a real education. Health care was in an apparently irreversible decline, but it was also free, and was only part of an all-embracing social security system. The country was surrounded by barbed wire, making travel difficult for decent and honest citizens, but also making it hard for international criminals to make contact with our domestic ones. The idea that it is the duty of the state to take care of its citizens became deeply embedded in the national psyche and was part of what I call the 'social culture'.

So, while people may have rebelled against the values which the system proclaimed and the culture it sponsored, they also unconsciously accepted many of its other features. I would even say they placed a high value on qualities which had become less important to people who grew up in conditions of freedom.

Expectations

People did suffer materially under totalitarian rule, but it is possible that they suffered more from mental and spiritual deprivation: from lack of freedom and lack of information, from the limitations that affected all spheres of life. The awareness that they were separated from the free world—which appeared to them in glowing colours as a place of abundance, affluence, freedom and endless possibilities—irritated them and filled them with a sense of futility largely because they believed that their society had no future. People felt disgust with totalitarianism and had an unqualified faith in the workings of a free society (despite the tireless efforts of the regime's propaganda), which they believed to be the solution to all human problems and the model for harmonious perfection. The United States, the most influential example of such an arrangement, became a symbol of that perfection, and all things American were greatly admired.

After 1989, it would have been too much to expect people to be alert to the poverty of consumer values, or to resist the invasion of mass culture from the free part of Europe. Culturally, most people were completely unprepared for the new conditions; they had not had the chance to develop the antibodies which would have protected them against the bacilli carried by the value system of a free-market society and its mass culture.

Curiosity

In the first months after the revolution there was a surge of interest in everything the former regime had forbidden. There was a huge and immediate demand for both the work of dissidents and Western best-sellers, as well as for pure trash—romances and action adventure stories. In the theatre, the work of Beckett and Ionesco drew big audiences, and so did a musical interpretation of *Les Misérables*. People were simply curious. They stood outside bookshops in queues a mile long for Havel's first book; the print-runs for works by other dissident authors were unbelievably large. But soon, Beckett disappeared from the repertoire of half-empty theatres, and books by the most famous domestic authors began to be printed in thousands rather than hundreds of thousands. Trash cut a victorious swathe through the culture. Curiosity had been satisfied, and average tastes, guided and enforced by no one, held sway.

Culture shock

The revolutionary changes touched all aspects of cultural life, including the value system. What had been certain yesterday was doubtful today. Yesterday's sins became today's virtues—and vice versa. Most people welcomed these changes, but not everyone was capable of adapting. Culture shock struck at every level of society.

People were accustomed to the simple schemata and precepts of the former regime (in all societies, people tend to be drawn by stirring slogans and simplistic solutions). They now cast about for a substitute ideology, for new superstitions which would help clarify the present situation. One of the most popular of these new superstitions is the claim that the market-place, left to itself, will solve all our problems. I am not an economist and so of course cannot judge to what extent this claim holds true in that field. But it does not hold true with regard to culture.

Uneasiness

Artists and intellectuals played a significant role in our revolution, and it gave them complete freedom, which could be considered the most essential element of creativity. Nevertheless, many of them are uneasy about the changes, as is a section of the cultured public.

I had a conversation recently with one of our most famous protest singers from the old days. I was astonished at how disgusted he was by the new situation. Behind all his arguments, I sensed a bitter personal disillusionment. He was barely tolerated by the old regime, but the thousands of young people who came to his concerts idolized him. Last time he played, it was to an audience of about thirty. His plight is identical to that of many artists, especially non-conformists, who used to be enormously popular for obvious reasons. Of course, and again for obvious reasons, that popularity has now evaporated.

Many people were nonplussed by the new reality because it was not what they had imagined. Most artists—actors, directors, would-be publishers, film-makers and television producers, radical

253

and conformist alike—had dreamt of what they would be able to accomplish if freedom returned. Tacitly, for the most part, they came up with the vague notion of a cultural 'third way': the state, they imagined, would continue as a patron of the arts, but now it would give complete freedom to the artists. At the same time it would work out how to limit the dissemination of endless trash. Very few grasped that freedom for them would mean freedom for everyone else as well. They hadn't reckoned on competition.

The market economy sprang up almost overnight, and it was all very different from the artists' dreams. The dreaded and familiar enemy, censorship, was replaced by the market-place. The market demands more than dreams; other requirements include capital, experience, courage, good judgement, talent and the outlay of enormous effort. Those who had dreamt of freedom possessed none or almost none of those qualities. The dreamers watched, amazed, as their fantasies of great, free, artistic creations that would be produced to huge public acclaim were elbowed out of the way by trash (and foreign trash at that). The public suddenly turned their backs; their preference, it seemed, was for the most banal forms of consumerism.

Losses

The triumph of the market-place, even if only for the time being, will undoubtedly be culture's loss. Disneyesque megakitsch has elbowed out Czech animation and puppetry, which was once among the finest in the world. The same is true of Czech children's literature, especially our long tradition of wonderful illustrated books. Czech cinema, which flourished in the sixties, is barely scraping by and for the most part produces only a kind of mongrel, comprising dumb comedy, pornography and action films. Our theatres try to survive by staging inane comedies and musicals. Many publishing houses (an incredible 2,000 sprang up after the revolution) have either gone bankrupt or are trying to survive by churning out rubbish. Magazines are folding one after the other.

A public unprepared for this sudden explosion of supply is bewildered and unpredictable. And the situation is complicated by the fact that the intelligentsia, which might have been able to influence the situation in the market-place to the benefit of true cultural values, are so badly paid they simply haven't the money to do it.

The present state of affairs does not fill me with enthusiasm. Even though I never had any illusions about the practicality of the 'third way', it is still disappointing to see that, despite having gone through so much as a society, we were capable of learning so little in the cultural field. But I'm convinced that in this apparently blind and ruthless process, an important winnowing-out is taking place. As illusions fade, those who make the culture will be able to assess without distortion their true position in the world.

And hope?

Society will of course recover from the state that I have called culture shock, and I believe that it will be able to draw the necessary conclusions from the past few years. Small countries need their own culture far more than large countries do, and at least a part of the Czech cultural public is aware of this and will continue to keep our culture alive. It is essential that their voices be heard.

Translated from the Czech by Paul Wilson

Notes on Contributors

Since *Money* in 1983, each of **Martin Amis**'s novels has first appeared in *Granta* as a work-in-progress. 'Author, Author' is from the novel he is currently writing, provisionally entitled *The Information*, which will be published in Britain next spring. **Neil Steinberg** works on the city desk of the *Chicago Sun-Times*. His humour pieces—'The Spelling Bee' among them—will be published in the United States in the autumn in *Complete and Utter Failure*. **Julian Barnes** is writing a collection of short stories occasioned by historical meetings between the English and the French; the collection will include his previous contribution to *Granta*, 'Dragons' (in *Granta* 32, 'History'). **Eugene Richards**'s photographs have regularly appeared in the magazine. 'In the Beginning' documents the birth of Jim and Sara Vogt's first child, Joshua, in Washington, DC. **Susan J. Miller** lives in Cambridge, Massachusetts. 'Never Let Me Down' is her first published work. **Bret Easton Ellis** has completed a new book of interconnected stories that will be published next year. His previous books include *Less than Zero* and *American Pyscho*. 'Buddy Carmody' is from **Jayne Anne Phillips**'s new novel, *Shelter*, that will be published in the autumn in the United States (by Houghton Mifflin) and in Britain next winter (by Faber & Faber). **Beverly Lowry**'s novel, *The Track of Real Desires*, was published last year in the United States. **David Owen** is the European Community's Mediator in the former Yugoslavia. **Jean Hatzfeld** is a foreign correspondent of the French newspaper *Libération*. He lives in Paris. **Gilles Peress**'s 'Compulsory Departures' depicts Muslim refugees fleeing Serbian troops in Banja Luka in Bosnia. The photographs will be included in *Farewell to Bosnia*, which will be published this summer by Scalo. They have also been included in an exhibition organized by the Corcoran Gallery of Art in Washington DC and the Fotomuseum Winterhur in Switzerland that is the second part of his ongoing project 'Hate thy Brother': a cycle of documentary stories describing intolerance and the re-emergence of nationalism in post-war Europe. The project has been supported by the Fondation de France. **Orville Schell** has written extensively about China; his previous contributions to *Granta* appeared issues 13 and 20. **Ivan Klíma** has completed his first novel since the collapse of the Communist regime in Czechoslovakia, *Waiting for the Dark, Waiting for the Light*. This, and a collection of his essays, *The Spirit of Prague*, will be published by Granta Books on the fifth anniversary of the 'Velvet Revolution' next November.